# Staging Shakespeare's Violence

# Staging Shakespeare's Violence

## My Cue to Fight – Domestic Fury

Seth Duerr and Jared Kirby

PEN & SWORD
HISTORY

First published in Great Britain in 2021 by
Pen & Sword History
An imprint of
Pen & Sword Books Ltd
Yorkshire – Philadelphia

ISBN 978 1 52676 240 5

Typeset by Mac Style
Printed and bound in India by Replika Press Pvt. Ltd.

Pen & Sword Books Limited incorporates the imprints of Atlas, Archaeology, Aviation,
Discovery, Family History, Fiction, History, Maritime, Military, Military Classics,
Politics, Select, Transport, True Crime, Air World, Frontline Publishing, Leo Cooper,
Remember When, Seaforth Publishing, The Praetorian Press, Wharncliffe
Local History, Wharncliffe Transport, Wharncliffe True Crime and White Owl.

For a complete list of Pen & Sword titles please contact

PEN & SWORD BOOKS LIMITED
47 Church Street, Barnsley, South Yorkshire, S70 2AS, England
E-mail: enquiries@pen-and-sword.co.uk
Website: www.pen-and-sword.co.uk

Or

PEN AND SWORD BOOKS
1950 Lawrence Rd, Havertown, PA 19083, USA
E-mail: Uspen-and-sword@casematepublishers.com
Website: www.penandswordbooks.com

# Special Thanks

*from Jared*

To Seth, my partner in crime. Thanks for hiring me almost twenty years ago and starting this friendship. We have had several incarnations of educating the world on violence in Shakespeare, and I am happy to tackle this version with you.

To Nicholas Martin-Smith and Susane Lee, collaborating on so many of these works with Hudson Warehouse has been a breath of fresh air every summer. Thank you for your trust and support.

To Paul Sugarman for running the Instant Shakespeare Company in NYC. I have met several people I have collaborated with for over a decade because of ISC.

To many of the fight directors who have had an impact on my learning and growth over the years.

Thank you, John Lennox, Kyle Rowling, Brad Waller, David 'Pops' Doersch, Ruth Cooper Brown, Rachel Bown-Williams, Michael Anderson, Donald Preston, Luis Rosa, Tim Ruzicki, Bryce Bermingham, J. David Brimmer, Ian Rose, Rick Skene, Anthony DeLongis, Luke Lafontaine, Bob Chapin, Scott Witt, Daniel Ford Beavis, Kev McCurdy, David Kessler, Daniel Levinson, Nigel Poulton, Dwight McLemore, and Chazz Menendez.

To all those who have trained with New York Combat for Screen and Stage over the last two decades, it has been a privilege to teach you and watch you grow in this art. Particular thanks to Kaitlyn Farley (aka 'Pepper'), Vincent Lane (aka 'Ram') and Tony Mita (aka 'Chopper').

To my son, Evan, for putting up with all those times that Daddy was on the computer working on this book. Your interest in screen/stage combat brings joy to my heart.

To my wife, Carol, for her love, patience, and support. I couldn't do this without you.

*from Seth*

I, too, would like to thank Jared's wife.

*Were it my cue to fight, I should have known it without a prompter.*

*Othello* (1.2)

*Just as real warriors perform an essential though anguishing service for society, actors also serve as courageous soldiers of the psyche. When we dig deep into the dark underbelly of the human ego and express our shadow selves truthfully in performance, we are helping the audience process that side of their natures, too. Society needs its stories in order to understand itself, and since drama is centered around conflict, violence lies at the heart of many great plays. Human beings kill. We make war. We rape, pillage, torture, and terrify. We can be brutal and animalistic. We even have the capacity to take joy in and revel in these horrors.*

Rocco Dal Vera, *The Voice in Violence*, 2001

# Violence by Play

BOLD CAPS = VIOLENCE WITH WEAPONRY
Bold = Violence without weaponry
*Italics = Potential moment of violence*

# Violence by Number of Participants

## 1w (woman)

AYL 4.3 Rosalind faints

E3 2.2 COUNTESS THREATENS SUICIDE

Ham 5.2 Gertrude falls and dies from poisoning

*1H6 5.3 Any self-harm by Joan to get the fiends' attention?*

John 3.3 Constance tears out her hair

*Mac 1.5 Blood sacrifice by Lady Macbeth?*

Mac 2.3 Lady Macbeth faints

## 1m (man)

CYM 4.1 CLOTEN DRAWS HIS SWORD

*1H4 2.3 Does Hotspur sustain a paper cut?*

*1H4 2.4 Does Francis trip on the slippery tavern floor with all the back and forth?*

1H4 5.3 FALSTAFF STABS HOTSPUR'S CORPSE AND THEN CARRIES IT

*2H4 2.4 Does Pistol purposely/accidentally discharge his pistol?*

2H4 4.2 The king faints

*2H4 5.5 How does Falstaff react to being disowned?*

*H5 3.6 Stage the hanging of Bardolph?*

2H6 3.2 Henry faints

2H6 3.3 The death of Winchester

3H6 2.6 Clifford talks himself to death

John 4.3 Arthur falls to his death

John 5.4 Count Meloon enters fatally wounded

John 5.7 John finally dies

LEAR 2.1 EDMUND SELF-WOUND

*M4M 2.2/4 Does Angelo self-flagellate?*

*MWW 2.3 How else does Dr Caius vent frustration?*

*MWW 4.2 Ford has been hurting himself in between scenes. Does it continue here?*

*R3 3.5 How does the mayor react to Hastings' severed head?*

## 1w/1m

*AWW 2.5 Does Bertram physically mistreat Helena?*

*AWW 3.4 Does the countess physically admonish Reynaldo?*

*AYL 1.3 Does Duke Frederick physically threaten Rosalind?*

*AYL 1.3 Or Celia when she tries to intervene?*

*Cym 1.2 Cymbeline manhandling of Imogen? Cymbeline and queen?*

*Cym 1.7 Does Iachimo get handsy? Does Imogen engage in self-defence?*

*Cym 2.3 What happens after Cloten requests Imogen's hand?*

**CYM 3.4 IMOGEN AND PISANIO PLAY HOT POTATO WITH A KNIFE**

**Cym 5.5 Posthumus strikes the disguised Imogen**

*E3 2.1 Does Edward get handsy with the countess?*

*Ham 3.1 Hamlet and Ophelia? Continuation of his offstage violence towards her before 2.1?*

*Ham 3.4 Hamlet and Gertrude? Potential grabs, slaps, shakes?*

*1H4 2.3 What will Lady Percy do to get truth out of Hotspur?*

*1H4 3.3 How flirty is the Falstaff/Hostess Quickly dynamic? Any of it physical?*

*2H4 2.4 Falstaff and Doll Tearsheet violence and/or SexyTimez™?*

*2H4 2.4 Does Doll Tearsheet attack Pistol?*

**1H6 1.2 JOAN OVERCOMES THE DAUPHIN IN SINGLE COMBAT**

**1H6 1.5 JOAN AND TALBOT FIGHT. TWICE**

**1H6 5.3 York captures Joan**

*1H6 5.3 Any physical kinks in the Margaret/Suffolk relationship?*

*2H6 1.3 How is the Margaret/Suffolk relationship physically developing when they are alone?*

*2H6 3.2 Margaret and Henry? After Suffolk's banishment, Henry and Margaret?*

*2H6 3.2 Final SexyTimez™ scene for Margaret/Suffolk (whilst he's alive anyway)*

*2H6 5.2 Margaret demands Henry fly*

*3H6 1.1 Margaret admonishes Henry*

*3H6 3.2 Are any of Edward's advances physical? Does Elizabeth reject them?*

*John 1.1 Does Lady Faulconbridge strike Philip?*

*John 2.2 Does Constance physically lash out at Salisbury?*

*Lear 1.1 Lear manhandling of Cordelia?*

*Lear 1.4 Lear violence towards Goneril?*

*Lear 2.2 Regan and Kent?*

*Lear 4.2 Albany and Goneril?*

*Mac 1.5 How does Lady Macbeth treat the help?*

*Mac 1.7 Does Lady Macbeth try any physical violence? Does Macbeth reciprocate?*

*Mac 2.2 Does Lady Macbeth use physical violence to get Macbeth to focus?*

*Mac 3.4 Does Lady Macbeth use physical violence to snap Macbeth out of his trance?*

*M4M 2.4 Angelo and Isabella?*

*M4M 3.1 Claudio and Isabella?*

**More 1.1 Francis de Barde hales Doll by the arm**

*More 1.1 Doll and Williamson? Doll and de Barde? Doll and Caveler?*

*More 2.2 Doll and Williamson?*

*MWW 3.3 How flirty is the Falstaff/Mistress Ford dynamic? Any of it physical?*

*MWW 3.4 Does Mistress Page physically intimidate or harm Fenton?*
*R3 2.4 Does Elizabeth have to physically silence her son?*
*R3 4.3 Mummy says goodbye*
*R3 4.3 The wooing of Elizabeth*

2w

2H6 1.3 Margaret gives Eleanor a box on the ear

2m

*AWW 2.3 Does the king physically threaten Bertram?*
*AWW 5.2 Does the clowne have to physically push Parolles away?*
*AWW 5.2 Does Lafew have to physically push Parolles away?*
AYL 1.1 Orlando strangles Oliver
AYL 1.2 Charles and Orlando wrestle
*AYL 3.1 Duke Frederick and Oliver?*
*Cym 1.2 Cymbeline manhandling of Posthumus?*
*Cym 2.4 Posthumus threatening Iachimo?*
CYM 4.2 GUIDERIUS AND CLOTEN FIGHT
CYM 5.2 POSTHUMUS AND IACHIMO FIGHT
*Cym 5.5 Does Posthumus strike Iachimo before knocking out Imogen?*
E3 1.1 EDWARD DRAWS ON LORRAINE
E3 4.5 French captain brings in the captured Salisbury
E3 5.1 Copland brings in the captured King David
*Ham 1.2 Claudius pulls Hamlet aside?*
HAM 3.4 HAMLET FATALLY STABS POLONIUS
*Ham 4.3 Hamlet and Claudius?; violence to get an answer from Hamlet?*
*Ham 4.5 Laertes' return? He's armed, does he use any force against Claudius?*
Ham 5.1 Hamlet grapples with Laertes
HAM 5.2 HAMLET/LAERTES DUEL; BOTH  FATALLY STABBED
BY POISONED FOIL
HAM 5.2 HAMLET FATALLY STABS CLAUDIUS
*1H4 1.3 Does Northumberland have to put Hotspur in his place?*
*1H4 2.4 Does the vintner beat Francis? Does Falstaff?*
*1H4 3.3 Does Hal play with Falstaff's boobs or guts?*
1H4 5.2 BLUNT (DISGUISED AS THE KING) IS KILLED BY
DOUGLAS
1H4 5.3 DOUGLAS FIGHTS THE KING AND IS ABOUT TO WIN
1H4 5.3 HAL TAKES OVER FIGHT WITH DOUGLAS WHO THEN
FLEES
1H4 5.3 HAL AND HOTSPUR FIGHT
1H4 5.3 DOUGLAS AND FALSTAFF FIGHT
2H4 2.4 Bardolph tries to get Pistol to leave

2H4 2.4 FALSTAFF FIGHTS PISTOL

2H4 4.1 COLEVILLE SUBMITS TO FALSTAFF

*2H4 4.2 Does the king beat the shit out of Hal?*

*H5 3.6 Pistol and Fluellen preview?*

H5 4.1 The disguised king and Williams exchange gauges

H5 4.4 PISTOL CORNERS A FRENCH SOLDIER

H5 4.8 Williams strikes Fluellen; *does Fluellen strike back?*

H5 5.1 FLUELLEN CUDGELS PISTOL; *is Pistol disarmed?*

1H6 1.4 SALISBURY AND GARGRAVE BLOWN TO BITS BY A CANNON

1H6 3.4 Vernon strikes Basset

1H6 4.1 Talbot strips Falstaff of his garter; *anything else?*

*1H6 4.5 How physical does the argument become between Talbot and his son?*

1H6 5.3 York fights Burgundy in hand-to-hand combat

2H6 2.3 PETER FATALLY STRIKES DOWN DRUNKEN HORNER

*2H6 3.2 Henry and Suffolk?*

2H6 3.2 WARWICK ACCUSES SUFFOLK; WEAPONS ARE DRAWN

2H6 4.10 IDEN FIGHTS AND KILLS CADE

2H6 5.2 RICHARD FIGHTS AND KILLS SOMERSET

*2H6 5.2 Young Clifford entreats Henry fly*

*3H6 1.2 How forcefully does York cut off Richard?*

3H6 1.3 CLIFFORD MURDERS RUTLAND

3H6 2.4 RICHARD AND CLIFFORD FIGHTUS INTERRUPTUS

*3H6 2.5 A son who killed his father, and a father who killed his son*

3H6 5.2 EDWARD BRINGS FORTH DYING WARWICK

3H6 5.6 RICHARD MURDERS HENRY

*H8 3.2 Surrey and Wolsey?*

*John 1.1 Does Robert strike Philip?*

*John 4.2 Does John attack Hubert?*

*John 4.3 Does Philip physically intimidate Hubert once they are alone?*

JOHN 5.6 PHILIP SCARES HUBERT

*Lear 1.1 Lear manhandling of Kent?*

*Lear 1.2 How does Gloucester get the letter from Edmund?*

*Lear 1.4 Lear violence towards Albany or the fool?*

Lear 1.4 Lear strikes Oswald

Lear 1.4 Kent trips Oswald

Lear 2.2 More Kent and Oswald

*Lear 2.2 Cornwall and Kent?*

LEAR 4.5 OSWALD AND EDGAR FIGHT

LEAR 5.3 EDMUND AND EDGAR FIGHT

*Mac 5.3/5 Does Macbeth beat any of the servants/messengers?*

MAC 5.7 MACBETH FIGHTS AND KILLS YOUNG SEYWARD

MAC 5.7 MACDUFF FIGHTS AND KILLS MACBETH

**M4M 1.3 THE ARREST OF CLAUDIO**

*M4M 2.1 How much of a rise does Pompey get out of Elbow?*

**M4M 5.1 Lucio and the duke scuffle**

*More 1.1 Does Caveler beat Williamson here or just before they enter?*

*More 1.1 Does Lincoln have to physically restrain George?*

**More 1.2 Lifter picks Suresby's purse**

*MWW 1.4 Does Dr Caius harm Simple upon discovering him?*

*MWW 1.4 Does Dr Caius mistreat Rugby?*

**MWW 2.3 DR CAIUS FORCES RUGBY TO DRAW**

**MWW 4.2 Falstaff is beaten out of doors by Ford**

*R2 1.1 Mowbray and Bolingbroke throw down their gauntlets*

*R2 1.3 Mowbray and Bolingbroke prepare to joust*

*R2 2.1 Gaunt and Richard?*

*R2 5.5 Richard beats the keeper?*

**R2 5.5 EXTON KILLS RICHARD**

*R3 4.2 Richard and Buckingham?*

*R3 4.2 Richard and Derby?*

*R3. 4.2/3 Time to have a chat about Richard and SexyTimez™*

**R3 4.3 Richard strikes a messenger**

**R3 5.4 RICHMOND FIGHTS AND KILLS RICHARD**

## 1w/2m

*AWW 5.3 Does the king physically threaten Bertram and Diana?*

*2H6 3.1 York and Somerset about to come to blows before Margaret steps in?*

*R2 2.2 Any physical intimidation towards the queen?*

## 2w/1m

*H5 5.2 Does Alice get in the way of the king and the princess?*

## 3m

*AYL 1.1 Does Adam physically attempt to separate Orlando and Oliver?*

*AYL 2.2 Duke Frederick and the lords?*

**Cym 5.3 Two captains arrest Posthumus**

**E3 4.8 The rescue of Audley by two squires**

**Ham 1.4 Horatio and Marcellus try to restrain Hamlet**

**H5 2.1 BARDOLPH DRAWS ON NYM AND PISTOL**

*H5 4.8 Does Gower intervene after Williams strikes Fluellen?*

*H5 5.1 Does Gower intervene after Fluellen cudgels Pistol?*

**2H6 5.2 WARWICK LEAVES YORK TO FIGHT AND KILL OLD CLIFFORD**

**3H6 3.1 HENRY IS APPREHENDED BY SOME RANDOM HUNTERS**

*3H6 4.1 Clarence and Somerset turn coat against Edward*
*H8 2.2 Does Henry physically intimidate or harm Norfolk and/or Suffolk?*
*Mac 3.1 Does Macbeth manhandle the two murderers?*
R2 5.5 RICHARD KILLS TWO OF EXTON'S MEN
R3 1.4 THE MURDER OF CLARENCE

## 1w/3m

CYM 3.7 BELARIUS, GUIDERIUS, AND ARVIRAGUS DRAW ON IMOGEN

## 4w

*Mac 3.5 How does Hecate's anger at the witches manifest?*

## 4m

*H5 3.2 How hard does Fluellen have to work to push Nym/Pistol/Bardolph into battle?*
*H5 3.2 An Englishman, a Welshman, an Irishman, and a Scot walk into a war zone*
*3H6 1.2 Edward/Richard/Montague physically fighting; Does York have to break them up?*
*3H6 2.3 How much shit does Richard give these folks at the watercooler?*
*R3 4.2 Show Dighton and Forrest murdering the princes?*

## 5m

3H6 2.6 THE YORKISTS PLAY WITH CLIFFORD'S CORPSE
3H6 4.5 THE RESCUE OF EDWARD
JOHN 4.3 PEMBROKE/SALISBURY/BIGOT DRAW ON HUBERT; PHILIP INTERVENES

## Group

AWW 4.1 PAROLLES IS CAPTURED
AWW 4.3 Parolles is interrogated
AYL 2.7 Orlando threatens Duke Senior and his followers
*AYL 3.1 Do lords and/or officers get involved in Duke Frederick's questioning of Oliver?*
CYM 5.2 BATTLE CONTINUES; CYMBELINE IS CAPTURED AND THEN SAVED
*E3 1.1 Who else gets involved after the king draws on Lorraine?*
*E3 3.1 Show some of the offstage battles during snacktime?*
*E3 3.3/4/5 Show any of Prince Edward's battles with the French?*
E3 4.9 King John, the Duke of Normandy, and Philip all brought in as prisoners
*2.1/2 Ham Hamlet's 'mad' scenes?*

*Ham 4.5 Ophelia's 'mad' scene?*

*Ham 5.2 Fortinbras' soldiers restrain the Danes who are still alive?*

1H4 2.2 FALSTAFF & CO ROB TRAVELLERS AND THEN ARE AMBUSHED

*1H4 5.3 Stage Douglas' fights with other counterfeits?*

1H4 5.4 Worcester and Vernon brought in as prisoners

2H4 2.1 THE ATTEMPTED ARREST OF FALSTAFF

*2H4 2.4 Anyone else harmed in the Falstaff/Pistol fight?*

2H4 4.1 REBELS ARE FOOLED AND ARRESTED; *possibly poisoned/ murdered?*

2H4 4.1 COLEVILLE IS LED AWAY TO EXECUTION

2H4 5.4 HOSTESS QUICKLY AND DOLL TEARSHEET RESIST ARREST

2H4 5.5 FALSTAFF & CO ARE ARRESTED

*H5 2.1 Any collateral damage keeping Nym and Pistol from fighting?*

H5 2.2 THE ARREST OF SCROOPE/CAMBRIDGE/GRAY

*H5 2.4 Does the dauphin physically get out of line? How is he put back in his place?*

H5 3.1 THE SIEGE OF HARFLEUR

H5 4.4 THE BATTLE OF AGINCOURT

H5 4.6 PRISONERS BROUGHT IN AND THEN SENTENCED TO DEATH

*H5 4.7 Show the murdering of the children? And is the boy discovered amongst them?*

H5 4.7 YOU GET A PRISONER! AND YOU GET A PRISONER! AND YOU…

*1H6 1.1 Any physical violence amongst the lords?*

1H6 1.2 THE ENGLISH DRIVE BACK THE FRENCH AT ORLEANCE

1H6 1.3 SKIRMISHES AMONGST GLOUCESTER'S AND WINCHESTER'S MEN

1H6 1.5 TALBOT DRIVES BACK THE DOLPHIN

1H6 1.5 JOAN DRIVES BACK THE ENGLISH

1H6 1.5 ENGLISH AND FRENCH SKIRMISH

*1H6 2.1 Does Charles lose it? How does Joan assuage him?*

1H6 2.3 THE TEMPORARY CAPTURE OF THE COUNTESS

*1H6 2.4 Any physical violence amongst the lords?*

*1H6 3.1 Any physical violence amongst the lords?*

1H6 3.1 MORE SKIRMISHES AMONGST G'S/W'S MEN BUT WITH PEBBLES!!!

1H6 3.2 MULTIPLE EXCURSIONS

*1H6 3.2 Do Joan and/or her cronies throw/drop anything at/on their enemies below?*

1H6 4.6 EXCURSIONS INCLUDING TALBOT RESCUING HIS SON

1H6 4.7 MORE EXCURSIONS; RIP TALBOT & SON

1H6 5.2 OH. LOOK. MORE FUCKING EXCURSIONS.

*M4M 5.1 Do the officers have to restrain Isabella?*

*M4M 5.1 Attempts to silence Lucio's ejaculations and later apprehend the disguised duke*

M4M 5.1 LUCIO IS CAPTURED WHEN FAILING TO SNEAK AWAY

MORE 1.2 LIFTER'S JUDICIAL HEARING

*More 2.1 On this week's episode of The Idiot Apprentice™…*

*More 2.2 Show any of the rioting/arsons?*

*More 2.2 Attacks on Sherwin's party?*

MORE 2.4 MORE NEGOTIATES WITH THE RIOTERS

MORE 3.1 TIME TO HANG SOME XENOPHOBES!!!

MORE 3.2 THE RUFFIAN AND THE HAIRCUT

MORE 4.1 THE MARRIAGE OF WIT AND WISDOM

MORE 4.2 THE ARREST OF ROCHESTER

MORE 4.4 ROCHESTER LED TO PRISON

MORE 4.5 THE ARREST OF MORE

MORE 5.1 MORE LED TO PRISON

*More 5.3 How severely does More's family plead?*

MORE 5.4 MORE PREPARES FOR EXECUTION

*MWW 1.1 Does any of the verbal onslaught become physical?*

MWW 3.1 THE DISARMAMENT OF DR CAIUS AND SIR HUGH EVANS

MWW 3.3 Falstaff hiding in the laundry basket is dropped; *on stage or off stage?*

MWW 5.5 FALSTAFF IS PINCHED AND BURNED BY 'FAIRIES'

*R2 3.1 Bushy and Greene are sentenced to death*

*R2 4.1 Most of the court throw down their gauntlets*

*R2 5.2 The Yorks are a bit much*

*R2 5.3 The Yorks are a bit much, part deux*

R3 1.1 OFF TO PRISON WITH CLARENCE

R3 1.2 THE WOOING OF LADY ANNE

*R3 1.3 The Dick & Maggie Variety Hour*

*R3 2.1 Richard continues shitstirring; Edward gets totes magotes angry*

*R3 2.2 An interruption during a very special episode of The Biggest Griever™*

*R3 3.1 Just to be clear – the little princes are assholes*

R3 3.3 RIVERS/VAUGHAN/GREY ESCORTED TO THEIR DEATHS

R3 3.4 RICHARD ORDERS STRAWBERRIES AND A BEHEADING

*R3 4.1 Desperate women v useless men*

*R3 4.2 Show the murder of Anne?*

*R3 4.3 What else does Richard do besides striking a messenger?*

R3 5.1 BUCKINGHAM LED TO EXECUTION

*R3 5.3 How does Richard engage in terms of paranoia and a desire to inspire/terrify?*

R3 5.4 EXCURSIONS

*R3 5.4 Um … so what happens with the corpse? (Asking for a sadist.)*

# About the Text

Almost half of the forty plays examined in these two volumes went unprinted in Shakespeare's lifetime –*All's Well That Ends Well; Antony and Cleopatra; As You Like It; The Comedy of Errors; Coriolanus; Cymbeline; Henry 6 Part 1; Henry 8; Julius Caesar; King John; Macbeth; Measure for Measure; The Taming of the Shrew; The Tempest; Timon of Athens; Twelfth Night; The Two Gentlemen of Verona* and *The Winter's Tale* had their initial printings in the First Folio of 1623, seven years after the playwright's death.

The First Folio was compiled by actors who worked with Shakespeare and his contemporaries. Whilst far from grammatical perfection, it is the least abused by editors of the texts we possess. We therefore have chosen to present the first-printed texts virtually unedited. Lineation, capitalisations, ever-changing character prefixes, and the majority of (seemingly) strange spellings remain intact. The protracted debate over whether or not these inconsistencies are clues for the actors in regard to characterisation at any given moment is not the focus of our book, but we will point out some instances of note as they occur. If you're looking for a deeper dive into First Folio technique, we recommend Neil Freeman's *Shakespeare's First Texts*.

For plays published prior to the First Folio, we may use excerpts from earlier printings, but generally still lean towards the First Folio. Plays such as *Hamlet*, *Lear*, and *Othello* conflict wildly from one version to another, and we will take some of those differences into consideration.

There is no telling what text you will be saddled with in rehearsal and, if you are a director, we beg you to stay away from those printings pillaged by editors who have never once stepped foot in a rehearsal room. These plays were written to be performed by actors, not 'corrected' by academics.

Finally, formal stage directions are incredibly rare in these early texts. For those directions which are violence-related, we will **embolden and colour them red**.

# About our Interjections

One of us will chime in every so often to share his individual thoughts, statements which will not necessarily be endorsed by the other. You will see these bracketed, colour-coded, and italicised with our respective initials – SD or JK. [*SD: Like this?!?!*] [*JK: Yeah, they get it.*] [*SD: Hamlet sucks.*] [*JK: I don't endorse your statement.*] We've chosen this device because we will sometimes disagree. That is a good thing. This book is not designed to give you the 'right' answer, as no such thing exists; we want you to think outside the box. We will simulate some healthy(ish) dialogue to have in the rehearsal room. Have these discussions yourself and figure out what works best for you. [*JK: Also, you shouldn't think that the last person to speak is some kind of winner.*] [*SD: Ignore him.*]

# Introduction

Research is a wake-up call. Drama can be a kind of dream, a kind of sleep, where we imitate art rather than life, believe in fiction's received ideas, fall for Hollywood's view of the world. Look at a street brawl: it's messy, the blows mostly miss, those that land rarely hurt or stun; it's nothing like what some fight directors encourage actors to do, delivering and taking blows with absurd grace – stylized, macho and pain-free – an insult to the victims of real violence. Look at real grief, too, or real drunkenness – it's not what you generally see on stage. We actors frequently copy previous interpretations of human behavior rather than the real thing. Research takes you back to the truth.

Antony Sher

*[JK: After working out all the choreography for the murder of Richard 2…] [SD: not my production, so don't blame me…] [JK: the director said that the knife didn't look real enough. There are plenty of stage weapons out there that don't resemble real ones, so … no worries. After being shown a variety of options, the director was convinced that only a real, sharp knife would do. All the dangers of such a decision were explained to him, yet he continued to insist. He had decided to make it 'safe' by fitting Richard with a wooden board over his chest, so that the knife wouldn't penetrate his flesh. After telling the director this would be too dangerous, the fight director was released from contract. The danger was explained to the producer (who thought it was fine!), who made sure the fight director's name was removed from the programme and website, and that there was no way to trace it to him. Before leaving, the fight director spoke privately with the actors about why they should not do this, even if they got fired over it (advice which obviously went unheeded). Several performances went along without incident, and the director likely felt fine and dandy about his decision. Then, the second week started. On one particular evening, the wooden board shifted slightly under Richard's costume. Compounded with the fact that Exton was slightly off-target that night, Richard was stabbed for real. He was rushed to the hospital for surgery. The actor lived to see another day; the show did not.]*

A writer utilises violence – like song or dance – in moments where the story requires more than just words. But addressing *how* the violence will be staged tends either to be neglected or utterly gratuitous. Both choices serve to separate the audience from the story, and kill the whole venture. The example above illustrates safety being thrown out the window, in a sorry exchange for a reality that ultimately is meaningless. How do we make the violence seem real, and evoke visceral reactions within the audience, whilst also doing so safely?

The answer rests in <u>approaching violence the same way we do scenework</u>. The addition of violence, or ballet, or a musical number may appear to be an altogether-separate beast from the basic text. Particularly to those who think poetry and violence are mutually exclusive concepts. But the plays of William Shakespeare seek to engage audiences with all of the characters' blood, tears, sweat, and guts. These works are not flowery poems meant to be mumbled in a classroom, or declaimed histrionically in frilly costumes. There is nothing light and fluffy about *rape* and *murder's rages*, or *carving* someone as a dish fit for the gods, or fighting till one's *flesh be hacked* from one's bones. As in subpar musical theatre productions when actors 'stop to sing', in ill-conceived Shakespeare productions they 'stop to fight'.

Making matters more complicated is the ambiguity (and sometimes complete lack) of formal stage directions. Modern texts typically possess clear directions whenever violence is to occur in the action, but playscripts were different four centuries ago. Such denotations were infrequent and inconsistent in Elizabethan and Jacobean printings. If you possess the text of a Shakespeare play with loads of overtly notated stage directions, it is usually because editors decided to insert them, not because Shakespeare or the first publishers of his plays put them on the page.

This book aims to catalogue and clarify each moment of violence demanded by the playwright, as well as highlight myriad instances of potential violence – implicitly or explicitly suggested – throughout the canon. With each chapter, we will reveal how the violence is not separate from the action, but borne out of it – essential for the story to move forward.

Deciding which potential moments to pursue in production comes down to the actors involved, how they match up with one another, and what types of violence exist within the vocabulary of the play and the world of any given production – specifically, yours. The potential violence we will examine is not appropriate for all productions or combinations of scene partners. We're here to question and inspire, rather than provide catch-all solutions. Actors, directors, fight directors, and intimacy consultants should work together to find the most effective way for their production to communicate the playwright's story to an audience.

It is rare that theatre, television, and film professionals spend a substantial amount of time considering how to incorporate violence as an essential part of performance. Many directors find the violence difficult to deal with, so they may procrastinate because they don't have 'the answers'. But this is central to the fight director's job – presenting the director with different options to tell the story through violence. All an actor or director need do is express their impulse in that moment, and a solid fight director will offer several options to convey it. [*JK: As a fight director with Art of Combat and NYC Combat for Screen and Stage, part of training new fight directors is getting them ready to do everything they need to do with only two hours of rehearsal. Often, the fights in a show are addressed as an afterthought – a fight director (if one was even budgeted) is asked to come in after the show has already been cast and commenced rehearsals, just to get that pesky moment or two of violence out of the way. Once, for an off-Broadway show no less, I didn't get the call until tech week. And, even then, I was only given an hour to prepare the fight.*]

You'll notice we keep saying fight *directors* and not fight *choreographers*. Yes, there may be an instance or two or seven like the above example, in which the producer or director will just expect someone to show up and force-feed fight choreography down the actors' throats. Whilst we may sympathise with this situation, and this publication will still be helpful to you, it is virtually impossible in this scenario for the actors to avoid pausing their character to fight. Ideally, there will be a fight *director*, involved from day one, who is as much a participant in the process as the actors, directors, designers, and technicians. You will get the most out of what we have to offer here if this is the type of process you and your collaborators pursue.

As you work with your colleagues in rehearsal to carefully select each moment of violence, and how to approach it – from the biggest battle down to the smallest slap, bite, ear-pull, kick, or spit – always consider the following criteria (distilled from *A History of Stage Swordplay* by Dr John Lennox):

• **Will it fit seamlessly within the parameters established by the playwright, as well as this particular production's vocabulary?**
  Kate and Petruchio's first meeting is obviously a physical scene, but individual directors will interpret it in different ways. Whatever you may feel Shakespeare calls for here, it certainly is not a five-minute sword fight [*JK: as I have once seen it performed*], unless the director has set the play in Amazonia, and wants to use this opportunity to show the audience Kate's badass fighting skills [*SD: ohdeargodno*]. Yes, the combat must be in accordance with the concept of the production. But, whatever this is, make certain that scenes containing violence build properly to the moment where a character has reached the ultimatum of 'fight or flight' and chooses *fight*. Consider the death of Cinna the Poet – the other actors typically taunt Cinna verbally, then kill him. This jump from A to Z doesn't enhance any production, it merely gets the violence over with. Now consider why the scene is part of the play – it is imperative that the audience witness an anxious and potentially lethal mob swarming in on Cinna merely because he shares a name with one of the assassins. Some productions accomplish this part of the equation but fail to consider the next building block of reality – whilst these people want to rip Cinna to shreds, no one wants to throw the first punch. Once someone finally does, they all join in and attack Cinna. But the suspense could – and should – be terrifying. The scene must realistically build towards the violence. Before, during, and after the violence, each character must react truthfully, so that the play's throughline (and that of each character) proceeds unabated.

- **Will it tell a story itself whilst helping to push the main story forward?**
  Each moment of violence has a dramatic structure with which you are already familiar – a beginning, middle, climax, and denouement. If approached this way, the violence will deepen the audience's understanding of each character, not suspend it. In the demise of Cinna the Poet, the audience have learned *through the violence itself* more about the fickle nature of the Roman mob. All of the microscopic moment-to-moment focus on the language during tablework should be applied to the violence just as diligently. Ask after each violent event – what do you know about the characters and their stories now that you didn't know before?

- **Will it be safe?**
  The fight director should work with the performers to ensure that all violence can be performed safely, and that it is repeatable from performance to performance. If it's not, then don't do it. There is never a reason to have real violence (even just a slap) on stage. However – and we cannot stress this enough – only those involved in the production need know the fight is safe. There are increasing numbers of professionals and amateurs alike who believe that the audience must know that the character is in danger but the actor is safe. This is ridiculous. There is not a single moment in production when the audience should be thinking about the safety of the actor. If the audience are considering the difference between the actor's safety and their character's safety, your staging has taken the audience out of the play, you have lost them, and everyone should bloody well go home. Again, *only those involved in the production need know the fight is safe.* Please let the audience fear for these people. This is the playwright's intention. [*SD: I know this because I asked him.*] The best way to ensure the fight is safe and well performed is to practise slowly at first. You've been told 'practice makes perfect', but this is incomplete; only '*perfect* practice makes perfect'. Practice, by itself, merely cements bad habits. If you practise slowly at first, and ensure safe distance whilst using the correct angles to hide the magic, you will be able to speed up the fight gradually throughout the rehearsal process, and eventually get it up to performance speed. Almost everyone wants to go faster before the fights are ready. That's because it feels 'more real' for the actor when you go faster, but it inevitably looks worse. The audience aren't giving their time or money for you to masturbate; the audience want and deserve a thrilling fight in a terrific show. Practise slowly and you'll learn quickly; practise quickly and you won't get beyond mediocre, if even that far. [*JK: Keeping everyone safe involves a great deal of partnering. One of the things I love about staged violence is that it requires 100 per cent cooperative energy to sell the illusion of conflict. Without significant and clear verbal communication throughout the rehearsal process, fight partners will never be able to develop the non-verbal communication necessary to sell the action. Everything we do requires the fighter to know what is coming and, at no point, should they be surprised. There will be more horror stories about this later.*]

- **Will it be well-acted?**

  It may seem we're opening up a can of worms with this particular question (which sounds result-oriented, and just begs for a judgmental rehearsal atmosphere), but the question is simple and reasonable. A 10-year-old can distinguish between good acting and bad. [*SD: Which is why student-matinee performances always reduce weak actors into puddles of abject humiliation, and one reason Bertolt Brecht invited children to view dress rehearsals.*] As with non-violent acting moments, the actions and reactions in the violent acting moments must be *appropriate*. The actors need to portray the pain involved, and how much or little it has affected their characters. More importantly, the actors must maintain their characterisation during the fight. If the actors drop character simply to execute paint-by-numbers choreography, the audience will never buy it. Nor should they. The leaps in suspension of disbelief already required of the audience are great enough without you asking them to pretend that rubbish acting is acceptable. Apply the same questions you would to moments of non-violence – *what* is the action? *Why* is it taking place? *When? Where? How?*

- **Will it follow the laws of physics?**

  Hopefully, your audience are not consciously thinking about this during performance. But if there is a punch to the right side of the face, and the victim spins in the wrong direction, a fundamental law of physics is broken. That's an obvious one, but even the most minimal violent act must obey these laws, or the audience will be pulled out of the play to process why it seemed incorrect. We acknowledge certain stories favour different laws of physics, but – once established by your production – the laws of your specific universe must be maintained.

- **Will it entertain?**

  A solid stage fight needs to hold the audience's attention, keep them involved in the story, and envelop them in the illusion. If it fails to do so, it is almost always due to violation of one or more of the principles listed above, which all are dependent on one another for success. Conversely, the possibility does exist of a fight being so good that it eclipses the production. This also will result in ripping the audience out of the story. When fights overshadow the rest of the production, this typically is due to weak acting, directing, dialogue, or an over-zealous fight choreographer. Rarely does a production have incredible acting, superb direction, and an excellent script, yet *still* get overtaken by phenomenal fight scenes. Our focus covers the works of Shakespeare, so you can depend on excellent scripts already being taken care of for you. [*SD: Well … most of them.*] This leaves *you* to provide acting, directing, and fighting worthy of the playwright's challenge.

A note regarding intimacy – whilst this book is not meant to be an exhaustive analysis of all the sexual situations in Shakespeare, those potential moments might overlap with violence. Even if they do not, we will examine many of them in these pages, as they still pose safety issues and bodily contact, and should be carefully staged. Until recently, if productions gave a damn about creating a safe environment for actors to explore not just potential violence but also sexual situations, the options on hand were to keep a closed rehearsal room with only the cast members involved, to have careful supervision by stage management, and to bring in the fight director in case the lines between sex and violence blur. In the last few years, however, a new resource has been introduced with greater frequency – intimacy consultants (sometimes intimacy coaches or intimacy directors). We encourage you to bring them aboard, as they are well versed in getting the most out of your actors during scenework whilst also ensuring comfortability and professionalism. If your production is outside the jurisdiction of union rules and/or you simply do not have the budget to employ an intimacy consultant, please at least take the steps outlined above so you can avoid traumatising your actors. Even if – like some producers – you have no moral compass, you will still want to avoid a lawsuit.

Finally, the onus is not only on a fight director or intimacy consultant to consider the checklist above; it is everyone's responsibility. If you truly collaborate and listen to each other's impulses and instincts, then the violence (physical, emotional, sexual, or otherwise) will be inseparable from the story, and help carry it forward to its inevitable and terrifying conclusion.

With this in mind, turn the page and let's get our hands dirty. (Consensually.)

*SD & JK*

Part 1

# Pesky Pagans

*David Garrick as King Lear.* James MacArdell (after Benjamin Wilson), 1761. (*Harris Brisbane Dick Fund, 1917*)

# Chapter 1

# King Lear

*''Tis worse than murther / To do upon respect such violent outrage.'* – Lear (2.4)

Imagine a senile and emotionally unstable old ruler, who cares about only one of his children, wastes taxpayer dollars going around the room asking everyone to declare how much they love him, and then proceeds to tear his country to pieces.

We may be writing this book in the United States in 2020, but the tyrant to whom we allude is a mythological king dating back three millennia, and his name is Lear.

Undoubtedly the greatest of Shakespeare's achievements *[JK: You're thinking of Chapter 3 – Hamlet.] [SD: I can assure you I am not.] [JK: Not even close to the brilliance of A Midsummer Night's Dream either!] [SD: The one where they drug a bunch of kids, and psychosexually manipulate them? Oh, yeah. Real brilliance. Surprised Polanski hasn't directed it yet.]*, this play contains tripping, stabbing, eye-gouging, myocardial infarction, poisoning, hanging, and is the perfect way for us to begin our adventure, staging Shakespeare's violence.

## Act 1  Scene 1[1]

The playwright drops us right into the action. We are immediately presented with the following questions, to which the author will never provide the answers: what has Lear's reign been like thus far? Given that he is 'fourscore and upward', how long has he been in power? When did he have his children? And where is their mother? Or multiple mothers? Asking questions like these during early tablework for your production will distinguish it from so many others.

Conclusions about what Lear has been like as ruler up until now do not immediately present themselves. At first blush, his decision to divide the kingdom and split it equally amongst his children – so that he can retire, and they can rule their subjects with fresh eyes – might seem clear-headed. But consider this exchange from his eldest and middle daughters, after the division of the kingdom:

> *Gon.* You see how full of changes his age is the obseruation we
> haue made of it hath not bin little; hee alwaies loued our sister
> most, and with what poore iudgement hee hath now cast her
> off, appeares too grosse.
> *Reg.* Tis the infirmitie of his age, yet hee hath euer but slen-
> derly knowne himselfe.

> *Gono.* The best and soundest of his time hath bin but rash,
> then must we looke to receiue from his age not alone the imper-
> fection of long ingrafted condition, but therwithal vnruly way-
> wardnes, that infirme and cholericke yeares bring with them.

Let's rewind. Consider some other questions that might arise in your staging. As mentioned in the Introduction, it is rare that Shakespeare or his contemporaries would provide stage directions for all the violence, explicit or implicit, and it is our task to explore possibilities when the stakes are so great, and this many people in one room – with weapons – experience increasing levels of aggravation. In the opening passages, ask if your Lear is not just a psychological tormentor but also a physical one. Does he beat the help? His children? The Earl of Kent? Does Lear send the Earl of Gloucester out of the room as a show of respect to the King of France and Duke of Burgundy or, for a more sinister reason, in an attempt to avoid any would-be interference with the 'darker purpose'? The chemistry of the room is constantly changing; each actor must gauge these changes, and adjust accordingly. And not just the principal performers. How do the guards react throughout? This detail may seem trivial, but it is a clear and efficient way to communicate to the audience whether we are in the presence of a brutal tyrant, a friendly fella who prefers to pick flowers in the garden and keep to himself, or something else entirely. The guards' reaction during the banishment of Kent will tell a specific story – if they are surprised, and slow to move in escorting Kent out, then Lear's behaviour is novel; if you have a Lear that moves to beat Kent, and the guards stand by idly, then the king acts like this quite often. The permutations are endless; a thorough and specific exploratory process is what will make your production sing. When we ask you to *see Glossary – Ensemble Readiness* throughout the book, this is the kind of questioning we want you to explore in rehearsal, and bring to life in performance.

Having received saccharine answers from Goneril and Regan on the question of love, Lear then turns to Cordelia – his 'joy' – but she has no desire to stick to the script, and what follows from Lear are the ramblings of someone who has spent their life in power and never been told 'no'.

> *Lear.* But goes this with thy heart?
> *Cord.*                                    I good my Lord.
> *Lear.* So yong and so vntender.
> *Cord.* So yong my Lord and true.
> *Lear.* Well let it be so, thy truth then be thy dower,
> For by the sacred radience of the Sunne,
> The mistresse of *Heccat*, and the might,
> By all the operation of the orbs,
> From whome we doe exsist and cease to be
> Heere I disclaime all my paternall care,
> Propinquitie and property of blood,

And as a stranger to my heart and me
Hould thee from this for euer, the barbarous *Scythyan*,
Or he that makes his generation Messes to gorge his appetite
Shall bee as well neighbour'd, pittyed and relieued
As thou my sometime daughter.
   *Kent*.                Good my Liege.
   *Lear*. Peace *Kent*, come not between the Dragon & his wrath,
I lou'd her most, and thought to set my rest
On her kind nurcery, hence and auoide my sight?
So be my graue my peace as here I giue,
Her fathers heart from her, call *France*, who stirres?
Call *Burgundy*, *Cornwell*, and *Albany*,
With my two daughters dower digest this third,
Let pride, which she cals plainnes, marrie her:
I doe inuest you iointly in my powre,
Preheminence, and all the large effects
That troope with Maiestie, our selfe by monthly course
With reseruation of an hundred knights,
By you to be sustayn'd, shall our abode
Make with you by due turnes, onely we still retaine
The name and all the additions to a King,
The sway, reuenue, execution of the rest,
Beloued sonnes be yours, which to confirme,
This Coronet part betwixt you.
   *Kent*.             Royall *Lear*,
Whom I haue euer honor'd as my King,
Loued as my Father, as my maister followed,
As my great patron thought on in my prayers.
   *Lear*. The bow is bent & drawen make from the shafte.
   *Kent*. Let it fall rather,
Though the forke inuade the region of my heart,
Be *Kent* vnmannerly when *Lear* is man,
What wilt thou doe ould man, think'st thou that dutie
Shall haue dread to speake, when power to flatterie bowes,
To plainnes honours bound when Maiesty stoops to folly,
Reuerse thy doome, and in thy best consideration
Checke this hideous rashnes, answere my life
My iudgement, thy yongest daughter does not loue thee least,
Nor are those empty harted whose low, sound
Reuerbs no hollownes.
   *Lear*.       *Kent* on thy life no more.
   *Kent*. My life I neuer held but as a pawne
To wage against thy enemies, nor feare to lose it

*(possible 'springboarding', in which Lear interrupts, and they share the third metric foot)*

Thy safty being the motiue.
   *Lear*. Out of my sight.
   *Kent*. See better *Lear* and let me still remaine,
The true blanke of thine eye.
   *Lear*. Now by Appollo,
   *Kent*. Now by Appollo King
thou swearest thy Gods in vaine.
   *Lear*. Vassall, recreant.

*See Glossary – Grabs; Strikes.*

Whether or not Lear is already cognisant of his 'crawle toward death'[2] as not just a physical decline but also a mental one is up to you, but Kent has concluded that Lear is succumbing to a 'foule disease'. And we mentioned that 'the best and soundest of his time hath bin but rash'. The question here then: what might occur when rashness meets madness? There is room for violence; Kent has stepped over a line – no matter how well-meaning – and Lear's repeated interruptions signal impatience. Whether this is a quiet argument [*JK: and why make that choice?*] or a loud exchange for all to hear, one possibility might be for Lear to strike Kent with the back of a hand on 'Vassall, recreant'. [*JK: If it is strong enough to fell Kent to his knees, you get a pretty little picture of Lear hovering over Kent as he pleads with Lear to see reason.*] [*SD: Leave the stage composition to me, ya sonofabitch.*] [*JK: I direct, too.*] [*SD: I directed and played Lear (in rotating repertory with* Coriolanus, Timon of Athens, *and* Henry 5, *directing and playing the titular roles in each) when I was 21.*] [*JK: You just wanted to say 'titular'. Also … 21? What is wrong with you?*] [*SD: Let's just say that classical actor-managers are ridiculous; Gielgud played his first Lear at 22, and I was feeling competitive. Also, it's my favourite play. Before Jared so rudely interrupted me, as Kent does Lear, I was going to say that I'd love to have knocked my Kent (the forceful, yet fluffy, Adam T. Perkins) to the ground, but opted to use the 'allegeance' card, so he would bow down merely from the force of my invocation. You can do this, or Jared's idea, or maybe a compromise – draw a weapon, or signal your guards to do so. Up to you. The point is to have these discussions, and figure out what works best for your production.*]

   *Lear*. Heare me, on thy allegeance heare me?
Since thou hast sought to make vs breake our vow,
Which we durst neuer yet; and with straied pride,
To come betweene our sentence and our powre,
Which nor our nature nor our place can beare,
Our potency made good, take thy reward,
Foure dayes we doe allot thee for prouision,
To shield thee from diseases of the world,
And on the fift to turne thy hated backe
Vpon our kingdome, if on the tenth day following,
Thy banisht truncke be found in our dominions,

*(a question mark was sometimes interchangeable with an exclamation point, as Lady Macbeth will demonstrate in Chapter 4)*

The moment is thy death, away, by *Iupiter*
This shall not be reuokt.
　　*Kent.* Why fare thee well king, since thus thou wilt appeare,
Friendship liues hence, and banishment is here,
The Gods to their protection take the maide,
That rightly thinks, and hast most iustly said,
And your large speeches may your deedes approue,
That good effects may spring from wordes of loue:
Thus *Kent* O Princes, bids you all adew,
Heele shape his old course in a countrie new.

Kent often delivers this to the assembled masses, and gracefully exits. But what if Lear has his guards forcibly remove Kent when he continues to overstep? He might exclaim those final lines whilst being dragged out.

If you opted for backhanding Kent, it may follow logically that something similar happens to Cordelia. If not, you still should contemplate the threat of violence here, an impulse to make things physical may manifest, but be held back from execution. [*SD: Again, I avoided physical contact. Of any kind. I would not even look at my Cordelia (the mercifully easy-to-carry-when-dead Jaime West) since my version of Lear withheld affection as a punishment. Your production may choose a different path, and that's okay because we are – each of us – the Flying Spaghetti Monster's precious meatball children.*] [*JK: How many glasses of scotch in are you right now, dude? We're only on the first chapter!*] [*SD: One. If I refill the same glass, it always counts as one.*]

The room is incredibly tense throughout, and the verse reflects this. Instead of the 'mighty line' of standard iambic pentameter (de-DUM, de-DUM, de-DUM, de-DUM, de-DUM) made famous by Christopher Marlowe, Shakespeare is now at the height of his powers (writing *King Lear* during a plague quarantine, whilst we pen this lesser work during the COVID-19 spring holiday), transforming the linguistic equivalent of classical music into jazz. Reviewing the scansion is amongst the mandatory first tasks for actors and directors. This is also a part of ensemble readiness – what do the shifts in rhythm and syntax tell you about the energy in the room at any given time? We'll come back to the experimentation with syncopation later on, especially in relation to Lear's final lines before death. #spoilers

## Act 1  Scene 2

*See Glossary – Grabs (maybe); Strikes (unlikely).*

It's fine to hand over the letter just because Gloucester asked. But, if Edmund [*JK: I just call both brothers Ed because I can never keep them straight*]. [*SD: \*insert Grindr joke here\**] really wants to sell that he loves his brother, it would be better to make the letter harder for Gloucester to obtain. We're not talking about a knock-down brawl, unless your production's Gloucester is naturally abusive; a small struggle is fine. [*JK: For example,*

*Gloucester can go for it and Edmund pulls it back; then Gloucester reaches again, and gets it, but Edmund holds on; then Gloucester has to use both hands to pry it from 'unwilling' Edmund. If you choose to have this struggle, perform your usual checks to ensure that it is safe; it's easy for an elbow to fly and hit someone in the jaw when struggling like this.] [SD: I'd propose here that Gloucester or Edmund might get a paper cut, but should save deployment of that comedic gem until Chapter 10 – Henry 4 Part 1 (2.3). Something to which we can all look forward, if you're still reading this book by that time.]*

## Act 1  Scene 4

*See Glossary – Ensemble Readiness; Falls; Grabs (maybe); Strikes (maybe).*

We are informed that one of Goneril's gentlemen was struck by Lear before the scene begins. What will he do here? Is Lear violent towards Albany? Other servants? The fool? How are the knights physically 'riotous'? Goneril gives us an idea later in the scene, and very well may be a victim of Lear's physical abuse during the sterility speech. These questions are for you to decide, but the playwright has determined, at the very least, that Kent (disguised as Caius) will trip Oswald.

> *Lear.* No more of that, I haue noted it, goe you and tell my
> daughter, I would speake with her, goe you cal hither my foole,
> O you sir, you sir, come you hither, who am I sir?
> *Steward.* My Ladies Father.
> *Lear.* My Ladies father, my Lords knaue, you horeson dog,
> you slaue, you cur.
> *Stew.* I am none of this my Lord,
> I beseech you pardon me.
> *Lear.* Doe you bandie lookes with me you rascall?
> *Stew.* Ile not be struck my Lord,

Lear must take a swing at Oswald to warrant the latter's line. You decide whether this is a swing and a miss (either because Oswald is capable enough to avoid it, or Lear is not particularly skilled), or if the hit lands (Oswald is not generally considered to be a skilled fighter, as will be evidenced later in the play, so it may as well be set up now). Depending on the choices you made earlier for Lear, he could start swinging on 'my Lords knaue'. This would mean Oswald absorbs multiple hits during the speech, and finally ejaculates 'I'll not be struck'. [*JK: You can tell Seth wrote this bit because he's the only person I know who would use the dated version of 'ejaculates'.*] Your decision here will highlight the tyranny, the comedy, or both. As always, consider each link as part of a chain of decisions – Oswald could be lucky enough to avoid the blow from Lear, only to be tripped by Kent.

The knights also play a part in this: are they supportive of Lear's violence? Do they participate? If you're highlighting Lear's toxic masculinity (a major theme of his five-act journey), the knights could be holding Oswald, even pushing him towards Lear, *etc.*

*Kent*. Nor tript neither, you base football player.
*Lear*. I thanke thee fellow, thou seru'st me, and ile loue thee.
*Kent*. Come sir ile teach you differences, away, away, if
you will measure your lubbers length a gaine, tarry, but away,
you haue wisedome.
*Lear*. Now friendly knaue I thanke thee, their's earnest of
thy seruice.

Kent's trip can be a small action that causes Oswald to stumble, or a big one that puts him on his ass/face. If you have an Oswald who can safely take the fall, go for it. It will give Lear more to work with in forming an opinion of 'Caius', insofar as he is useful not only for security detail but also entertainment.

Further violence may occur as Kent ushers Oswald away. If you're going for the laugh, a chase could facilitate this. A note of caution regarding your decision-making process: if Kent attacks Oswald *ad nauseam*, there is a risk of damaging Kent's dramatic function as the conscience of the play. Walk this tightrope by balancing out Kent's violence with Oswald's deserving of it.

## Act 2  Scene 1

Performances in Shakespeare's time were typically in modern dress, but would utilise period-appropriate weapons, armour, or costume pieces to lend a flavour of history to the proceedings. There are few productions of Lear set circa 800 BC because everyone has a gimmick these days. [*JK: Or … \*gulp\* … 'concept'. (Sorry. Sometimes my inside voice becomes my outside voice.)*] [*SD: I only have an outside voice.*] Shakespeare's works are often produced with some kind of ulterior motive – directors think they have something to say, and proceed to shoehorn the play into serving that purpose, tending to make the production one-dimensional and otherwise poorly conceived. There are occasional exceptions. [*JK: I'll talk about one in* Romeo and Juliet.] [*SD: Which is part of* Volume Two. *Nice work selling pre-orders, pal!*] Your production may have switchblades or automatic pistols rather than period weapons, so take care your Edmund wounds himself with a sensical implement from the era in which you set the play. In 2.2, his weapon is described as a rapier. The earliest references to rapiers are in the late fifteenth and early sixteenth centuries. You can go with one of those, or just consider 'rapier' synonymous with 'sword', and choose something specific to your production's setting. If you do go circa 800 BC, note that ironworking techniques reached Britain around this time, and were used for making tools and weapons. This took bronze (a softer metal) into a realm of new possibilities. Swords continued being made in a leaf shape, but of now-stronger iron. The swords were either flange-hilted or full-hilted. Spears and knives followed a similar trajectory.

*See Glossary – Blood; Draws.*

Here is an opportunity to reveal more about Edgar's character, merely by how he draws his weapon: if smooth and effortless, this shows skill from training with that weapon; if awkward and jumbled, then he spent more time reading than fighting. The weapon may not even get out of Edgar's sheath, adding more urgency to Edmund's 'flie brother flie'. If you do opt for a novice Edgar, you'll have to suss this out by the fifth act, when he manages to beat Edmund in combat. (This doesn't give Edgar the status he attains by the end of the play, so it's probably wise to have him be at least moderately skilled.)

We'll incessantly revisit the concept of violence revealing character. Here, we learn more about Edmund based on how he cuts himself. Does he really commit to the injury, with a slice to the flank in order to ensure Gloucester thinks horribly of Edgar; or does Edmund opt for a superficial wound, because he can't bring himself to cut himself too deeply? Furthermore, what is his martial awareness? [*JK: I would have him take a cut to the middle of the left forearm, near the ulna. This is a good defensive wound since most right-handed people will cut from their right to left, which would deliver this blow to Edmund's left arm if he held it up to defend himself. This is an area where the damage is superficial – something a trained fighter would know.*] Whichever damage you select, ensure it is something the actor can play for the next few acts. It doesn't serve your production for Edmund to stab himself in the leg, unless there is some reason you want him limping around like Richard 3 for the rest of the performance. [*JK: Never allow your actors to forget to play their wound/pains throughout the show; it's like watching* My Fair Lady *and they drop the British dialects to sing the songs.*]

Blood is referenced several times in the scene. You can get away with just a little if the wound is superficial. If you want to avoid a blood pack, a bloody handkerchief hidden in Edmund's pocket can be pulled upstage, out of the audience's sightline, until Edmund turns around and the handkerchief is on the wound. (If you want to show the blood coming from the wound, *see Glossary – Blood Packs*. Alternatively, you can rent a knife/dagger that is rigged with a small pump, which will make it appear like blood is running from the wound in real time.)

## Act 2  Scene 2

*See Glossary – Arrests; Binds; Draws; Ensemble Readiness; Falls; Knees; Strikes.*

We know from Oswald's later report that he was tripped from behind, and railed at on the ground by Kent. [*JK: This could start with a push, which makes Oswald fall. In this position, Kent can advance on Oswald, who does a crabwalk to get away. In one of my favourite versions, Kent took off his belt to start giving Oswald a spanking. Oswald eventually got up, and Kent started to chase. Something like this lets the actors use the entire stage, and adds comedy to the scene. The choice of a flexible weapon will give you a variety of ways to attack: Kent could be trying to whip and snap the belt like a towel in a locker room; comedically swings and misses; then moves into restraints and chokes, as well. It's important that all this comes across like Kent teaching Oswald a lesson for impertinence, rather than a penchant for mortal harm, thereby reinforcing Kent's desire for justice. Note that your Oswald doesn't have to take this lying down. When ducking a swing, he might try to punch Kent in the guts. Oswald could run to grab the belt, and struggle over possession of it, before either character gets an elbow to face. Things like this will add a bit more of a spine to Oswald, if necessary for your specific production.]*

*Enter Edmund with his rapier drawne, Gloster the Duke and Dutchesse.*

When a gentleman comes out with a weapon drawn, commoners must stop in their tracks. Anything Edmund might perceive as threatening to himself, his father, Cornwall, or Regan could be dealt with by a fatal blow. Either Kent and Oswald see Edmund coming and freeze, or the struggle is staged in such a way that neither Kent nor Oswald holds off fighting. It is also possible only one of them pauses, whilst the other continues fighting, confused by the other's sudden cessation. Oswald, upon realising the threat, would drop to his knees in fealty, but your Kent might forget his Caius guise for a moment, then realise he also needs to kneel. A delay of even a second or two reveals to the audience that Kent is not used to lying.

Kent may have been goading Oswald this entire time into drawing first, so that Kent could claim his own draw was in defence. Or, if fully inside his Caius persona, he may have cut to the chase and drawn. You could toy with a delay in Oswald brandishing his own weapon, due to a combination of nerves and incompetence. Once they are drawn, it's up to you whether Edmund knocks both blades away with his own. *[JK: A bit dramatic, if you ask me, because it makes Edmund look heroic. Not the direction I recommend, but definitely a possibility.] [SD: Isn't he still putting on an act for his father? And it could be a turn-on for Cornwall and Regan, both of whom later confer powers on Edmund.]*

> *Bast.* How now, whats the matter?
> *Kent.* With you goodman boy, and you please come, ile
> fleash you, come on yong maister.
> *Glost.* Weapons, armes, whats the matter here?
> *Duke.* Keepe peace vpon your liues, hee dies that strikes a-
> gaine, what's the matter?

Someone, by this point, has landed at least one strike – Cornwall's line would otherwise be unjustified. You decide whether it was only Kent, or others also, as well as the total number of strikes.

If your production's Regan has the impulse for violence, here is an optimal moment against Kent – a backhand, a push to the ground, a kick whilst he's down. If your Regan is more of a puppetmaster, Cornwall could perform any one of these abuses for his wife's delight, looking to her after each to confirm she is pleased. Your choices here will distinguish between their marriage and the milquetoast remains of Goneril and Albany's.

*Kent.* I am too old to learne, call not your stockes for me,
I serue the King, on whose imployments I was sent to you,
You should doe small respect, shew too bold malice
Against the Grace and person of my maister,
Stopping his messenger.

The stocks were a wooden structure used to punish petty offences. The ankles, wrists, and sometimes neck were secured between movable boards. The imprisonment could range from a few hours to several days. The alleged criminal would be exposed to public abuse, such as rotten food (and other waste) being thrown at them.

Kent can struggle a bit as he is put in the stocks, but not so much he would compromise his disguise. Remember that the actor being abused should always be in control of his safety. The servants will place hands on Kent to make it look like he is struggling, but the actor playing Kent will technically place himself in the stocks. Never use real locks – just mime the locking of the stocks, so the actor playing Kent can get free in case of an emergency, such as your theatre being set on fire because your audience are bored.

Finally, when Lear arrives and sees his man in the stocks, how physical does Lear get with Cornwall and/or Regan and/or Oswald in retaliation?

## Act 3  Scene 4

*See Glossary – Grabs (maybe); Strikes (maybe).*

Lear may attempt to get naked on 'Off, off you Lendings: Come, vnbutton here'. The fool protests verbally, but does he also physically try to stop Lear? Does Edgar intervene? How forcefully does Lear resist any of these attempts?

## Act 3  Scene 7

*See Glossary – Arrests; Binds; Blood; Blood Packs.*

*Enter Gloster brought in by two or three.*

We will mention this more than once throughout our time together – never play the end of the scene at the beginning. Gloucester thinks he will get away with his plan, as hosts and guests were bound by a sacrosanct etiquette. See Chapter 4 – *Macbeth* (1.7). In order to maximise the dramatic and visceral impact of the violence, Gloucester (as the audience's representative in this scene) should not see any of this coming. [*SD: Like the 2016 election results.*] [*JK: Oooo, too soon, it still hurts. Plus, we shouldn't be political in this book.*] [*SD: Why not? It's a British publisher, and they already think Americans are stupid, and we are, and an in-depth study of Shakespeare can't be apolitical, and this sentence is too long.*]

*Corn.* Bind him I say,
*Reg.* Hard hard, O filthie traytor!
*Glost.* Vnmercifull Lady as you are, I am true.
*Corn.* To this chaire bind him, villaine thou shalt find---
*Glost.* By the kind Gods tis most ignobly done, to pluck me
by the beard.
*Reg.* So white and such a Traytor.

Regan will need to pluck some hairs from Gloucester's beard, if you keep this exchange. This is done the same way we perform hair-pulls or ear-grabs – the aggressor will move their hand just in front of the beard, making sure not to actually grab it, and then close their fingers. By pressing against the chin, it will look like Regan has Gloucester's beard. With a jerking motion, and a yelp from Gloucester, the illusion will sell to the audience. For added effect, if the theatre is intimate enough, Regan can palm some hairs from your props department before doing the grab. Regan would then drop the hairs when opening her hand after completing the pull.

*Corn.* Seet shalt thou neuer, fellowes hold the chaire,
Vpon those eyes of thine, Ile set my foote.
*Glost.* He that will thinke to liue till he be old
Giue me some helpe, O cruell, O ye Gods!

[*JK:* See Appendix – Bursting the Bubble. *Cornwall will need to be close to Gloucester's eye, so that the gouging is safer to perform, and also to make it look like Cornwall is really putting his back into this. The best way is to apply pressure to the supraorbital ridge, which is bone and safe.*] [*SD: 'Supraorbital ridge'… seriously?*] [*JK: I let you get away with 'myocardial infarction' several pages back, bro.*] [*SD: As you were.*] [*JK: Moving on, think about petting the eyebrow. If the audience are in close proximity, Cornwall will also need to make it look like his thumb went in. This is done by laying the thumbnail on the eyebrow and pushing on the supraorbital ridge, so the proximal phalanx is in line with the ocular cavity. For your reference, it takes the same amount of pressure to pop an eyeball as it does to penetrate the skin of an orange, which, unsurprisingly, is used by the US military for operant conditioning training drills. When the eye-pop happens, I cannot stress enough the need for blood. The easiest way to do this is for Cornwall to have a blood pack hidden in his hand and, as he pushes on the supraorbital ridge, squeeze the blood pack to pop it. This will spray everywhere unless you make it a directional pack. I personally prefer to make it even more disturbing, to heighten the action. Using his bare hands, or a spoon, you can dig out the first eye. I tend to make a fake eyeball out of hair gel in a small plastic bag. You may be able to hide the fake eyeball in a tray of blood by building it into the chair to which Gloucester is bound. The servants holding the chair are also in position to help Cornwall with the magic. Cornwall can grab the fake eyeball from the tray, as he acts digging out the real one. Once Cornwall has the eyeball in hand, he can drop it on the ground, which will result in a sickening plop. If Cornwall stomps on it, a nice visceral effect should develop in your audience based on the combination of the splatting sound and oozing gel. In one production I worked on, several audience members went white and passed out. The director's husband left the performance, and never saw the second half of the show.]*

    *Reg.* One side will mocke another, tother to.
    *Corn.* If you see vengeance---
    *Seruant.* Hold your hand my Lord
I haue seru'd euer since I was a child
But better seruice haue I neuer done you, than now to bid you hold.
    *Reg.* How now you dogge.
    *Seru.* If you did weare a beard vpon your chin id'e shake it
on this quarrell, what doe you meane?
    *Corn.* My villaine.

***Draw and fight.***

    *Seru.* Why then come on, and take the chance of anger.
    *Reg.* Giue me thy sword, a pesant stand vp thus.

***Shee takes a sword and runs at him behind.***

    *Seruant.* Oh I am slaine my Lord, yet haue you one eye left to
see some mischiefe on him, oh!

*[JK: We should amend 'fight' here to 'scuffle'. I've never understood how this could be a long fight. It would be a rare servant who could match a gentleman, so make sure your servant has the kind of skill to not only mortally wound Cornwall, but also last long enough for Regan to get involved. Maybe this servant was the king's fencing-master's son, or some other backstory of your choosing. Another option is for the servants to be more like personal guards – Gloucester was just brought in 'by two or three', who could be trained fighters.]*

    *Corn.* Least it see more preuent it, out vild Ielly.
Where is thy luster now?

*[JK: See the earlier trick with the directional blood pack for the second eye. If you pulled out the first one, it is a change to gouge out the other, and you can get much more of a blood-spray effect going here.]*

    *Glost.* All darke and comfortles, wher's my sonne *Edmund*?
*Edmund* vnbridle all the sparks of nature, to quit this horred act.
    *Reg.* Out villaine, thou calst on him that hates thee, it was he
that made the ouerture of thy treasons to vs, who is too good to
pittie thee.

*Glost.* O my follies, then *Edgar* was abus'd,
Kind Gods forgiue me that, and prosper him.
    *Reg.* Goe thrust him out at gates, and let him smell his way to
Douer, how ist my Lord? how looke you?
    *Corn.* I haue receiu'd a hurt, follow me Ladie,
Turne out that eyles villaine, throw this slaue vpon
The dungell *Regan*, I bleed apace, vntimely
Comes this hurt, giue me your arme.

*See Glossary – Carries.*

[*JK: There are additional tortures you could include, depending on the kink level of your Cornwall and Regan. In one production, we broke Gloucester's pinkie finger. Add a snapping sound effect, and you'll get a delicious reaction from the audience. Then we ripped off a fingernail with pliers. Use a press-on nail that isn't really adhered to the fingernail and, after ripping it off, use thick blood under the arm of the chair to smear on the real fingernail. Cornwall and Regan made out in between each moment of inflicting pain, and got close to simulating sex on stage.*] [*SD: For my production, Paul Rubin delivered a heart-breaking Gloucester. He decided to immediately follow Regan's direction of 'let him smell his way to Douer'. Regan, the super-terrifying-on-stage-but-perfectly-approachable-off-stage Heather Murdock, kicked Gloucester whilst he was down. Paul collected himself, and soldiered on. I thought it would add to the pathos to put the interval here, in such a way that there would be no applause. As the sightless Gloucester crawled off stage, through the aisle bisecting the house, the lights came up slowly to reveal a paralysed audience.*]

## Act 4  Scene 2

*See Glossary – Grabs (maybe); Strikes (maybe).*

The language may be venomous enough between Goneril and Albany without having to physicalise it, but there are opportunities for a slap, or maybe a blow that Albany avoids. He remains unwilling to physically attack her, but he might stop an attack from her and simply choose not to escalate. [*JK: Albany really should read more of Shakespeare's plays if he thinks Goneril deserves protection because of her 'womans shape'. Go spend a night at Castle Macbeth, and see how that logic works out for ya.*] [*SD: Shakespeare's characters don't know that Shakespeare wrote them.*] [*JK: Wow. That's actually quite deep.*] [*SD: Shut up.*]

## Act 4  Scene 5

There are several ways to play this scene – once the gentlemen seize Lear, he can writhe, wriggle, and flail, so they have a hard time holding on to him. Lear eventually slips free and runs away. Another option is to 'play dead' when they grab him. If he acts old and all 'woe is me', the gentlemen might relax their guard, allowing Lear to break free and run away. If your Lear was a trained soldier, he could use some ancient technique to break free, with the gentlemen standing there in temporary shock before resuming chase. Whichever your choice, ensure the gentlemen remove distance and stay in contact with Lear – this will help avoid injury, whilst making the struggle look realistic. *See Appendix – Bursting the Bubble.*

*Enter Steward.*

*Stew.* A proclamed prize, most happy, that eyles head of thine was framed flesh to rayse my fortunes, thou most vnhappy tray-tor, briefly thy selfe remember, the sword is out that must de-stroy thee.
*Glost.* Now let thy friendly hand put strength enough to't.
*Stew.* Wherefore bould pesant durst thou support a publisht traytor, hence least the infection of his fortune take like hold on thee, let goe his arme?
*Edg.* Chill not let goe sir without cagion.
*Stew.* Let goe slaue, or thou diest.
*Edg.* Good Gentleman goe your gate, let poore voke passe, and chud haue beene swaggar'd out of my life, it would not haue beene so long by a fortnight, nay come not neare the old man, keepe out, cheuore ye, or ile trie whether your coster or my bat-tero be the harder, ile be plaine with you.
*Stew.* Out dunghill.

*They fight.*

*Edg.*  Chill pick your teeth sir, come, no
matter for your foyns.
*Stew.* Slaue thou hast slaine me, villaine take my pursse,
If euer thou wilt thriue, burie my bodie,
And giue the letters which thou find'st about me
To *Edmund* Earle of *Gloster*, seeke him out vpon
The *British* partie, ô vntimely death! death.

*He dies.*

Whilst Oswald has to stop and deal with Edgar, Oswald's primary objective is to kill Gloucester. [*JK: Here's one possible version – Oswald draws and moves to strike down Gloucester but Edgar runs in with a heroic parry, or he beats away the weapon before Gloucester is hit; Edgar grabs Gloucester's right arm with his left hand to move Gloucester to safety; Oswald decides to attack by feinting to Edgar's right, so Oswald can actually get to*

*Gloucester on Edgar's left; Oswald starts that swing but Edgar puts Oswald on point, and they have a standoff (if Oswald kills Gloucester, then Edgar will kill Oswald in the same moment). This is a strong position to show Oswald has had enough, and he can then beat away Edgar's blade on 'Out dunghill'. The fight can be over quickly or be more substantial, depending on the story you want to tell.] [SD: Bear in mind that your choices here will add to or subtract from the suspense in the climactic battle with Edmund in the next act.] [JK: To be done quickly, Oswald simply sees a peasant, underestimates him, and is bested in the blink of an eye. For something more complex, Oswald can proceed with caution, especially if Edgar has already shown some skill when saving Gloucester.]*

## Act 4  Scene 6

*See Glossary – Carries.*

> *Enter Lear in a chair carried by servants.*

## Act 5  Scene 1

*See Glossary – Intimacy.*

Set aside rehearsal time with your intimacy coordinator to explore how Edmund manipulates those who can elevate his status. He clearly gains the affections of Goneril and Regan. How much are these exchanges physicalised? Edmund might have even seduced Cornwall or Oswald before they died. We won't spend much time on the concept here, but take a peek at Chapter 17 – *Richard 3* (1.2; 4.2; 4.3) for further discussion of psychopathic adaptability in the sexual arena.

## Act 5  Scene 3

*See Glossary – Arrests; Binds; Blood; Ensemble Readiness; Grabs; Intimacy; Strikes; ALL OF THE THINGS!!!*

> *Enter Edmund, with Lear and Cordelia prisoners.*

Lear and Cordelia enter as prisoners, so you should have them bound. Edmund has no care for them and isn't going to pretend otherwise. They can be dirty, bruised, and bloody. Note that a front-bind would allow for Lear to console Cordelia (*e.g.* wipe away her tears).

*Bast.*                          Take them away.

Edmund has to repeat himself, and might smack a guard for not having complied immediately. There shouldn't be much struggle from Lear, as he makes it clear he's happy to head to prison with Cordelia. If the guard is particularly annoyed about being beaten, he could take it out on Lear and Cordelia by pulling hard on their restraints/ bindings to get them going. Unless the guard's reason for the delay was pity for the former monarchs, rather than being distracted or confused. Note that your guards, soldiers, and other background characters need to be on their toes throughout this scene to sell it. They always should be, of course, but a scene like this will quickly expose any actors daydreaming about their after-show meal instead of being present in the scene. The kingdom is upside down and, with multiple nobles claiming power over one another, allegiances are confusing and continually shifting.

> *Alb.*                    Sir by your patience,
> I hold you but a subiect of this warre, not as a brother.
> *Reg.* That's as we list to grace him,
> Me thinkes our pleasure should haue beene demanded
> Ere you had spoke so farre, he led our powers,
> Bore the commission of my place and person,
> The which imediate may well stand vp,
> And call it selfe your brother.
> *Gono.* Not so hot, in his owne grace hee doth exalt himselfe
> more then in your aduancement.
> *Reg.* In my right by me inuested he com-peers the best.
> *Gon.* That were the most, if hee should husband you.
> *Reg.* Iesters doe oft proue Prophets.
> *Gon.* Hola, hola, that eye that told you so, lookt but a squint.
> *Reg.* Lady I am not well, els I should answere
> From a full flowing stomack, Generall
> Take thou my souldiers, prisoners, patrimonie,
> Witnes the world that I create thee here
> My Lord and maister.
> *Gon.* Meane you to inioy him then?
> *Alb.* The let alone lies not in your good will.
> *Bast.* Nor in thine Lord.
> *Alb.*                    Halfe blouded fellow, yes.

There is a possible tug-o'-Edmund here, since Goneril and Regan have no regard for Albany as being any kind of an equal. This is an oversight, now that Albany has found a spine and aims to put Edmund's powerplay to an end.

> *Bast.* Let the drum strike, and proue my title good.
> *Alb.* Stay yet, heare reason, *Edmund* I arrest thee
> On capitall treason, and in thine attaint,

This gilded Serpent, for your claime faire sister
I bare it in the interest of my wife.
Tis she is subcontracted to this Lord
And I her husband contradict the banes,
If you will mary, make your loue to me,
My Lady is bespoke, thou art arm'd *Gloster*,
If none appeare to proue vpon thy head,
Thy hainous, manifest, and many treasons,
There is my pledge, ile proue it on thy heart
Ere I tast bread, thou art in nothing lesse
Then I haue here proclaimd thee.
 *Reg.* Sicke, ô sicke.
 *Gon.* If not, ile ne're trust poyson.

Goneril probably poisoned Regan with aconite or hemlock. Aconite poisoning begins with gastrointestinal problems, such as stomach pains and nausea. The victim may feel a burning sensation in the mouth. These are symptoms the actor playing Regan can exhibit before she exits. She ultimately dies, either of respiratory paralysis or irregular heartbeat. If you go with hemlock, the acting choices are similar – the victim experiences gastrointestinal burning, trembling, and muscle pain, whilst the heart rate swings between rapid increases and decreases. Prior to death, there can also be convulsions and loss of speech, but Regan would be off stage before any of that. With either poison option, the gastrointestinal issue could lead to her coughing up some blood on 'Sicke, ô sicke', if that's something you fancy.

 *Bast.* Ther's my exchange, what in the world he is,
That names me traytor, villain-like he lies,
Call by thy trumpet, he that dares approach,
On him, on you, who not, I will maintaine
My truth and honour firmely.
 *Alb.* A Herald ho.
 *Bast.*    A Herald ho, a Herald.
 *Alb.* Trust to thy single vertue, for thy souldiers
All leuied in my name, haue in my name
tooke their discharge.
 *Reg.* This sicknes growes vpon me.
 *Alb.* She is not well, conuey her to my tent,
Come hether Herald, let the trumpet sound,
And read out this.
 *Cap.* Sound trumpet?
 *Her.* If any man of qualitie or degree, in the hoast of the
army, will maintaine vpon *Edmund* supposed Earle of *Gloster*,
that he's a manifold traitour, let him appeare at the third sound
of the trumpet, he is bold in his defence.

Albany has most likely thrown down his gage on 'There is my pledge'. Once Edmund tosses his on 'Ther's my exchange', he sets up the possibility of a judicial duel (or trial by combat). The formalities, having been a part of European culture for a thousand years, were well-known to Shakespeare's audience. See Chapter 9 – *Richard 2* (1.1) for clarification on gages and an in-depth discussion of this process. (Nothing so formalised existed in 800 BC.)

Edmund and Edgar can prepare for the fight during their speeches. Since this is formal, there should be a salute before the fight begins. This shows both parties are ready, and then the duel begins immediately. In some cultures, the duel would begin as soon as both drew their weapons.

Albany tells us later that he suspected the masked man was noble ('thy very gait did prophesy / A royal nobleness'). If Albany picks up on this from the way Edgar enters, Edmund may detect the same. If so, he would not underestimate this stranger. This doesn't mean he is tentative; as a recently victorious general, Edmund is still high on success.

Before beginning to choreograph this fight, you'll need to be clear on how Edgar is approaching it – is he in control of himself, or clouded by revenge? You also need to be clear about Edgar's skill level in relationship to Edmund's. If you decide Edmund is the better fighter, then Edgar should attack first. Many historical masters believe that, if the adversary is better than you, you should focus on attacking, as defence requires more practice and skill. If Edgar attacks to try and end this quickly, it would allow the audience to see Edmund's skill in defence. After this initial onslaught, Edmund can turn to offence for the second phase of this fight. One way to distinguish their competency would be if Edmund, as a more skilled fighter, can trust his parries; Edgar can parry, but will also choose to avoid attacks by stepping back or away. This will embolden Edmund in the middle of the fight, as it will feel like he is winning. For the final phase of the fight, you can have Edgar best Edmund through skill or luck. We'll ignore the latter because it's dumb. If Edgar has gained more skill during his time as 'Poor Tom' – due to people and locales with which Edmund would never be acquainted, and picking up skills neither of them would have learned in any shared training in their youth – the fight can turn on its head. If you used the Oswald fight to foreshadow Edgar's unorthodox bag of tricks, then pay it off here.

Whichever way you approach this fight (or any other), the clearer you are about the characters and their level of training, the more your fight director will be able to help you express it in the choreography.

[*JK: Research trial by combat for the time period in which you set the play. One of the most memorable versions I did was set in the States, so we used a version common to the American South – a bound duel. The fighters both held the end of a length of cloth, armed with a knife. This was sometimes with no distance (literally bound together), or with several feet of slack. We chose at least six feet, as it allowed for a dynamic fight with more choreographic options.*]

*Alarums. Fights.*

*Alb.* Saue him, saue him,

  *Gon.* This is meere practise *Gloster* by the law of armes
Thou art not bound to answere an vnknowne opposite,
Thou art not vanquisht, but cousned and beguild,

  *Alb.* Stop your mouth dame, or with this paper shall I stople
it, thou worse then any thing, reade thine owne euill, nay no
tearing Lady, I perceiue you know't.

  *Gon.* Say if I do, the lawes are mine not thine, who shal arraine me for't.

  *Alb.* Most monstrous know'st thou this paper?

  *Gon.* Aske me not what I know.

*Exit Gonorill.*

*Alb.* Go after her, shee's desperate, gouerne her.

The fact that Albany says 'Saue him, saue him' has been dealt with by scholars in different ways. Some suggest Albany is attempting to stop Edgar from killing Edmund with a final blow, some just give the line to Goneril. Another option is to use the fight choreography to make sense of this. If the fight seemingly ends with Edgar beating Edmund down and disarming him, Edgar can make the classic mistake of victoriously turning his back on Edmund. Albany (and the audience) can see Edmund pick up his weapon, and charge towards Edgar's back. This would trigger Albany to yell 'Saue him, saue him' in reference to Edgar, who could turn at the last moment, duck, and avoid the attack. Whilst he was gentlemanly enough not to deliver a fatal blow in the formal duel, he may have no choice here but to permanently dispatch Edmund. This could help trigger Edmund's attack of conscience in his dying moments. Something that curiously eluded him until *after* his final battle (as opposed to Macbeth or Richard 3).

*See Glossary – Carries.*

*The bodies of Gonorill and Regan are brought in.*

  *Kent.* Alack why thus.

  *Bast.*                 Yet *Edmund* was beloued,
The one the other poysoned for my sake,
And after slue her selfe.

  *Duke.*               Euen so, couer their faces.

  *Bast.* I pant for life, some good I meane to do,
Despight of my owne nature, quickly send,
Be briefe, int toth' castle for my writ,
Is on the life of *Lear* and on *Cordelia*,
Nay send in time.

  *Duke.*         Runne, runne, O runne.

*Edg.* To who my Lord, who hath the office, send
Thy token of repreeue.
    *Bast.* Well thought on, take my sword the Captaine,
Giue it the Captaine?
    *Duke.*                 Hast thee for thy life.
    *Bast.* He hath Commission from thy wife and me,
To hang *Cordelia* in the prison, and to lay
The blame vpon her owne despaire,
That she fordid her selfe.
    *Duke.* The Gods defend her, beare him hence a while.

*Enter Lear with Cordelia in his armes.*

    *Lear.* Howle, howle, howle, howle, O you are men of stones,
Had I your tongues and eyes, I would vse them so,
That heauens vault should cracke, shees gone for euer,
I know when one is dead and when one liues,
Shees dead as earth, lend me a looking glasse,
If that her breath will mist or staine the stone,
Why then she liues.

Your Lear may be unable to carry the dead Cordelia. This is unfortunate, as the tableau is one of the most visceral in the history of theatre. If you must do something other than a carry, at least employ a method that can take everyone by surprise. The 2019 Broadway production had the hanged Cordelia drop from the flyspace. For the mechanics of this approach, see Chapter 18 – *Sir Thomas More* (3.1). Whatever you decide, do not allow the audience to get ahead of you, as in other productions, where Cordelia was slowly hauled in atop a burlap sack, or wheeled in a barrow. This is not just a visual cue, but also an audio one – any silence after Albany's line and before Lear's will give the game away.

    *Lear.* And my poore Foole is hang'd: no, no, no life?
Why should a Dog, a Horse, a Rat haue life,
And thou no breath at all? Thou'lt come no more,
Neuer, neuer, neuer, neuer, neuer.
Pray you vndo this Button. Thanke you Sir,
Do you see this? Looke on her? Looke her lips,
Looke there, looke there.

*He dies.*

[SD: *We've been using the First Quarto for most of this chapter, but switch now to the First Folio. In this version, there are five nevers rather than three, forming a full line of trochaic pentameter – DUM-de, DUM-de, DUM-de, DUM-de, DUM-de – the complete inversion of iambic pentameter's healthy heartbeat. This is mostly subconscious for an audience but – if you've heard a majority of lines in iambic pentameter for hours at a time – significant departures from this rhythm can and should be jarring.*]

As Gloucester's 'flaw'd heart / (Alacke too weake the conflict to support) / Twixt two extremes of passion, ioy and greefe, / Burst smilingly', Lear dies from a combination of the heartbreak reflected in the language, and one final hallucination that Cordelia may still be alive. This raises the question of what Lear may have been doing throughout the scene to try and revive Cordelia; in desperation, Lear might shake or even lightly slap his daughter. This should be carefully choreographed with the fight director in advance, so that any shaking is controlled, as is any contact from a slap (a gentle patting as if she merely fainted). This will allow consistency across each performance, so that the actress playing Cordelia is not only safe but also never surprised – the last thing you want at the end of your tragedy is a flinching corpse. Or maybe you do. We don't know you very well yet.

# *from Joseph Mydell*

*In the 2008 Globe Theatre production of* King Lear, *I played Gloucester. The theatre workshop created life-like eye sockets, with dangly bits of muscle, for the blinding of Gloucester. After Cornwall took out the first eye, he held it up to show it dripping with blood, before hurling it into the upstage wall, to the gasp of the audience. Regan then straddled me and, with her nails, yanked out the other eye. My task as the actor was to find just the right sound and volume for each extraction. I then was escorted by a groom, along the runway through the standing audience, to the exit. Quite often, the actor playing the groom would whisper to me 'punter just fainted in front of you', steering me, blood pouring from my eyes to the exit, as the lights go down on the first half of the show. And a stunning exit it was. Perhaps too stunning, for one night a couple I knew was in the audience, and the husband fainted, had to be rushed to hospital, and have stitches to his head. Luckily, his wife was a nurse and could assist him, but not before sending me a note backstage to tell me what had happened!*

# Chapter 2

# Cymbeline

## Act 1  Scene 2

*See Glossary – Grabs (maybe); Strikes (maybe).*

There is only one other 'King of Britain' in the canon, and he ain't nearly as interesting or well known as Lear. You should seize any and all opportunities from the outset for the actor playing Cymbeline to make clear what kind of king he is, and what kind of father. Does he manhandle Posthumus, but draw the line at physically harming Imogen? Or, when it comes to beatings, is this king an equal-opportunity abuser? Maybe words are his primary weapons. This is a friendly reminder that your choices have consequences, must be tailored to the cast you have constructed, and will serve to distinguish your production from others. If your Cymbeline is inclined towards physical violence, then perhaps he gives a backhand slap to Posthumus before sending him on his way, and/or shakes Imogen to her senses.

Does Cymbeline harm the queen on 'Thou foolish thing'? And is 'Away with her, And pen her vp' to the queen, or his lords? Whether or not they respect him enough to begin to comply before the queen intervenes is another way to clarify your production's version of the title character.

Some minor housekeeping – there is mention of an offstage scene in which Cloten tried to start a fight with Posthumus before the latter was exiled, but we hear it was stopped by others. Whilst 1.3's main purpose is to set up Cloten as an entitled idiot, we should carry into that scene the feeling and event of the offstage confrontation. Cloten could have messed-up hair or a shirt partly untucked – something to make clear he was in the midst of an attempted altercation, and was physically restrained.

We also point your attention to 1.6, in which the queen has requested specific drugs from Doctor Cornelius, in the hope of designing a poison for Imogen. Cornelius does not trust the queen and, without her knowledge, prepares a sleeping potion to simulate death. Poisons and their mimics occur multiple times throughout the canon. You should detail each poison, and how it would course through the veins of your actors' portrayals. This will provide them with specific, actable choices. [*JK: There are few known poisons still around, such as hemlock and aconite discussed in Chapter 1 – King Lear (5.3), but I think the best choice for this play is a poison derived from the yew tree. King Cativolcus used it to commit suicide in 53 BC. It would, in proper amounts, induce a sleep-like state, causing the heart to slow. Death results when the heart fails to pump blood quickly enough to meet the body's needs. Another option is dwale, a concoction dating back to medieval times (thus anachronistic), which was a mix of herbs in alcohol, used as a surgical anaesthetic. There are many manuscript recipes for dwale, calling for the same ingredients – boar bile, wild lettuce, opium, henbane, bryony, mandrake root, hemlock, and vinegar. These would be boiled and, before an operation, three spoonfuls would be added to a drink. These cocktails were just as likely to kill the patient as render them unconscious but, when faced with biting down on a stick or a chug of the drug, there wasn't much of a choice at all.*]

## Act 1  Scene 7

*See Glossary – Grabs (maybe); Intimacy; Strikes (maybe).*

Iachimo seems rather confident Imogen will relent, so he might go in for the kiss, and possibly even make contact. She is clearly not having it, so the question is whether she rebuffs him with words, or if there is a physical repulsion. Also up for debate is when and whether Iachimo ends his advances. Imogen describes what Iachimo has done as 'thy Assault', but Iachimo blows it off later as allegedly just a test; it is for you to decide how far this pupil is being examined. Imogen calls for Pisanio no fewer than three times. At a minimum, Imogen is uncomfortable being alone with Iachimo. Depending on the gauntlet you want Imogen to run, you will have to make decisions here accordingly, and consider how they will contrast with her potentially creepier experiences in 2.3 with Cloten. As we mentioned in the Introduction, we encourage you to have an intimacy consultant on hand, in tandem with a fight director.

## Act 2  Scene 2

*Iachimo from the Trunke.*

Please ensure the actor playing Iachimo can never actually be locked in the trunk. Either have latches that can be manipulated from the inside, or a false back (so the actor can get out, should there be any issues emerging from the top). There also needs to be some type of ventilation, so your actor doesn't die in the event the foregoing measures were somehow overlooked. We realise this all sounds obvious, but you might be surprised by the depths of idiocy we have encountered in the last few decades. Stay out of court, friends. And morgues.

## Act 2  Scene 3

*See Glossary – Grabs (maybe); Intimacy; Strikes (maybe).*

And, now, back to slimy sex stuff. Cloten's wooing of Imogen should be distinct from Iachimo's. It begins with a tame request for Imogen's hand (as opposed to Iachimo leaping straight to a kiss), but the text has more swings back and forth between the speakers, and you need to decide how much Cloten's stupidity and desperation will come into play. Again, how does Imogen react, and what does her admirer/attacker do in response? How will it advance character and plot in your production?

Imogen might try to pull her hand away, and her wrist is grabbed by Cloten to force the kiss of the hand. This is one possible justification for Imogen's 'you lay out too much pains'. As the scene progresses, how entitled is Cloten? How far is Imogen willing to go beyond words in repelling the son of a king, on whose shit-list she already holds a high position? Does her self-control eventually reach boiling point at 'which I had rather / You felt, than make't my boast'?

## Act 2  Scene 4

*See Glossary – Ensemble Readiness; Grabs (maybe); Strikes (maybe).*

The degree and manifestation of Posthumus' anger here is proportional to his love for Imogen. How much, and of what variety, does your production's Posthumus love her? As we will examine with Leontes in *The Winter's Tale* (available next year in Volume Two!), there is a possessive love at play – more selfish than selfless in the early acts. Posthumus could grab Iachimo by the lapels, pin him against a wall, maybe choke him, or hold a fist in the air barely able to restrain from punching Iachimo. (This also gives the actor playing Iachimo more to work with as he explains why he's not the bad guy here.) Posthumus might also direct violence at himself, or the furniture, or Philario. It doesn't seem as though Philario has to physically intervene, but that is another decision you get to make.

## Act 3  Scene 4

*See Glossary – Draws.*

Imogen steals Pisanio's weapon on 'I draw the Sword my self'. As she says 'take it, and hit / The innocent Mansion of my Loue', she can try to force him to wield it. He refuses, and they can struggle a little, until Pisanio knocks it out of her hand on 'Hence vile Instrument'. Alternatively, he can take it from her when she says 'take it', and she can put herself on point, but he would toss it away on 'Hence vile Instrument'. There is an opportunity for her to pick it up again on 'Come, heere's my heart', and he

*Iachimo Claims his Wager.* Engraving by C. W. Wilson, date unknown. (After painting by Richard Westall, 1796.) (*Public domain*)

*Pisanio and Imogen.* Robert Thew (after John Hoppner), 1801. (*Gertrude and Thomas Jefferson Mumford Collection, Gift of Dorothy Quick Mayer, 1942*)

could take it away from her and sheathe it. When she says 'Wher's thy knife?,' she is demanding he pull it out again. Or, if he tosses the knife far enough away originally, then her 'Wher's thy knife?' can be her looking around to find it. After finding it, she can pick it up and – having earlier dismissed the idea of suicide – give him the instrument and put herself on his point. Explore these options in rehearsal, and how each might reveal character in the strongest way for your production. Also note (this will sound obvious) your actors should not forget that the blade, in real life, would be sharp. As such, they should treat it as dangerous during the struggle, even though it's only a stage weapon.

## Act 3  Scene 7

*See Glossary – Draws; Ensemble Readiness; Grabs (maybe).*

To find a stranger in your home cannot be taken lightly; assume the worst, and hope for the best. All must draw their weapons when Imogen appears. Belarius has the right to march Imogen out of the cave on dagger point, or drag her out by the collar. It's on the gents in this scene to keep the stakes high with the threat of violence, so that Imogen has a sense of urgency when pleading her case.

## Act 4  Scene 1

*See Glossary – Draws.*

This is a great opportunity to display Cloten's incompetence, and buy yourself some laughs: he could try to draw on 'out Sword' with his non-dominant hand first, and fail; then try drawing without grabbing hold of the scabbard, so the weapon gets stuck; then look down at the hilt as he draws, but hold the scabbard and hit himself in the face with the pommel.

## Act 4  Scene 2

This fight is another opportunity to reveal character: does Cloten, in his arrogance, underestimate Guiderius? If so, how quickly does Cloten recover and take Guiderius seriously? Is Cloten's fighting style formalised and measured, or untrained and rash? Contrast with Guiderius, whose approach might be more intuitive, depending on how much Belarius passed down to the boys. For their own safety, Belarius might have avoided teaching them a style similar to his own, back when he was a general in Cymbeline's armies; if the boys learned a military style, they could be suspected of desertion, or form a breadcrumb trail straight back to Belarius.

*Imogen Found in the Cave of Belarius.* George Dawe, circa 1809. (*Purchased from P. M. Hill* [*Grant-in-Aid*], *1965*)

*Fight and Exeunt.*

When Guiderius returns with the head of Cloten, we know that Cloten had his sword against Guiderius' throat, and Guiderius disarms Cloten to use his own sword to behead him. [*JK: I'd prefer you not exit, and instead stage the decapitation. See Chapter 4 –* Macbeth *(5.7).*]

*See Glossary – Carries.*

*Enter Aruiragus, with Imogen dead, bearing her in his Armes.*

*See Glossary – Carries.*

*Enter Belarius with the body of Cloten.*

## Act 5  Scene 2

*Enter Lucius, Iachimo, and the Romane Army at one doore: and the Britaine Army at another: Leonatus Posthumus following like a poore Souldier. They march ouer, and goe out. Then enter againe in Skirmish Iachimo and Posthumus: he vanquisheth and disarmeth Iachimo, and then leaues him.*

[*JK: In our polite theatre world, it's common to quiet the background noise for monologues or scenes during battles; the whole battle sometimes just fades off stage so the audience can hear the actor(s) better. This does not serve the production. Once there is a battle going on, the battle should continue on stage throughout until it is over – nonstop fighting. Bring the armies in from every possible entrance, so the audience get to feel the chaos of battle. Bring soldiers down every aisle, and see if there is any way to surprise the audience. For example, 'They march ouer, and goe out' is typically assumed to mean that they all exit, and then Iachimo and Posthumus re-enter by themselves. Try reading 'They' as just the named characters. This way, the battle can carry the named characters off stage but continue on stage. This battle should start off showing Iachimo and Posthumus leading the initial charge of the armies on their respective sides. Each can fight other adversaries before ending up together for a fight, which eventually carries them off stage. To maintain the intensity, have Posthumus charge at Iachimo in a murderous frenzy. Posthumus can take out his anger on Iachimo in such a way that Iachimo flees after Posthumus' initial onslaught. Posthumus chases after him, with the battle raging on a bit before they return. This way, it feels like they have been fighting for a while. Ultimately, we see Posthumus beat Iachimo and disarm him. Posthumus can start to swing a finishing blow, but stop himself in a moment of clarity that it is not solely Iachimo's fault, and so Posthumus leaves this particular fight. Left on stage disarmed and beaten, Iachimo's self-loathing gives the actor playing him plenty of catalyst into his speech. Whilst Iachimo can find some corner of the stage to do this (with the battle still going on behind him), his words should have to be said over the sounds of conflict. Explore the option of Iachimo having a few fights, as he speaks, before he exits. This will be much more exciting and engaging for your audience.*]

> *Iac.* The heauinesse and guilt within my bosome,
> Takes off my manhood: I haue belyed a Lady,
> The Princesse of this Country; and the ayre on't
> Reuengingly enfeebles me, or could this Carle,
> A very drudge of Natures, haue subdu'de me
> In my profession? Knighthoods, and Honors borne
> As I weare mine) are titles but of scorne.
> If that thy Gentry (Britaine) go before
> This Lowt, as he exceeds our Lords, the oddes
> Is, that we scarse are men, and you are Goddes.

> *Exit. The Battaile continues, the Britaines fly, Cymbeline is taken:*
> *Then enter to his rescue, Bellarius, Guiderius, and Aruiragus.*

This kind of detailed battle direction is rare in Shakespeare, so make sure to follow it. There are also implied directions in the text – accounts of the battle that can provide you with specific staging. Some things to incorporate from descriptions in 5.3:

- 'A narrow Lane, an old man, and two Boyes.'
- 'Some mortally, some slightly touch'd, some falling.' This gives you myriad options to craft individual assaults in the battle. During warfare, fighters tend to focus more on their own survival than killing others already incapacitated. Successfully cleave a sword-arm? Fantastic. Move along to your next opponent! Shakespeare sometimes notes how certain soldiers freeze ('falling/meerely through feare').
- A 'strait Lane' and 'strait passe was damm'd / With deadmen, hurt behinde, and Cowards liuing' very close to the battle. For Belarius' line to make sense, you need to create a narrow gauntlet the fighters are trying to run. If you want to dress it up, we know it is 'ditch'd, & wall'd with turph'. By funnelling the adversary into a narrow area, the space can be held by fewer men.

Cymbeline's capture offers another opportunity to reveal character: is he a seasoned war veteran? If so, you could surround him with half a dozen enemies, and maybe he wounds or kills a few before being taken. Or maybe he was skilled but has been out of practice, so the capture isn't as difficult. Be specific about what you want from this moment.

You can include the trio in the initial battle, and show their prowess as they fight the others off stage and then re-enter. Or, the trio can come in just for this section of the battle. Either way, keep them together in a tight formation. The decisions you made earlier with the Cloten fight need to be carried through in Guiderius' fighting style here – and now we get to see the rest of the family mirror that style (or not).

*Bel.* Stand, stand, we haue th' aduantage of the ground,
The Lane is guarded: Nothing rowts vs, but
The villany of our feares.
  *Gui. Arui.* Stand, stand, and fight.

*Enter Posthumus, and seconds the Britaines. They Rescue Cymbeline, and Exeunt.*

Here, Posthumus must be the deciding factor as the trio fight Cymbeline's captors. Feel free to reinforce the Roman ranks to make it a difficult fight; the trio should be holding their own (but not really winning) when Posthumus arrives. As described in 5.3, he comes in a silly habit, and yet he tips the scale. Victory needs to be theirs before the Britaines enter as reinforcements.

*Then enter Lucius, Iachimo, and Imogen.*

*Luc.* Away boy from the Troopes, and saue thy selfe:
For friends kil friends, and the disorder's such
As warre were hood-wink'd.
  *Iac.* 'Tis their fresh supplies.
  *Luc.* It is a day turn'd strangely: or betimes
Let's re-inforce, or fly.

*Exeunt.*

The battle is waning, but Lucius, Iachimo, and Imogen can fight some random soldiers before running right back off stage.

## Act 5  Scene 3

*See Glossary – Arrests; Strikes (maybe).*

*Enter two Captaines, and Soldiers.*

  1. Great Iupiter be prais'd, *Lucius* is taken,
'Tis thought the old man, and his sonnes, were Angels.
  2. There was a fourth man, in a silly habit,
That gaue th' Affront with them.
  1. So 'tis reported:
But none of 'em can be found. Stand, who's there?
  *Post.* A Roman,
Who had not now beene drooping heere, if Seconds
Had answer'd him.

[JK: *Those who grab Posthumus should be rough, although he probably offers no resistance.* See Appendix – Bursting the Bubble. *The closer they are to Posthumus, the more violent*

*the arrest will look whilst being safe. If any of the arresting officers are particularly brutal, a*
*gut punch or right cross could be justified in their minds (as soldiers coming from battle taking*
*out their anger on a prisoner), but they are not allowed to kill him since he has surrendered.*]
[*SD: And because he has more lines to deliver.*]

2.                              Lay hands on him: a Dogge,
A legge of Rome shall not returne to tell
What Crows haue peckt them here: he brags his seruice
As if he were of note: bring him to'th' King.

*Enter Cymbeline, Belarius, Guiderius, Aruiragus, Pisanio, and Romane Captiues.*
*The Captaines present Posthumus to Cymbeline, who deliuers him ouer to a Gaoler.*

## Act 5  Scene 4

See *Glossary – Binds*.

Posthumus is described as having his 'shanks, & wrists' 'fetter'd' in 'Manacles' with 'Lockes' and a 'Bolt'. This is very specific direction, and seems like overkill for one prisoner, but we should oblige the playwright(s). It's possible that these many restraints signify the value of the target; if the captors consider him a great warrior and/or useful hostage, they wouldn't want to take any chances on him getting free.

See *Glossary – Knees*.

*Iupiter descends in Thunder and Lightning, sitting vppon an Eagle:*
*hee throwes a Thunder-bolt. The Ghostes fall on their knees.*

[*JK: Um … yeah … have fun staging this. To do this all out, you will need a professional*
*rigging team to fly Jupiter down, and ensure that the 'Thunder-bolt' is safely aimed away*
*from any of the actors. Probably wise to toss it off stage, and have some lighting and sound*
*effects. Or, just cut this moment since it's dragging out the end of the show. I want to go home,*
*and regret ever having left.*]

## Act 5  Scene 5

See *Glossary – Arrests; Binds*.

*Enter Lucius, Iachimo, and other Roman prisoners, Leonatus behind, and Imogen.*

How were the prisoners treated? Were they beaten and tortured, or are they in a similar state to how they were thrown in the dungeons? Either way, they probably should be bound and guarded as they are brought in.

*See Glossary – Ensemble Readiness; Falls; Strikes.*

As Posthumus is about to reveal himself, does he physicalise any of his wrath towards Iachimo? Does anyone attempt to restrain Posthumus? You can choose if he is held back by others, if Posthumus fights against them to try and get to Iachimo, and even if Posthumus gets a few punches to land before being pulled away. This will get him flailing about enough that Imogen can be knocked down in the crossfire, forgetting she is dressed as a boy and therefore just another person in Posthumus' way. He can punch, kick, backhand, or otherwise maul Imogen to a point of unconsciousness. Whichever you decide, ensure it supports her later line ('throw your wedded Lady').

# Part 2

# Countries Norway Doesn't Seem to Like Very Much

John Barrymore and Sidney Mather in Hamlet. Francis Bruguière, 1923. (*E.V. Brewster Publications Inc, Sep 1922–Feb 1923*)

# Chapter 3

# Hamlet

*'And he, most violent author'* – Claudius (4.5)

Easily the most-discussed work in the canon [*SD: I don't like it.*] [*JK: It's my second favourite!*] [SD: *You've only read two Shakespeare plays?*], *Hamlet* has succumbed to the same impotency plaguing its Danish prince. Productions have moved further and further away from the compact revenge tragedy of the 1603 First Quarto, inching ever closer to four hours of conflating each folio, quarto and bastardised text of the play ever since. This play (along with *King Lear* and *Othello*) proves particularly difficult with regards to an authoritative text. Each printing has been radically different – *e.g.* character names (Corambis is eventually renamed Polonius), and famous lines (it originally was 'To be or not to be, aye, there's the point'). [SD: *Amongst the many sins of my actor-manager predecessors over the centuries is their search for the maximum possible lines they can utter. In the case of this play – conflation of all the available texts, including a 242-minute cinematic exercise in audience torture.*]

The potential for violence is particularly high in this play; the inciting action is the suspicious death of a king – amidst a war no less – and crowns are moving about left and right. All hell breaks loose, much as it will after Duncan's murder in Chapter 4 – *Macbeth* and the death of the eponymous titular character in Chapter 13 – *Henry 5*. These are people with immense power, scrambling not only to survive but flourish. Add greed, guilt, and the fact that many of these folks are related, and you have a recipe for disaster. What makes the tragedies and histories particularly rich is that *virtually every scene has life-and-death stakes*. Considering this, let's find ways to reclaim the visceral action of the play, so we can counter the title character's existential inaction.

## Act 1  Scene 2

*See Glossary – Grabs (maybe); Strikes (maybe).*

Prince Hamlet has been an embarrassment at his uncle Claudius' court throughout the scene, and it is for the actors and director in any given production to decide how much of Claudius' speech is public or private. Describing Hamlet's behaviour as 'sweet and commendable' is uncomfortable enough for Claudius that he requires a pause to collect himself. He then continues, with increasing levels of verbal abuse, to belittle Hamlet's grief. It is possible that Claudius is a reasonable guy who killed his brother to save the country, and is just trying to give Hamlet perspective on why it's trivial to care about his loss, when the world is so very old and large, and all of us insignificant in the larger scheme of things. But the likelier case is that Claudius is attempting to neutralise a threat, in much the same way Brutus fears Caesar is 'a Serpents egge, / Which hatch'd, would as his kinde grow mischievous'. See Volume Two – *Julius Caesar* (2.1).

Most contemporary audiences know that Claudius murdered his brother, so adding his nephew to the body count is certainly on the table (which Claudius later attempts). Bear in mind that Claudius not only deprived Hamlet of a father, but also of a claim to the crown. The Denmark of this play seems to follow the historical elective monarchy – meaning Claudius, Hamlet, and others were all potential candidates. Hamlet even mentions this system in his dying moments – 'I do prophesie th'election lights / On *Fortinbras*, he ha's my dying voyce'. Despite the theoretical flexibility of this system, crowns almost always passed to the eldest male heir. Hamlet was more likely to receive the crown had he not been off doing nerd stuff in Wittenberg. Whether or not he'd have wanted the crown, and how that might change the fibre of the play, we'll never know. Claudius robbed Hamlet and the audience of such possibilities. At the end of the play, after he has dispatched Claudius, Hamlet is presumed to be king in the brief moment before his death, such that he is allowed to name (or, at the very least, recommend) his successor, and chooses Fortinbras.

But back to the beginning – this is the first time the audience see Hamlet and Claudius interact; the more suspense, the better. Depending on the dynamic between the two actors, it may be extremely powerful for Claudius not only to take Hamlet aside from the court, but to do so forcefully. As the eldest male heir of the prior monarch, Hamlet will always be a threat to Claudius. How quickly/harshly would Claudius address this problem? Particularly since the only clues he has to what may or may not be Hamlet's motives are his passive-aggressive replies.

Be specific. If Claudius starts by motioning for Hamlet to move aside for 'a chat' and Hamlet blows him off, it makes sense for Claudius to grab Hamlet by the arm and pull him aside. If Hamlet isn't looking at Claudius when spoken to, Claudius could grab Hamlet's face and force eye contact. If Claudius doesn't feel he's being listened to, he could grab his nephew's ear. In anything set early twentieth century and prior, this kind of physicalising of Claudius' intention(s) would not be out of place, or even considered abusive. In fact, a slap could be justified due to Claudius' severe stress as a new king (let alone the magnified paranoia induced by having murdered the last one). And what of 'beseech you, bend you to remaine'? Is this just a turn of phrase, or a physical action to force Hamlet to drop out of school and stay in Elsinore under careful monitoring? Claudius could be holding Hamlet's hand, say 'beseech you' loudly enough for the court to hear, and then start twisting his fingers on a whispered 'bend you'.

A less-contained Claudius could lose his cool in front of the court for a moment, and possibly feel bad about it afterwards, either genuinely or to save face. He can never know what each member of his court truly feels, and there very well may be those who would rather see the prince on the throne.

Another possibility is that Claudius uses these words, at full volume, to humiliate Hamlet in front of the entire court. The question for any production: will this choice help tell your story better than a private moment with Hamlet?

[*SD: Claudius' potential violence need not be comprised solely of reactions to Hamlet's actual behaviour but also to* perceived *behaviour. It is Claudius' fate that, so long as he lives, he will always have to look over his shoulder. The level of his psychological distress can immediately be set up in how he handles his biggest threat. I was Claudius to Timothy D. Stickney's prince, an actor far more charming and physically powerful.*] [*JK: Which isn't saying much.*] [*SD: True. My particular choice was to gently bring him out of the court's earshot, and avoid any physical violence. Gaining this apparently respectful privacy, I used the text to terrorise him. The court had no idea what I was doing, and I could send a clear message to Hamlet that he should obey my every fucking whim. An added bonus to this choice was that the court probably assumed I was consoling Hamlet, trying to protect him from embarrassment. This is the type of work encouraged throughout this book – legitimately consider the given circumstances of how your scene partners match up with you physically, mentally, psychologically, emotionally,* etc., *and make moment-to-moment decisions which will lead to the most fireworks for your particular combinations. Had I a tinier, younger, or more dimwitted Hamlet, I would have made different choices.*]

## Act 1  Scene 4

*See Glossary – Grabs.*

> *Ham.*                                    Hold off your hand.
> *Hor.* Be rul'd, you shall not goe.
> *Ham.*                                    My fate cries out,
> And makes each petty Artire in this body,
> As hardy as the Nemian Lions nerue:
> Still am I cal'd? Vnhand me Gentlemen:
> By Heau'n, Ile make a Ghost of him that lets me:
> I say away, goe on, Ile follow thee.

You'll notice there is no formal stage direction, but Hamlet says 'Hold off your hand' and 'Vnhand me Gentlemen'. [*SD: These implied directions are typical throughout each of the plays, and we'll continue to draw your attention to them. You may thank the authors of this publication for doing so by sending them single malt scotch and cuddly-yet-judgemental stuffed animals.*] The urgency is made clear by the shared lines, as Hamlet immediately replies to each of their pleas.

There are myriad ways Hamlet can be restrained, depending on the story you want to tell. Marcellus and Horatio can each grab an arm and hold Hamlet back. Be certain with any performed violence, such as a restraint, that the victim (Hamlet in this moment) is always in control. Marcellus and Horatio should not be pulling on Hamlet's arms, as this could lead to a dislocation. They should be bracing their shoulder or body against Hamlet's chest (specifically, where the deltoid and pectoralis major meet), so that Hamlet has a good base to push against when trying to follow the ghost. Though, if a guard manhandled a prince, even for his own good, the guard could be fired or killed. A stronger choice is to have Hamlet try to get by Horatio during the 'Flood' speech. This will lend more urgency to Horatio's questions, and he can start holding Hamlet back. First, Horatio might just hold up his hand, then actually grab Hamlet and, in a short struggle, put him in a bear hug or some other kind of restraining hold. This will help feed Hamlet's desperation for 'It wafts me still', as he can push against Horatio's restraint. Marcellus can then get in front of Hamlet whilst he is being held from behind by Horatio. It is up to you to decide to whom 'Hold off your hand' is barked. There is the added dilemma of differing texts: the First Quarto assigns Marcellus' 'you shall not goe' to Horatio, with no prompt about 'hand' or 'hands' from Hamlet; the Second Quarto has Hamlet say 'hands', not 'hand'. If only Horatio is restraining Hamlet, give Horatio the line; if Marcellus has just stepped in front of Hamlet and pushes him back, then Marcellus can keep the line and Hamlet can remind Marcellus of his place.

It is important to be clear about how Hamlet gets out of the hold. This tells the audience a lot about him, and it is their first glimpse of his battle prowess (or lack thereof). If you use a martial arts move, you convey his skill; if Hamlet strikes his best friend in the stomach to get free, it shows how desperate Hamlet is to follow the ghost. Hamlet can bite an arm, stomp a foot, or even twist out in a way that hurls the holder to the ground. Just ensure this matches the skill level of the Hamlet being portrayed in your production. [*JK: I once saw a Hamlet drop into a karate stance after getting free, and deliver the lines commencing with 'My fate cries out'. Putting aside my curiosity as to when exactly Hamlet travelled to Japan, great confusion came later in the grave – Hamlet seemed to forget all his magical martial arts training when grappling with Laertes. Furthermore, when Hamlet was pulled from the grave, the attendant used the same hold Hamlet had been put in at the beginning of the play but, for some reason, Hamlet couldn't get out of it this time. No martial artist forgets. They get rusty without practice, but they don't forget how to ride the proverbial bike.*]

## Act 2 Scenes 1 and 2

Much has been discussed (in countless volumes, for many centuries) as to whether Hamlet is or is not mad, and what this may actually mean. Our remit is not to debate such questions, but it is worth noting that Hamlet's proclivity towards violence is on a gradually increasing trajectory – from verbal violence, to light physical violence with Ophelia off stage, to the murder of Polonius, to the battle with Laertes in the grave and subsequent duel, to the murder of Claudius.

Ophelia gives a detailed depiction of Hamlet's appearance and behaviour, as well as the physical violence towards her person (which seems to be a first in their relationship).

It's up to the actress playing Ophelia to determine how much physical violence she has experienced in her life. In this particular moment, she should, at the very least, have a bruised wrist and sore arm, and still be dealing with the shock of what has occurred.

This specific violence is the first we hear of Hamlet's new behaviour. How might his psychological imbalance (affected or not) manifest when he discovers Rosencrantz and Guildenstern are spies? Or that Polonius is doing Claudius' dirty work?

## Act 3  Scene 1

*See Glossary – Falls (maybe); Grabs (maybe); Intimacy; Knees (maybe); Strikes (maybe).*

Whatever the legitimacy of Hamlet's madness, his direct address to the audience in the 'To be, or not to be' soliloquy is more than philosophical debate. Whether or not the production concept allows for the actor to hold a loaded gun to his head, see Chapter 11 – *Henry 4 Part 2* (2.4), the performance of the speech should telegraph this immediacy to the audience. You could, theoretically, choose to have your Hamlet aware of the presence of Claudius and Polonius from the beginning – in which case, this is just for the sake of performance – toying with them, letting them believe he might just end it all and magically solve their problems for them. If all this is real, however, we'll never know if he'd have elected suicide, as Ophelia interrupts him.

As we learned from Ophelia in 2.1, Hamlet has already committed physical violence towards her.  What might he do now? One of the only people he could depend on for the truth has turned liar. And what if he deduces that her father and the regicidal/fratricidal king are listening in on this conversation? And that she's lying at *their* behest? Hamlet demands, multiple times, that she 'go'. Do these demands escalate beyond the verbal? If she communicates her anxiety to her father in 2.1, merely as the result of being grabbed by the wrist and held hard, what must Hamlet do here, in front of her father and the king, to elicit the reaction in her soliloquy after Hamlet storms out? He is clearly off balance, and resorts to speaking in uncharacteristic prose. This is a major indicator for a classical actor – pattern recognition, as clinical as it may sound, is essential to the work.  Notice when your characters deviate from their own norms, and dig until you find reasons why.

There are plenty of possibilities for violence that will enhance this scene: pushing, grabbing, throwing Ophelia to the floor, messing with her makeup (if you go with the quarto versions – 'God has given you one *"face"*, and you make yourselves another', as opposed to the First Folio's '*pace*'). Even slapping or choking could be deployed, especially in interpretations where Hamlet suspects, or indeed knows, that Polonius and Claudius are in the room, and abuses Ophelia to try and force them out of hiding. Note that this is a two-way street, and Ophelia could attempt something physical (violent and/or sexual) to try and get through to Hamlet. Bring in your fight director and intimacy consultant, and spend proper rehearsal time exploring the best version of this scene for your production.

With regards to Polonius and Claudius, all that is mentioned is they 'withdraw'. We know little else about the nature of the room. Depending on where they are hiding, Hamlet may or may not do violence to their method of cover (*e.g.* a door, a one-way mirror, *etc.*). [*SD: Timothy's Hamlet brilliantly terrorised Polonius and me, taking his 'Those that are married already, all but one shall live' directly to the upstage arras hiding us. It took a great deal of effort for me to restrain from bursts of laughter behind the tapestry, as the actor playing Polonius – Broadway veteran Arthur French – liked to use this time to take a brief nap whilst we were hidden from view, and Timothy scared him awake every damned night.*]

## Act 3  Scene 4

*See Glossary – Blood; Blood Packs (maybe); Falls (maybe); Grabs (maybe);* ~~Intimacy~~*; Knees (maybe); Strikes (maybe).*

Hamlet confronts his mother about the murder of his father. Yet again, Polonius is eavesdropping. As with Hamlet and Claudius in 1.2, the potential violence here will come down to the mixture of actors in your production, and how far each feels they need to go to get through to the other.

> *Qu.* What wilt thou do? thou wilt not murther me?
> Helpe, helpe, hoa.
> *Pol.* What hoa, helpe, helpe, helpe.
> *Ham.* How now, a Rat? dead for a Ducate, dead.
> *Pol.* Oh I am slaine.

> *Killes Polonius.*

What triggers the queen's cries for help? Just Hamlet's language? Doubtful. She is clearly disturbed by her son's opening gambit, and attempts to leave the room ('Nay, then Ile set those to you that can speake'), either for fear of him, despair at his labelling ('your Husbands Brothers wife'), desire to get him help, or some combination thereof. Hamlet is, at a minimum, barring her exit – quite possibly physically restraining her ('you shall not boudge') – as her comments elevate in intensity. She summoned him here, yet almost immediately tries to leave. What has happened? For her line to make sense, Hamlet must be threatening her or doing something that would make a mother think her son has the capacity to kill her in this moment. Was it just an invitation for her to sit down, or did he force her to do so?

There are plenty of opportunities for violence – *e.g.* when Hamlet retorts 'Mother, you have my Father much offended', she could slap the attitude out of him. [*JK: I was actually slapped in a callback once by the actress with whom I was reading. The director, knowing I was a fight guy, stopped us and asked if that was staged. It wasn't. Just the way I said the line had pulled that out of her, and it was a surprise to me. Needless to say, the actress was released by the director. The lack of self-control and partner communication made it clear to the director that he would not want to work with her, even in non-violent scenes.*] Remember that Hamlet now knows Claudius is guilty, but has yet to discover to what extent his mother was involved. This justifies a fair amount of violence (manhandling, shoving, choking, *etc.*), as his curiosity and rage would be hard to suppress. [*JK: If the director is going with the Freudian angle …*] [*SD: Nope. Absolutely not. Shut your stupid mouth.*] [*JK: Whoa, cowboy. I agree it's overdone, and a bit ridiculous, but give it some thought.*] [*SD: Okay. Fine. It's unlikely that such an interpretation is of value. Besides the obvious reasons, the character prefix for Gertrude throughout the scene is 'Queene'. She is not designated 'Mother' (as Lady Capulet is sometimes titled in Volume Two –* Romeo and Juliet*), or even something as familiar as her first name (the Second Quarto, not even attempting to hide its uselessness, does have her switching between 'Queene' and 'Gertrude' quite a bit). The choice of character prefix was fluid from scene to scene in these initial publications, and even changed line by line within a scene. From a First Folio technique viewpoint, we might take her title in this scene to signify a detachment or distance from her son, and that her royal position outweighs her filial one. Though, it's possible his being titled something other than 'Prince' may mean he desires to bridge that gap. After all, he does commence the scene with an argument about what she should be called. Happy now?*] [*JK: Sorry, wasn't paying attention; I was too busy scrolling job postings for productions of* Oedipus Rex.]

Next, Hamlet focuses on the rat behind the drapery. The feeling of stabbing someone for the first time can run the gamut of reactions, based on how the actor/character has built to this moment. If it happened in blind rage and Hamlet charged the curtain, that anger may immediately subside as he gets hit with the realisation of what he's done. If he crosses to the curtain more deliberately, he conveys determination and cold-bloodedness.

For Polonius' death, be clear about where on the body he is struck. There are significant differences between a victim experiencing shock, becoming unconscious, and then dying. We typically only care about unconsciousness, so that the character is no longer able to speak. [*SD: You don't want to hear random gurgling and shrieking from Polonius during the rest of the scene? It surely will be better than most of the text, or what I've seen actors do to it over the years.*] [*JK: From a stab wound, it would take a while for Polonius to lose consciousness, so there are several ways to ensure he never utters another word. Hamlet could repeatedly stab him (on 'farewell' or 'take thy Fortune'), but understand what this might say about Hamlet to the audience (e.g. living out the particular fantasy of how he'd kill Claudius if ever getting the chance). Don't just do it to kill Polonius quickly. Psychological shock from a traumatic wound can also precipitate rapid unconsciousness. Your fight director should be versed in internal anatomy, be able to tell the actor exactly where he is hit, what happens to his body as he is dying, and roughly how long it would all take.*]

The important thing to remember is that *dying is a long way from dead*. What Polonius does as he expires can enhance the production in different ways – whilst Hamlet usually pulls back the arras to find a corpse, what would it be like if Polonius was near passing out but still conscious? Hamlet could deliver those lines to Polonius as he is dying, and even have Polonius' literal blood on his hands.

Note that the stage direction occurs *after* Polonius says 'Oh I am slaine'. Whilst this could be a typographical error, it does leave open the possibility that Polonius is speaking aloud his realisation of the inevitable just before it happens. Neither of the quarto texts inserts a stage direction, and the First Quarto intriguingly has Corambis (Polonius) call out 'Helpe for the Queene', more clearly a selfless plea than the generic 'What hoa, helpe, helpe, helpe', which could just be for his own safety.

Having committed his first murder, Hamlet finds himself alone in a room with yet another woman he loves lying to his face. [*SD: The queen's language falls off the rails. She maintains regular meter for the first question, but drops to prose. She then switches to the 'springboard' verse Shakespeare employs throughout the second half of his career, whereby one character leaps onto a line of verse before the other has a chance to finish, and vice versa. This is not just a shared line in the traditional sense, wherein there are no pauses; these are two people speaking simultaneously for a second or two, on multiple occasions, throughout. Not unlike the works of David Mamet during the twentieth century, back when his existence was useful to our species.*] Does he physically force her to look at the pictures of her two husbands? Or the ghost only he can see? And what about the blood that will start to pool from Polonius' wounds? Imagine it slowly filling up the room, and Gertrude's possible attempts to stay clear of it. What would happen if it touches her? What if Hamlet drags her into it? Questions along these lines will strengthen your production, and may lead you to better questions. Please embrace the corporeal nature of these plays – flesh, bones, blood, piss, shit. If you're going to utilise the blood, don't treat it like stage blood. Again, the audience should never have a chance to consider that it's just some fake concoction. [*JK: Don't forget it has to be cleaned up. In one production I worked on, the director actually had a servant on all fours with a bucket of water, trying to mop it up in the background of the following scene. Whilst initially performed out of necessity (an outdoor theatre that couldn't go to blackout), it turned out to be a brilliant choice, as it added realism whilst also making the killing more immediate to the scene. If Rosencrantz and Guildenstern aren't ready for the blood, it could also be a funny reason for them to get the hell out of there after entering with the king in the next scene.*] [*SD: I'd really have enjoyed getting to play off of that. I was already going apeshit as Claudius – not concerned for the death of the man who put me on the throne, but because Hamlet could have killed meeeeee! I can only imagine what the hell I'd have done if I saw his blood everywhere.*]

*See Glossary – Carries.*

Whether the blood is cleaned up or not, the body will have to be moved.

> *Ham.* This man shall set me packing:
> Ile lugge the Guts into the Neighbor roome,
> Mother goodnight. Indeede this Counsellor
> Is now most still, most secret, and most graue,

Who was in life, a foolish prating Knaue.
Come sir, to draw toward an end with you.
Good night Mother.

*Exit Hamlet tugging in Polonius.*

Most directors don't think about this scene when they are casting a rotund Polonius alongside an emaciated Hamlet, who only started hitting the gym last week. Benchpressing hundreds of pounds is hard enough – dead weight (and the awkward position required to drag it) further impedes the endeavour. Whilst you can get away with going to blackout to avoid most of this, the audience need to see Hamlet at least start to drag the body away. To do this safely, the actor playing Hamlet should get under the body sufficiently to use leg strength, and not rely on back muscles. He should also secure Polonius' head, so there is no chance of a concussion.

The more awkward the drag, the funnier the scene. (The tragedies are the real comedies.) If the production is using stage blood, that can get all over Hamlet as well. This would add a new layer to the scene when Rosencrantz and Guildenstern come to Hamlet to find out where Polonius' body is. You normally see this staged as a regular conversation, but imagine the horror when they finally find Hamlet, and he turns around to reveal blood all over his clothes and hands. We're not saying you must make any of these choices, just that you consider each of the circumstances and follow them through to conclusions logical for your production. Basic questions like these can invite spectacular answers.

# *from Dakin Matthews*

*Once, while playing Polonius, I thought on first preview night of what might be a clever piece of business. We had practiced the death stab through the curtain quite religiously, so I was not concerned about that, but what if, what if, I thought, I died facing downstage with my eyes open? How cool would that be for a death scene! How spooky for the audience! And so I did, completely oblivious (at first) to the excruciating fact that there was a rather lengthy mother/son scene to be yet played out. And there I lay open eyed and in extreme ocular discomfort through it all. I made sure to fall facing upstage for the remainder of the run.*

## Act 4  Scene 3

*See Glossary – Blood (maybe); Grabs (maybe); Strikes (maybe).*

What is more frustrating than finding out someone tried to murder you, killed your best friend instead, and then having to argue with the murderer about where the hell he's hidden the body? Like the possibility of Claudius' physical violence towards Hamlet in 1.2, what might happen here with the intensity now through the roof? What tactics are available to Claudius after Hamlet continuously ignores the questioning, using it as yet another opportunity to publicly embarrass his uncle? [*SD: I made the choice early on that my performance would rarely show its hand with excessive volume, because I knew everything was leading up to this scene in which I had two choices: manhandle Hamlet in some fashion (which, as I mentioned earlier, would just be silly considering Timothy's six-pack Hamlet); or make his ears (and the audience's) bleed with 'Where is Polonius?' I chose the latter.*] Also consider that Claudius may have upped his own security and entered with some guards (his 'Switzers'), who might put Hamlet on point to force disclosure of the cadaver's location. Something clearly changes after 'other place your selfe', and before 'but indeed'. It is your task to figure this out.

## Act 4  Scene 5

*See Glossary – Ensemble Readiness; Grabs (maybe); Strikes (maybe).*

As if events couldn't go to hell in a handbasket with any more celerity, Ophelia is now '*distracted*', and her brother Laertes has gathered an army to possibly usurp and/or kill the king. Ophelia resorts to sexual innuendo with Claudius, but also may become violent. Like Hamlet, it is questionable how much of her behaviour is in her own control. Her condition will stoke Laertes' ire over the course of the scene, once he arrives with his soldiers and breaks the doors, thirsting for answers and revenge.

   This is another highly charged scene with no formal stage directions for violence. Yet the physical nature is obvious from the start: a messenger has just declared that Laertes has apparently amassed an army, who clamour for him to take Claudius' throne (which would have to happen through regicide or forced abdication); Claudius states 'The doores are broke' (Laertes and some or all of his soldiers have either pushed through the guards, or quite literally broken the doors themselves); and Claudius pleads 'Let him go *Gertrude*'. At the very least, Laertes has stormed into the room, and Gertrude attempts either to stand between her husband and Laertes, or possibly lay hands on him. His power made clear, Laertes orders his men to stay without and guard the door. It has the feeling of a formal parley (which we'll discuss in depth during the history plays) – the threat of violence is crystal clear, but tightly leashed. Much of the suspense derives from what Laertes and his men *might* do, making Claudius and Gertrude the audience's representatives in this particular scene; whatever Laertes does or does not do to the monarchs should simultaneously have the same effect on the audience.

Should Laertes decide to manhandle Claudius after getting past Gertrude? Does Laertes throw Claudius up against a wall, forearm against his throat? Will Claudius let him? How do each of these choices deepen your audience's understanding of the characters?

Matters get even worse when Ophelia enters – singing – and proceeds to distribute flowers that may or may not be imaginary. How will Laertes react to this? He immediately devolves into prose. This represents a loss of control, made even more dangerous by his possession of an army. Claudius will have a great deal of work to do in his mission to harness Laertes, and the potential violence is worth exploring both here and in the private scene between Claudius and Laertes that ends the fourth act. Just in case the stakes still aren't high enough, Shakespeare kills off Ophelia and we'll get to see how all these folks will interact at her funeral.

## Act 5  Scene 1

*See Glossary – Ensemble Readiness; Grabs (maybe); Strikes (maybe).*

*Leaps in the graue.*

The fight should convey how much Laertes blames Hamlet for Ophelia's death, which may be confusing to Hamlet, who only just learned Ophelia is dead. Laertes clearly '*leaps in the grave*', but the ensuing scuffle must build to a point where Hamlet asks Laertes '*prythee take thy fingers from my throat*'. The king orders the attendants to '*pluck them asunder*'. Do they try? Are they successful? To whom is the queen pleading '*for love of God forbeare him*'? Is it a cry for Laertes to ignore Hamlet, or for Hamlet to let go of Laertes? And what of Hamlet's invitation/challenge '*Come show me what thou'lt doe*'? This chaos must occur in concert with the words. Otherwise, you just have a bunch of actors standing around, waiting for the fight to end before their next line. Consider also the juxtaposition of violence in a place of serenity. This moment is a step forward for Hamlet, after his earlier struggle to kill Claudius in a sacred venue: Hamlet's willingness to engage with Laertes puts the question of holiness to rest; should Hamlet meet Claudius in the chapel again, he'd likely not make it out alive.

## Act 5  Scene 2

*See Glossary – Blood; Blood Packs; Ensemble Readiness; Grabs; Strikes; MANY OF THE THINGS!!!*

Circumstances, circumstances, circumstances. Most revenge tragedies culminate in a final scene with a massive body count, but let's examine the elements particular to this play – '*Hamlet, Horatio, and young Osricke*' are already present when the following people (and props) join the fray: '*King, Queene, Laertes and Lords, with other Attendants with*

*Foyles, and Gauntlets, a Table and Flagons of Wine on it.*' How might each of these be utilised within the fight?

> *King.* Giue them the Foyles yong *Osricke*,
> Cousen *Hamlet*, you know the wager.
>     *Ham.* Verie well my Lord,
> Your Grace hath laide the oddes a'th'weaker side.
>     *King.* I do not feare it,
> I haue seene you both:
> But since he is better'd, we haue therefore oddes.
>     *Laer.* This is too heauy,
> Let me see another.
>     *Ham.* This likes me well,
> These Foyles haue all a length.

*Prepare to play.*

> *Osricke.*                              I my good Lord.
>     *King.* Set me the Stopes of wine vpon that Table:
> If *Hamlet* giue the first, or second hit,
> Or quit in answer of the third exchange,
> Let all the Battlements their Ordinance fire,
> The King shal drinke to *Hamlets* better breath,
> And in the Cup an vnion shal he throw
> Richer then that, which foure successiue Kings
> In Denmarkes Crowne haue worne.
> Giue me the Cups,
> And let the Kettle to the Trumpets speake,
> The Trumpet to the Cannoneer without,
> The Cannons to the Heauens, the Heauen to Earth,
> Now the King drinkes to *Hamlet*. Come, begin,
> And you the Iudges beare a wary eye.
>     *Ham.* Come on sir.
>     *Laer.* Come on sir.

*They play.*

> *Ham.* One.
> *Laer.* No.
> *Ham.* Iudgement.
> *Osr.* A hit, a very palpable hit.
> *Laer.* Well: againe.
> *King.* Stay, giue me drinke.

*Hamlet*, this Pearle is thine,
Here's to thy health. Giue him the cup,

*Trumpets sound, and shot goes off.*

   *Ham.* Ile play this bout first, set by a-while.
Come: Another hit; what say you?
   *Laer.* A touch, a touch, I do confesse.
   *King.* Our Sonne shall win.
   *Qu.*                He's fat, and scant of breath.
Heere's a Napkin, rub thy browes,
The Queene Carowses to thy fortune, *Hamlet.*
   *Ham.* Good Madam.
   *King. Gertrude*, do not drinke.
   *Qu.* I will my Lord;
I pray you pardon me.
   *King.* It is the poyson'd Cup, it is too late.
   *Ham.* I dare not drinke yet Madam,
By and by.
   *Qu.* Come, let me wipe thy face.
   *Laer.* My Lord, Ile hit him now.
   *King.*             I do not thinke't.
   *Laer.* And yet 'tis almost 'gainst my conscience.
   *Ham.* Come for the third.
*Laertes*, you but dally,
I pray you passe with your best violence,
I am affear'd you make a wanton of me.
   *Laer.* Say you so? Come on.

*Play.*

   *Osr.* Nothing neither way.
   *Laer.* Haue at you now.

*In scuffling they change Rapiers.*

   *King.* Part them, they are incens'd.
   *Ham.*               Nay come, againe.
   *Osr.* Looke to the Queene there hoa.
   *Hor.* They bleed on both sides. How is't my Lord?
   *Osr.* How is't *Laertes*?
   *Laer.* Why as a Woodcocke
To mine Sprindge, *Osricke*,

I am iustly kill'd with mine owne Treacherie.

    *Ham.* How does the Queene?

    *King.*                 She sounds to see them bleede.

    *Qu.* No, no, the drinke, the drinke.

Oh my deere *Hamlet*, the drinke, the drinke,

I am poyson'd.

    *Ham.* Oh Villany! How? Let the doore be lock'd.

Treacherie, seeke it out.

    *Laer.* It is heere *Hamlet.*

*Hamlet*, thou art slaine,

No Medicine in the world can do thee good.

In thee, there is not halfe an houre of life;

The Treacherous Instrument is in thy hand,

Vnbated and envenom'd: the foule practise

Hath turn'd it selfe on me. Loe, heere I lye,

Neuer to rise againe: Thy Mothers poyson'd:

I can no more, the King, the King's too blame.

    *Ham.* The point envenom'd too,

Then venome to thy worke.

*Hurts the King.*

    *All.* Treason, Treason.

    *King.* O yet defend me Friends, I am but hurt.

    *Ham.* Heere thou incestuous, murdrous,

Damned Dane,

Drinke off this Potion: Is thy Vnion heere?

Follow my Mother.

*King Dyes.*

    *Laer.*             He is iustly seru'd.

It is a poyson temp'red by himselfe:

Exchange forgiuenesse with me, Noble *Hamlet*;

Mine and my Fathers death come not vpon thee,

Nor thine on me.

*Dyes.*

    *Ham.* Heauen make thee free of it, I follow thee.

I am dead *Horatio*, wretched Queene adiew,

You that looke pale, and tremble at this chance,

That are but Mutes or audience to this acte:

Had I but time (as this fell Sergeant death
Is strick'd in his Arrest) oh I could tell you.
But let it be: *Horatio*, I am dead,
Thou liu'st, report me and my causes right
To the vnsatisfied.
    *Hor.*           Neuer beleeue it.
I am more an Antike Roman then a Dane:
Heere's yet some Liquor left.
    *Ham.* As th'art a man, giue me the Cup.
Let go, by Heauen Ile haue't.
Oh good *Horatio*, what a wounded name,
(Things standing thus vnknowne) shall liue behind me.
If thou did'st euer hold me in thy heart,
Absent thee from felicitie awhile,
And in this harsh world draw thy breath in paine,
To tell my Storie.

*March afarre off, and shout within.*

What warlike noyse is this?

*Enter Osricke.*

    *Osr.* Yong *Fortinbras*, with conquest come from Poland
To th' Ambassadors of England giues this warlike volly.
    *Ham.* O I dye *Horatio*:
The potent poyson quite ore-crowes my spirit,
I cannot liue to heare the Newes from England,
But I do prophesie th'election lights
On *Fortinbras*, he ha's my dying voyce,
So tell him with the occurrents more and lesse,
Which haue solicited. The rest is silence. O, o, o, o.

*Dyes*

    *Hora.* Now cracke a Noble heart:
Goodnight sweet Prince,
And flights of Angels sing thee to thy rest,
Why do's the Drumme come hither?

*Enter Fortinbras and English Ambassador, with Drumme, Colours, and Attendants.*

This is a great deal for a fight director to consider. Firstly, not all of the passes are labelled clearly. There is obviously a second pass, which occurs somewhere during Hamlet's 'Ile play this bout first, set by a-while. / Come: Another hit; what say you'. Having established where the passes occur, the fight director must layer in the details known by the audience, to make certain that the fight supports the script.

For example, Laertes is the better fencer. This is discussed earlier in 5.2 (Claudius has given Hamlet a three-touch handicap, and Hamlet then tells Horatio 'I shall win at the odds', implying Hamlet can't beat Laertes outright), and once again at the beginning of this scene, so it is important the audience witness this firsthand in the initial exchange. Notwithstanding, Laertes fails to hit Hamlet in the first or second pass. How is this possible? The issue is generally resolved in performance by Hamlet magically gaining awesome fighting skills and getting the better of Laertes, despite the direct contradiction with the text. But what if Laertes is hesitant to hit Hamlet with the envenomed foil? For a man who has probably never killed before, and certainly not murdered anyone (for the distinction between killing and murder, see Chapter 4 – *Macbeth* (1.7)), it could be difficult for Laertes to follow through with his inclination to kill Hamlet.

Hamlet notices Laertes holding back, and says so before the third pass. This choice also makes Laertes' line, 'And yet 'tis almost 'gainst my conscience', far more appropriate. Shakespeare left a clue for the actor, of course – for this to scan, 'conscience' must be pronounced with three syllables, pointing out to the actor the depth of Laertes' struggle in this moment, and his need to convey that to the audience. Shakespeare could have employed the two-syllable version (as with Hamlet's 'Thus Conscience does make Cowards of vs all'), but wanted the word drawn out here. Whether it is a fear of murdering Hamlet, or a growing doubt as to the veracity of Claudius' claims, Laertes is terrified of what is to come, and his decision to proceed is made with a heavy heart.

The first two passes can be as short or long as the director would like, but we caution you to keep them from becoming five-minute fight extravaganzas. Whilst this can be entertaining (yet rarely is), remember that the past two hours (or three or seven) have led up to this final scene. This fight has the ability to enhance your story with a thrilling climax or, by making just one gratuitous decision, you can destroy all of your work. No pressure.

After the second pass, the queen drinks from the poisoned cup. It's important that the actor playing Claudius decide how much he knows about the properties of the poison used. It's clear that the poison has no obvious taste, but the effects are painful enough that the queen understands she has been poisoned (there are some poisons that just help you to a sleep from which you never wake). The audience must understand why Claudius doesn't run from the room at that moment. Is it the same poison he used to kill the last king? If so, the ghost gave us details in 1.5 that the actor playing Gertrude can use in the portrayal of her death:

With iuyce of cursed Hebenon in a Violl,
And in the Porches of mine eares did poure
The leaperous Distilment; whose effect

Holds such an enmity with bloud of Man,
That swift as Quick-siluer, it courses through
The naturall Gates and Allies of the Body;
And with a sodaine vigour it doth posset
And curd, like Aygre droppings into Milke,
The thin and wholsome blood: so did it mine;
And a most instant Tetter bak'd about,
Most Lazar-like, with vile and loathsome crust,
All my smooth Body.

It seems unlikely, however, that Claudius has used the same poison. Some reasons for this: the apothecary from whom Claudius (or one of his representatives) procured the original poison was probably mortally silenced, so who knows what goods the next apothecary might have; suspicion could arise if the corpses of King Hamlet and his son were to show the exact same effects; and Gertrude would have to be pretty strong to endure this terrible poison longer than her dead husband. Earlier in this scene, Claudius states:

The King shal drinke to *Hamlets* better breath,
And in the Cup an vnion shal he throw
Richer then that, which foure successiue Kings
In Denmarkes Crowne haue worne.

Some texts amend 'union' to 'onion', but it's confusing why an onion would ever be worn in a crown. He more likely means a pearl of some sort, which has been poisoned. That poison could be hebenon and, maybe because it's coated on the pearl and distilled in the wine, instead of being poured undistilled into someone's ear, Gertrude could last longer. You could also go with aconite or hemlock, as discussed in Chapter 1 – *King Lear* (5.3) and Chapter 2 – *Cymbeline* (1.6). Whichever you choose, make sure its effects are specific and sufficient enough that Gertrude knows it's poison *in extremis*, but it's distilled enough so she can survive to say the lines. There's some speculation about whether hebenon is even a real thing. There are differing opinions on whether it existed in Shakespeare's day, or if it's hemlock, or if it's just something Willy invented to pass the time (which he often did). Ensure that you set strict characteristics for whatever it may be in your production.

When the fencing match begins, the stage direction is 'They Play', but the third pass is 'in scuffling'. This suggests a distinctly less-refined feel. Additionally, both fighters get wounded with the envenomed blade during the pass. This is typically executed by Laertes finally wounding Hamlet (something quite shocking to everyone in the room who assumed the fight was with foiled blades), and Hamlet charging at Laertes, forcing a *corps-à-corps* in which 'they change Rapiers'. This will allow Hamlet to wound Laertes with the same envenomed sword. It's imperative that the actor playing Hamlet decide if/when he realises he has been poisoned before Laertes confirms the same. [*JK: I have seen Hamlet stab Laertes in the torso with the sword, which makes no sense unless Hamlet knew right away that he had been poisoned. It's more likely that he is so angry over being wounded that he loses control, allowing the fight to spiral into a chaotic mess in which punches could be thrown.*] Claudius notes that they are 'incensed', so the fight director should modulate the fight from gentlemanly play at fencing to infuriated men fighting tooth and nail.

The body count that follows should happen rapidly. There is a tendency, since the play is coming to an end, to drag out the scene so that everyone can have a showy death. This isn't melodrama though, it's Shakespeare. [*SD: Admittedly, there's some overlap.*] Once Laertes tells Hamlet that the king is to blame, Hamlet should whirl around and thrust the sword through Claudius. If Hamlet stalks slowly up to the king, at least a few guards could come to his aid and Hamlet would have to kill them as well. It doesn't matter who's right/wrong, the soldiers would protect their king, whether or not they like him. It's a choice, but we don't like it. As with our recommendation in Chapter 1 – *King Lear* (5.3) that Lear enters howling, with the dead Cordelia in his arms before the audience can sense it coming, you have a similar weapon at your disposal here – we have spent hours waiting for this moment. The audience should be just as shocked as Claudius at how quickly the stab occurs, and how irreversible it is. <u>Taking away the audience's time to process the sequence of tragedies is the way to land visceral punches.</u>

Keep the speed at a clip in this otherwise-molasses-laden play – Hamlet grabs the cup, and pours the poison down the king's throat. The large dose ingested by Claudius (including the poison from the sword) would kill him quickly, given that a mere sip did in the queen.

Note that you also need to be specific about the type of poison applied to the sword. It should be different from the poison in the drink because it was procured by Laertes, who told Claudius in 4.7 that it is:

> an Vnction of a Mountebanke
> So mortall, I but dipt a knife in it,
> Where it drawes blood, no Cataplasme so rare,
> Collected from all Simples that haue Vertue
> Vnder the Moone, can saue the thing from death,
> That is but scratcht withall:

The actors playing Hamlet and Laertes should discuss the poison's qualities, so that they exhibit similar symptoms whilst dying. Again, this needs to move quickly.

After Horatio's eulogy, Fortinbras enters with his troops. [*JK: Probably not, since almost every production cuts this aspect of the show (much like Paris and Romeo's fight in Volume Two).*] Who knows what Fortinbras has been expecting? Probably not four corpses in the throne room (or more if you opted for Hamlet to slaughter some of the king's guards). The shock of this scene would give Fortinbras pause for at least a second. After this, does he remain frozen? Does he 'snap to', and send his troops to secure all the doors, seizing any other folks who can tell the story? How does he address Horatio, who is probably still holding on to Hamlet's corpse? [*SD: Are we finally done with this terrible play?*]

## from Estelle Kohler

*I was playing Ophelia to David Warner's Hamlet for the RSC at the Aldwych Theatre in the '70s. Michael Jayston, playing Laertes, used to do a bit of business where he jumped down into the grave to lift Ophelia's body from her coffin. On the night in question, his foot slipped as he jumped and he went right through the coffin lid, landing on top of me. He spent the rest of the scene whispering apologies to me, between his Laertes' lines. I wasn't hurt, but was corpsing (literally!) throughout.*

MaConnia Chesser, Cristina Carrión, and Jerilyn Sackler as the Weird Sisters; Seth Duerr as Macbeth. (*The York Shakespeare Company, 2010*)

# Chapter 4

# Macbeth

*Th' expedition of my violent love / Outrun the pauser, reason'* – Macbeth (2.3)

*[JK: Many productions begin the play in battle. I enjoy this not just because it's more violence for me to choreograph, but it's also a great opportunity to show Macbeth and Banquo working together. I've always envisioned them as best friends. Staging the battle gives you opportunities to show this in action, and also justifies their description as badasses in the captain's report.]* *[SD: We differ on this, and not just because friendship makes me gag. The captain's speech contains some of Shakespeare's richest imagery. I prefer that the audience do the heavy lifting early on, so we can build up Mackers one scene after another, but never actually see him in action until the final act, by which point we will be in serious doubt as to whether his physical prowess remains intact given his severe mental decline. The answer, as young Seward will unfortunately find out in real time with the audience, is a bloody and resounding 'yes'. There was an audible gasp most evenings in late 2010 when my Scottish king dispatched the overeager kiddo within seconds, my first onstage kill after two hours of being lauded but never actually seen in battle. Quite different from my Coriolanus in 2002, who was bathed in blood from carving corpses for the first half-hour of the evening. I can understand Jared's inclination for a big set piece at the top of the proceedings given the entertainment value, and to illustrate the relationship between Macky and Banqy, but the text already does the latter and most popular television/film can give you the former. This is one reason why Shakespeare rarely translates well into film – a production can show or it can tell, but it easily descends into overkill when it does both. A cinematic experience is twenty-four frames per second of onscreen visuals, versus the theatrical experience of thousands of images in your head as the playwright conjures them. As we'll revisit below, this play is obsessed with the corporeal. Not just in fight mode, but all bodily functions. From the porter's sexual disappointments, to a staggering number of references to food throughout each act, to the ultimate dissertation on substance versus shadow, let the language land the imagery more often than not, and the few physical manifestations will have more impact than if you stage a non-stop visual horror show.]*

## Act 1  Scene 2

*See Glossary – Blood; Blood Packs.*

Be specific about the wounds the bloody captain has sustained. We know he has 'gashes', which is to say more than one gash. There are myriad places he could be hit without immediate need of a surgeon. The head is a good choice since the scalp bleeds a lot but, unless the skull is fractured, there is little damage done; though it is difficult to get bleeding to subside without stitches. You could also go with a cut to the abdominal area or extremities. This will allow for muscles to be sliced, which will not be life-threatening but will produce a lot of blood and will definitely need to be stitched. Again, not the most urgent patient in triage, except perhaps in terms of the immense amount of pain involved. Whatever the injury, the captain is working through it as best he can, sticking to relatively normal verse at first, but slowly disintegrating to the point that the king finally allows surgery.

Note that this character is referred to as 'Captaine' in the stage direction but is called 'Serjeant' by Malcolm. These are very different ranks. [*SD: \*cue live studio audience\* HOW DIFFERENT ARE THEY?*] [*JK: Definitely anachronistic titles from the sixteenth century, as they didn't exist in the eleventh. A captain in the sixteenth century would have been in charge of 100-200 men, whilst a sergeant is lower than a lieutenant, which is under a captain.*] Decide whether it is the author's mistake or Malcolm's. If Malcolm's, do the other warriors notice the difference, and are they tempted to correct him? Shakespeare clearly did not serve battle time. The physics required for any kind of weapon to cleave a man right up the middle, from the groin to the jaw, do not exist outside of a blockbuster action flick. Unseaming in the other direction is more believable, as Macbeth would have gravity on his side, but would still require a tremendous amount of force. This isn't particularly a problem given the play's constant nods to the supernatural/superhuman. Shakespeare has created a stunning image for the audience, and we're probably meant to focus on what it tells us about the character, and the mood it conveys, rather than the physics.

Macbeth's next action – decapitation – would be more straightforward. Whilst the spine serves as an impediment to cleaving off the head in one fell swoop, a few blows from a backsword, longsword, or most cutting weapons of the time would be able to sever the head.

Note that the actor playing Banquo should exhibit a skill level on par with Macbeth, as the captain reports they are both kicking serious ass in this battle. Banquo could also have performed some next-level kills, but we're not hearing about them. Thus, the king is not hearing about them. The laurels that the king puts on Macbeth are because of this report. [*SD: I directed the 2010 production mentioned above, in which I played the titular role, and hired Jared to do the fights and play Banquo. My suspicion has now been confirmed – his inner voice was incessantly whingeing about not being talked up as much I was by the captain.*] [*JK: Will you please stop saying 'titular'?!*]

The importance of decapitation and putting a head on a spike is that it becomes a public proclamation of a traitor's death and dishonour. This tradition was well established in Shakespeare's time.

## Act 1 Scene 3

*See Glossary – Draws; Ensemble Readiness.*

*Banq.* Were such things here, as we doe speake about?
Or haue we eaten on the insane Root,
That takes the Reason Prisoner?
 *Macb.* Your Children shall be Kings.
 *Banq.*        You shall be King.
 *Macb.* And *Thane* of Cawdor too: went it not so?
 *Banq.* Toth'selfe-same tune, and words: who's here?

      *Enter Rosse and Angus.*

We cannot tell you how many times we have seen Rosse/Angus enter, and Macbeth/ Banquo stroll on over and say howdy. These are warriors who just finished a vicious battle, and are then told they'll have control over the throne for generations by some bizarre strangers, who may or may not exist. When Rosse/Angus arrive, Macbeth/ Banquo – already raw bags of nerves – should immediately prepare a physical defence, even though it will quickly be proved unnecessary.


## Act 1 Scene 5

*See Glossary – Strikes (maybe).*

Time to deal with the dead baby.

 In 1.7, Lady Macbeth will try any number of tactics to convince her husband to murder Duncan. Macbeth is receptive to none, except the last – his wife's mention of having breastfed a child, and a willingness to murder it if she knew her husband would prove so weak. As we mentioned at the top of Chapter 1 – *King Lear*, Shakespeare will often present us with questions to which he will never provide the answers. This one is pivotal. Lady Macbeth could have nursed some other person's child, but this makes little sense for our dramatic purposes. (She historically had a son from a former marriage, who became the stepson of Macbeth and ascended to the throne. But he was considered incredibly inept, and was usurped and assassinated by Malcolm. Shakespeare omits these details.)

 The story we propose is that the Macbeths had a child, who died just before Mr went to war. Mrs has been alone in their huge castle this entire time and, as the entitled granddaughter of a former king, is unable to connect with the help. Now, after slowly losing her mind in the eleventh-century version of COVID-19 self-isolation, there is not only the hope of greeting civilisation again, but hosting its most powerful representative. This would give her the opportunity to eliminate him, and assume what she believes to be her rightful place on the throne.

 *Mess.* The King comes here to Night.
 *Lady.*        Thou'rt mad to say it.

This psychological swing could easily be enough to warrant slapping the messenger, out of shock and joy.

> Come thick Night,
> And pall thee in the dunnest smoake of Hell,
> That my keene Knife see not the Wound it makes,
> Nor Heauen peepe through the Blanket of the darke,
> To cry, hold, hold.

*See Glossary – Blood (maybe).*

Okay, so what is the 'keene Knife'? Does Lady M have one on her person? Is she using it to cut herself in this incantation? Or does she mean a knife she will use to kill Duncan? It would make sense if Lady M thought she would have to do the deed (should her husband arrive too late), but the messenger makes clear Lord M is on his way. So why does Lady M feel compelled to unsex? Has she already determined the low odds of her husband being up to the task of regicide? It's a reasonable assumption, given the result of his soliloquy in 1.7.

If you do opt for ritual here, the kind of knife Lady M wields will reveal more about her character: it was not unusual for people during this time to have a standard knife for eating and other utilitarian functions; if you decide Lady M is something of a sorceress, and not just dabbling in this as a novice, she may be in possession of something more ornate. The wound would typically be to the hand, but you may want to go for the forearm (see Chapter 1 – *King Lear* (2.1)); or the thigh (see Volume Two – *Julius Caesar* (2.1)). These locations are easier to bandage, and you won't have to show the audience that she is healing if these areas are covered (assuming you want to hide the wound). Neither of us has seen a production that opted for a wound to the hand and bandaged it in subsequent scenes. It could make for a deliciously awkward 1.6 if Lady M has to hide the thing from Duncan, who says at the end 'Giue me your hand', and the other bozos who have no business running the kingdom.)

[*SD: My 2010 Lady M (Chicago-badass-and-noted-corgi-whisperer Jenn Remke) and I discussed these possibilities, but decided to scrap an actual knife or drawing any blood, as it would place her too much in the world of the weird sisters, and we both wanted Lady M to function as a separate influence on Mackers, rather than end up diluted in some cosmic conspiracy. We were on the same page at each point during tablework anyway, since Jenn used a Lady M speech in an audition for a different play in 2009, and I chimed in with M's next line. Not missing a beat, she continued to play the scene. I told her afterwards that, whilst not the fit I was looking for in that production (Portia in* Merchant, *partly because of how impossible it would be to find a Bassanio she wouldn't see through from the very start), she would be top of my list whenever I got to work on Mackers. And she was.*]

*See Glossary – Intimacy.*

[*SD: The Macbeths provide the most microscopic examination in the canon of a couple disintegrating. (Antony and Cleopatra come close, but there are constantly servants around; the Macbeths almost always confer privately.) The concept of an intimacy consultant is relatively new. Please hire one. For the 2010 production, I closed off early rehearsals of these private scenes so that only Jenn, the stage manager, and I were in the room. Any physical intimacy was choreographed. Whether or not you have the budget for a consultant, you can at least take these basic steps. Something Jenn and I agreed early on was that, in the short period after their child died and before M went off to war, they absolutely did not discuss the death of their child in any depth. As a distraction, they may still have been 'fucking' but never 'making love'. This was reflected in our choices for their first intimate encounter here, after what must have felt like eons. The death of a child will severely impact any marriage. A divorce is almost a best-case scenario, considering what happens to the Macbeths. Note that anyone playing the Scottish couple, or directing the production, should watch one of my all-time favourite films – Todd Field's* In the Bedroom *(2001) – to get a sense of just how granular the examination of a marriage is in this play, and the power of what goes unspoken.*]

## Act 1  Scene 6

*Banq.* This Guest of Summer,
The Temple-haunting Barlet does approue,
By his loued Mansonry, that the Heauens breath
Smells wooingly here: no Iutty frieze,
Buttrice, nor Coigne of Vantage, but this Bird
Hath made his pendant Bed, and procreant Cradle,
Where they must breed, and haunt: I haue obseru'd
The ayre is delicate.

[*JK: I played Banquo at least three times before doing it for Seth's production in 2010. Not once had anybody included this passage. So, when I received my script, I was pretty sure he'd made it up. Turns out he hadn't, and this weather forecast was Shakespeare's idea. It took some time to understand that it's important to set up how all of nature is harmonious in the world of this play because Duncan is still alive, and how that will be juxtaposed with the post-regicide reports by Lennox – 'The obscure Bird clamor'd the liue-long Night. / Some say, the Earth was feuorous, / And did shake' – and then Ross, regarding Duncan's horses eating each other. Violent discord in nature, as a reflection of disturbances to the monarchy, is a device used throughout the canon. If you hear a character discussing how beautifully everything is going, you can be sure it's all about to collapse in short order.*]

## Act 1  Scene 7

*See Glossary – Grabs (maybe); Intimacy; Strikes (maybe).*

Jenn Remke as Lady Macbeth and Seth Duerr as Macbeth. (*The York Shakespeare Company, 2010*)

[*JK: I use* Macbeth *as a perfect example of the difference between killing and murder. Humans are not naturally inclined to kill each other. There are exceptions but, on the whole, we are not wired that way. Training is required to kill another human, and that training can come in many forms (military training, watching/living in violence). For example, the Human Resources Research Office (HRRO) of the US Army revolutionised combat training in the mid-1900s. In Korea, the rate of fire for a US soldier had been approximately fifty-five per cent. That means about forty-five per cent of soldiers would not pull the trigger when an enemy was in their sights. They had only practised firing at bullseye targets in basic training, so forty-five per cent of people couldn't kill even if it meant their own death. The HRRO worked to identify training elements that could increase the fire rate and found the most success by using realistic, man-shaped, pop-up targets that fall when hit. This kind of operant conditioning is the only way to reliably influence the midbrain processing of a frightened human being. According to Dave Grossman, in his book* On Killing, *similar application and perfection of these basic conditioning techniques increased the rate of fire to around ninety-five per cent in Vietnam. This is just an example of how difficult it is for a trained soldier to kill someone, even when their life is on the line. Premeditated murder is much harder, because it's in cold blood. The psychological aftermath of murder cannot be overstated. Shakespeare is clear at the beginning of this play that Macbeth has killed hundreds, if not thousands, of people. But this would be his first murder. The distinction is not trivial. Having a noble cause, such as 'defending your country', provides a human justification to commit these acts. Murdering someone for personal gain will have a major psychological effect.*] [*SD: It's not just personal gain. I'll explain later in the scene the Macbeths' reasons for removing a sweet but useless monarch.*] [*JK: To murder someone for ANY reason will have a major psychological effect. Jesus, are you happy?!*] [*SD: Never. But you may proceed.*] [*JK: This psychological impact is not the same for everyone. The play brilliantly depicts two very human and distinct responses to committing murder, whatever their excuses were at the time. A major part of the guilt that will plague our soon-to-be-miserable couple is the responsibility of a host (and of a guest). We alluded to this in Chapter 1 –* King Lear *(3.7). These obligations were clearly spelled out by Shakespeare's time. The etiquette would have been known by rich and poor alike. When someone was your guest, they were yours to protect and feed. You could not take advantage of them, nor they you. A host would roll out their version of the red carpet if someone of a higher station were to visit – there was no 'hey, you can crash here and help yourself to the fridge'.*]

Your Macbeths may have a very physical relationship. See Chapter 1 – *King Lear* (3.7) to compare and contrast with Cornwall and Regan's next-level kink. You'll need to decide how much of this works for your production. As we mentioned earlier, Lady M deploys many tactics before playing the dead-baby trump card. It's not unreasonable for Lady Macbeth to move from the verbal to the physical with a slap; not to beat the crap out of her husband, just to wake him up. Or, if you want to establish that this is part of their relationship, you could have her start to slap him and he catches her wrist.

There are plenty of moments for Lady M to smack his chest, arms, *etc.*, and for him to either pull her into a bearhug (so her arms are pinned), or push her away. She can push him back, and he can grab her face on lines such as 'Prythee peace'. Make sure to have your fight director and intimacy coordinator on hand here and give this scene proper rehearsal time.

We discussed earlier that Macbeth keeps saying 'no', until the dead child is mentioned and then the reply is 'maybe'. You should build your own backstory on why this strategy works on Lord M. [*SD: Jenn and I looked to history. Lady M's grandfather had been king until he was murdered by Duncan's father. This is not specifically mentioned in the play, but neither my Lord M nor Jenn's Lady M found Duncan particularly competent (this is different from kind, which we considered a deficit). And we were not pleased with his judgment in confirming heir-apparent Malcolm McFuckstick, whose forename was shared with the dude who killed Lady M's granpappy. If the idea of Mackers finding Duncan 'cleere in his great Office' seems at odds with this assessment of his rule, revisit 1.4 (in which Mackers told Duncan how a king should behave – 'Your Highnesse part, is to receiue our Duties' – despite not consciously trying to overstep; Duncan probably would have been too dumb to notice anyway, having 'built / an absolute Trust' on the prior Thane of Cawdor). This gets back to Jared's earlier point that what gives the couple pause is their personal connection to Duncan, not a political one – Mackers has affection for Duncan, notwithstanding his strategic missteps, and Lady M thinks Duncan looks like her dead father.*] As everyone knows, 'maybe' means 'yes'. Now that the couple is on the same page, work with your intimacy coordinator. The innuendos are not accidental – 'screw your courage to the sticking place' and 'bend vp each corporall Agent' – nor is Macbeth's 'Bring forth Men-Children only' mere moments after Lady M used a dead child as leverage. [*SD: This was, for Jenn and me, the eleventh-century Scottish equivalent of couples therapy – we were politically going to assume power to stabilise the kingdom, but personally doing it in some deranged attempt to save our marriage. This was also our workaround in answering a famous question presented by the play – if you believe the witches' prophecy will come true, why not just wait and let it happen? Our wish to rush the process along was reinforced not only by the need to repair a marriage we thought would fail without immediate intervention, but was also in the normal course of events for the Scottish throne at this time. It was typical to kill the current king, and take his crown. Shakespeare does, however, leave this fact out, so that 2.3 is more dramatic. Otherwise, that scene would basically just be the couple shouting 'We did it and now we get the crowns! Peace out, losers.'*]

## Act 2  Scene 2

*See Glossary – Blood; Grabs; Intimacy; Strikes (maybe).*

> *Macb.* I haue done the deed:
> Didst thou not heare a noyse?
> *Lady.* I heard the Owle schreame, and the Crickets cry.
> Did not you speake?
> *Macb.*            When?
> *Lady.*            Now.                    (<------*looks like a staircase!*)
> *Macb.*                    As I descended?

Time to get your fight director and intimacy consultant again. We'll spend the next four acts watching this marriage deteriorate. The power of this scene, and some of the comedy, is in the shared lines. Everything should feel as though it's happening too quickly and – given that it takes most of the scene before Lady M even notices her husband is holding onto the bloody daggers – it probably is. She might try to soothe him, to get him to calm the hell down, but it's not going to be successful. Again, she's in control of herself (with the help of some booze lifted off the groomsmen), and her husband is a complete mess. (They will reverse positions over the course of the play, but these are still early days.)

If you're struggling to find reasons Lady M fails to see the daggers from the top of the scene – besides psychological distress, adrenaline, inebriation, and a husband bathed in blood – you could try a combination of dim lighting and positioning the daggers such that Mackers holds both in one hand but in reverse grip (*i.e.* with the blades running along his forearm). [*JK: It's valuable for the actor playing Macbeth to sit down with the fight director, and discuss in detail how the murder of Duncan went down. Your fight director should be able to talk you through where all this blood has come from when stabbing/slashing the king. By creating specificity in the murder, this scene will play out more believably. The first question – why is Macbeth smothered in blood? The plan was to get enough blood to smear the groomsmen. Did something go wrong? It could be that Macbeth botched the first stab, which woke Duncan, causing Macbeth to panic and make a bunch of haphazard stabs, forcing blood to spray everywhere. If Duncan woke and tried to defend himself, Macbeth could have a bloody handprint on his clothes, or bloody fingermarks on his cheek. Or did Macbeth cut Duncan's throat first, severing both carotid arteries and spraying Macbeth with blood? A plan like this has the benefit of making it impossible for Duncan to scream out for help. Another silencing method would be if Macbeth covered Duncan's mouth, and plunged a dagger into his heart. Whichever path you choose, Macbeth would have to stab Duncan's corpse multiple times to make it look like he was killed by the groomsmen. This, alone, would do a real number on Macbeth's psyche. The more horrifying his experience, the easier it will be for the actor playing him to refuse to go back to Duncan's chamber.*]

When Macbeth declines to return and place the daggers, Lady M could switch from soothing to punishing on 'Infirme of purpose'. Smack, push, shove, whatever floats your boat. It should be in line with the vocabulary you set up in 1.5 and 1.7. They will eventually get to a point where even physical abuse will be missed, as they drift apart in Act 3, and don't meet at all in Acts 4 and 5.

# from Harriet Walter

*We act so much that is beyond our experience that inevitably what we do on stage is a mere imitation of an imitation of what we have seen other actors do in movies or on stage. We clutch our hearts and writhe and gasp when we 'die', we grunt and groan as we thrust swords and parry usually at quite a slow choreographed pace, nothing like the speeded-up insane flailing you sometimes see in a street brawl outside a pub.*

*I actually find Shakespeare sword fights quite boring. Usually you know who is going to win: Tybalt, then Romeo, Henry Tudor, Prince Hal or whatever, so it is just a case of sitting back admiring the co-ordination of the actors and the inventiveness of the fight director staging Hamlet v Laertes for the fifteenth time in his (usually) career.*

*So we watch with complacence. We let drop our suspension of disbelief and the plot that we have up to now been caught up in becomes flat or, at worst, silly. But that may just be me.*

*For this reason I was very grateful that during rehearsals for Macbeth at the RSC in 1999, Antony Sher suggested to the director, Greg Doran, that we should rehearse the scene after the murder of Duncan using real sharpened daggers and real blood just once to see how it made us behave physically, if at all differently. So one evening the three of us and the stage management team stayed on after the rest of the cast had left and we rehearsed as described.*

*People talk about the 'taste of fear' and Macbeth is a play about fear as much as it is about anything else, and that evening we tapped into a fear that we had only been counterfeiting before. We spoke in panicky whispers huddled in a small alcove of the rehearsal room looking at and smelling the blood on our hands and passing those sharp dripping blades back and forth to one another as if they were hot coals. I never took the handling of those weapons for granted again. Each night I had to climb a spiral staircase in a long dress carrying the two knives up to Duncan's chamber and in my imagination's memory I believed they could at any minute have gashed my thighs.*

*Another slightly more bizarre result of that rehearsal was that when I went out to supper that same night, my friend remarked that I kept rubbing my hands. Unconsciously I was exactly carrying out Lady M's handwashing motion because, despite many washes, my hands could still feel the viscous coating of that blood, in this case lamb's blood and believe me it is nothing at all like Kensington Gore.*

## Act 2  Scene 3

*See Glossary – Draws; Ensemble Readiness.*

The king is dead and the killer(s) unknown. Who is armed? Who isn't? How does a group of humans behave when the murders could continue from any direction? Ringing the bell will alert the entire castle to present danger. They don't know if there is an enemy threat outside the walls, a fire inside, or something else. It makes sense that each character is getting dressed, armed, *etc.* When they get the news that the king is dead, all must raise their guard levels even higher; there is every reason to believe they could be next. This doesn't mean community-theatre-type mugging, but rather an alertness born out of survival instinct.

Primogeniture has not yet been adopted in Scotland and, as we mentioned, it was common for kings to be usurped and killed. The naming of Malcolm as heir in 1.4 would strike several people as bizarre, for a variety of reasons, but now Mackers can use it to his advantage since Malcolm seems the likeliest suspect. (Maybe not everyone leaps to this conclusion in the game of whodunnit – Macbeth not waiting for the witches' prophecy to come true is, on its own, just as impulsive as Malcolm not waiting for his father to die – but most will soon subscribe to this belief when Malcolm flees the kingdom.) [*JK: When I played Banquo, Mackers was the first suspect that came to mind. Banquo is the only other person to know about the witches' prophecy. That doesn't mean I thought Mackers did it, but I sure as hell didn't think Malcolm would have the guts. I spent most of the scene trying to make eye contact with Macbeth. Mostly to just say 'brah, maybe you'll be king' but, when he wouldn't look at me, my wheels started to turn. That gave me a catalyst to cross to Lady M, with this same question in mind and, lo and behold, she goes and faints.*] [*SD: I'm glad not to have looked upon you.*]

*See Glossary – Faints.*

> *Lady.*                              Helpe me hence, hoa.

Work with your fight director to stage Lady M's fall safely. She should be as low to the ground as possible before gravity takes over. Avoid any bony bits; always land on muscle. If you need to make it even safer (due to any prior injuries or conditions your actress may have), position one of the other actors near Lady M, so she can be caught and helped to the ground.

## Act 3  Scene 1

*See Glossary – Ensemble Readiness.*

Make sure to fill in your backstory – act breaks weren't just an opportunity centuries ago for stagehands to trim candles, but also for leading characters to catch their breath whilst contemplating kiddie murder.

*Macb.* To night we hold a solemne Supper sir,
And Ile request your presence.
   *Banq.* Let your Highnesse
Command vpon me, to the which my duties
Are with a most indissoluble tye
For euer knit.
   *Macb.* Ride you this afternoone?
   *Ban.* I, my good Lord.
   *Macb.* We should haue else desir'd your good aduice
(Which still hath been both graue, and prosperous)
In this dayes Councell: but wee'le take to morrow.
Is't farre you ride?

*(Does M jump in to share B's line, or is there a pause before M asks his question and B jumps in to answer?)*

We don't anticipate violence in the first part of this scene, but your ensemble should be on edge. Macbeth, like Richard 3, has no idea what to do with the crown once he obtains it, other than hurl himself into the paranoia pool and hire some assassins. Macbeth spends most of the third act incredibly uncomfortable in the role of monarch (later described as 'a Giants Robe / Vpon a dwarfish Theefe'). The question for your ensemble is whether Mackers is a threat or simply nervous. [*JK: Playing Banquo opposite Seth's Macbeth was a great time each evening. Please don't tell him I said so.*] [*SD: Remember when there was only one set of footprints in the sand? It was then that I carried every scene partner I ever had.*] [*JK: Wow. Moving on. This whole scene is just so awkward for Banquo. He's wrestling with what the witches have said, his own potential rise to power, and it's easy to feel somewhat guilty around Macbeth. I told myself Macbeth had just been avoiding me with all the coronation stuff going on, so we hadn't had time to catch up. Yeah ... that's why we hadn't talked lately. Now, we finally get to chat, and Seth would take pauses that felt like forever. He took three metrical feet of silence after 'For euer knit'. When he finally asked, 'Ride you this afternoone?', I jumped right in to make that a shared line. I wanted to be helpful and even tried to reply to 'Councell', to say I would cancel my plans. No friggin' pause there! Then, back to questions about my ride.*]

Note that there are three metrical feet of silence before Banquo answers Macbeth's second question. Your production's Banquo will have to figure out why. [*JK: I took the pause, thinking 'WTF, Mackers, why are you so interested in my travel plans'?! I hadn't really been scared of him until this interaction. In the back of my brain, I did wonder if he was the murderer. If so, he's the only one who knew the witches' prophecy about my family. What would he do with me and my children? Never mind. Everyone would be fine! We've been friends forever, and he knows I always have his back. No reason to be scared. I stumbled a bit with 'As farre, my Lord', but then cracked a joke about my horse's competency. This attempt at lightening the mood resulted in five metrical feet of silence from Seth.*] [*SD: Macbeth's four-syllable 'Faile not our Feast' is typically the end of a six-syllable shared line Banquo started. Banquo then has five syllables of silence he can disperse before, amongst, or after 'My Lord, I will not'.*]

    *Ban.* As farre, my Lord, as will fill vp the time
'Twixt this, and Supper. Goe not my Horse the better,
I must become a borrower of the Night,
For a darke houre, or twaine.
    *Macb.* Faile not our Feast.
    *Ban.* My Lord, I will not.

[*SD: By the third act, my Macbeth was not particularly a fan of open-mic nights. Instead of jumping in with the shared line, I darted ten syllables of deadpan silence in Jared's direction.*]

    *Ban.* As farre, my Lord, as will fill vp the time
'Twixt this, and Supper. Goe not my Horse the better,
I must become a borrower of the Night,
For a darke houre, or twaine. --------------------
    *Macb.* ----------------------- Faile not our Feast.
    *Ban.* My Lord, I will not.

*See Glossary – Grabs (maybe); Intimacy (maybe); Strikes (maybe).*

[*JK: Hiring a commoner to kill a nobleman on the road goes back hundreds of years by Shakespeare's time. The tradition of bringing seconds to a duel actually sprang from this concept. Nobleman A would challenge Nobleman B to a duel, and then arrive early. Along the road to the duelling ground, Nobleman A would have hired men in position to kill Nobleman B on his way to the duel. After waiting an appropriate amount of time, Nobleman A would declare that Nobleman B did not show up for the duel, and therefore is disgraced. Meanwhile, Nobleman B is dead in a ditch.*] [*SD: Must you quote Boris Johnson?*] [*JK: It then became the norm to bring seconds along to a duel, to ensure you actually arrived in one piece.*]

    You'll have to decide what Macbeth is like in the interviewing process. Does he abuse/ seduce either of the murderers? He asks about their manhood, the second murderer mentions 'blowes', the first says 'tugg'd', and Mackers speaks of 'thrusts' and 'I to your assistance doe make loue'.

    [*JK: If you pursue any physical avenue here, especially of a sexual variety, make sure to have an intimacy consultant on hand with your fight director. Whenever coming into contact with another actor, it is important you're not actually grabbing their hair, ears, naughty bits, or anything else Macbeth might pursue here. You will place your hand in front of the area, and the victim pulls that against themselves, to make it look like you are grabbing the appropriate part(s). When we're talking about nether regions, you can often place the hand on the thigh and it will look like you've grabbed the groin. It's also important to have a conversation with both actors before making a choice like this. As a fight director, the physical safety of the actors is only part of the job. Psychological and emotional well-being is also key. All actors need to be comfortable with the choreography and, more importantly, understand how the action furthers the story, so it comes across in the performance. Otherwise, it's merely gratuitous. We'll discuss this again during the murder of Lady Macduff (4.2).*]

## Act 3　Scene 2

*See Glossary – Grabs (maybe); Intimacy (maybe); Strikes (maybe).*

[*SD: Continue to track the fracturing of this relationship. They've now switched positions in terms of who is pushing for violence and who is retreating: Lady M contemplated one murder and one only; Lord M will likely never stop since, like Claudius in Chapter 3 –* Hamlet, *he is destined to spend the entirety of his reign looking over his shoulder. The language reflects this marital discord – the shared lines, so common to this couple before, are virtually absent here.*] [*JK: Not unlike how Seth and I started this chapter in a unified voice but now just write asides to you, dear reader.*] [*SD: Macbeth decides here to keep his wife in the dark from now on – 'Be innocent of the knowledge, dearest Chuck.' You can explore with your fight director and intimacy consultant how the physical language also devolves. As this act proceeded, I recall choosing to avoid physical contact with Jenn, for fear of getting any of my paranoia and death on her. I kept this secret from her, despite our openness in rehearsals, just to see what she might do with it. A decade after our production closed, Jenn told me she had her own secret – an entire thought process about why I avoided touching her throughout our final scenes together. This made the scenes richer, as we were being driven away from each other by our own private guilts.*]

## Act 3　Scene 3

[*JK: I miss Seth. Maybe this is where our voices can become unified again. Over the years, I have done some fun things with the murderers. Many productions choose the third murderer to be Macbeth in disguise.*] [*SD: I hate this idea. Bye now.*] [*JK: *sigh* See ya. I also particularly like the use of the three witches (in magical disguise). The murderers have a job to do and it's pretty clear their capabilities are in question. To prove themselves, it is in their interest to go overboard in slaughtering Banquo. In choreographing the fight, we have a clear report from the first murderer in the next scene about what he and his accomplices did to Banquo. Your production's choices will reveal the murderers' characters – the fight either matches the description in 3.4, or it is exposed to the audience as a lie. The murderers can be cold-blooded killers, who actually give Banquo 'twenty trenched gashes on his head' and slit his throat. Or they could be overselling it, in the hope of getting paid a gnarly bonus. If you make the latter choice, the murderers can stab Banquo a few times, and run away. Either option is valid, but I rarely see the latter. Whichever you choose, you have a decision to make about Fleance's age and capability. Does he attempt to stay and fight? How much does Banquo then have to focus on protecting his child, particularly if he is not battle-ready? If Fleance receives a small wound, this would be a good catalyst for Banquo to yell 'Fly'. It's very difficult to defend yourself from a properly planned and executed assassination. The surprise in the first moments is the perfect time to land a few of the trenched gashes on Banquo.*] [*SD: On his head? That's what the murderer claims.*] [*JK: No, I don't think the murderers counted the injuries inflicted on Banquo generally, let alone the ones to his head. The murderers just cut Banquo up like a Christmas turkey.*] [*SD: You know I don't celebrate holidays of any kind.*] [*JK: I'm saying the murderers land some hits on Banquo, but nothing life-threatening before he orders Fleance* *to run. Once he's gone, Banquo can have a substantial fight, exhibiting his great martial skill referenced at the beginning of the play. He can get a few hits in on the murderers before being overwhelmed but, especially if he is injured before Fleance runs, it will make sense that the murderers eventually defeat Banquo. This fight is at dusk, hence the need for torches. Make sure the production team works through their plans in advance. I once choreographed this fight, and rehearsed it for a month. When we got to this scene during tech, it was pitch black. I asked the lighting designer to bring up the lights for the fight. That's when I found out the whole scene was going to be in darkness, with just a single torch on stage. I understood then that the vision was for the audience to feel what Banquo is feeling, by being in complete darkness. This removed any reason to stage a fight. We scrapped the choreography and played a game of tag in the darkness. Banquo would yell out each time he was tagged.]* *[SD: What if Fleance is skilled/lucky? I couldn't help but notice each evening in 3.4 that only one of my murderers returned, and it wasn't the one I sent to chaperone my original hires.]* *[JK: This is why I like working with you. Few people give much thought to Fleance and just let him run off. If you want to show Fleance has training, he can stay and fight back to back with Daddy at the top. This is an interesting choice, but will require a catalyst in the fight to scare Banquo enough that he orders Fleance to run. For example, Fleance might be about to get hit, but Banquo jumps in between to take the wound instead. This could be enough to make him realise the fight is a lost cause, and his son should save himself.]* *[SD: This is where a design team might freeze the action and reprise some music/effects from the witches' prophecy, just to give your Banquo a kick in the pants about his children being kings but not their pappy.]* *[JK: That could be cool. And I recommend that one of the murderers chase after Fleance. It may seem like a small detail but it's important to play the reality of the scene, which includes a very clear mandate from Macbeth that Fleance also be erased. Only one other production I worked on sent someone after him, which lets it be a two-on-one fight for Banquo, and more reason he can hold his own. In that production, the murderer failed to catch Fleance, and then returned, making a three-on-one fight that finally overpowered Banquo.]*

# from Elizabeth Swain

*The Scottish Play – NY State Theatre*

*We observed all the rules about not saying the name or quoting* etc. *and were very proud of an entire rehearsal period without incident.*

*So we come to final dress tech.*

*The murder of Banquo.*

*Murderer One trips, falls, and the set takes a slice out of his nose. One of the witches quickly retrieves the nose slice, puts it on ice and it is sewn back on in the emergency room.*

*I guess we weren't going to get away entirely scot free! Smooth sailing after that.*

## Act 3  Scene 4

*See Glossary – Grabs (maybe); Intimacy (maybe); Strikes (maybe).*

[*SD: If you thought Mackers was awkward in 3.1, boy oh boy is he out of place here. I was able to get a solid laugh each evening on 'Our selfe will mingle with Society', since 'mingle' did not sound remotely like a turn of phrase that would have been in his vocabulary (even though 'multitudinous Seas incarnardine' in 2.2 did). He's been trying on the idea of what kings do since his instructions to Duncan in 1.4, and failing ever since.*]

Upon hearing of Fleance's escape, it's possible Macbeth might get violent with the murderer – throw him up against the proscenium arch, or some such thing. If you went with the sexual route earlier, maybe a knife to the balls. Find your bliss!

*See Glossary – Ensemble Readiness; Grabs (maybe); Strikes (maybe).*

[*JK: The weight of murder on Macbeth's psyche should not be underplayed. Too many productions place emphasis on his having killed a king; it was the act of murdering a human being that starts Macbeth's downward spiral. You can now add to that the guilt of murdering his best friend.*] [*SD: I'll ignore your desire to direct me in retrospect. I am, however, curious why you keep calling them best friends. Where do you see this in the text?*] [*JK: It's not. It's in my mind's eye, Sethratio.*] [*SD: That's deeply offensive. Not just due to the inferior wordplay, but also because Horatio only has 277 lines.*]

For the banquet itself, will your production gain more from the audience seeing the ghost or not? Rupert Goold's production for the Chichester Festival Theatre in 2007 famously played the scene both ways, separated by an interval. If you show the ghost, you place the audience in Macbeth's headspace; if you don't, the audience experience the scene alongside Lady M and all the guests. Both options can be terrifying. Choose wisely. [*SD: I loved Jared's work as Banquo in this scene.*] [*JK: I don't remember being on stage when we … oh, I see.*]

Lady Macbeth's reactions to Macbeth's hallucinations should be in line with the choices you've made in earlier scenes regarding physicality and brutality. She could smack some sense into him, grab his face to try to get his attention, *etc.* But they're not alone this time. She not only has the presence of the lords to deal with, but also any PTSD her husband may be experiencing; she cannot allow him to expose their regicide, but also has to be careful of a warrior hallucinating or having a flashback.

This is a stellar scene for the actors in your ensemble, each of whom should be scared shitless, given that there's basically nothing they can do to get control over this situation other than leave, which Lady M forbids. They may also have to avoid dinnerware and furniture being hurled at them, if Mackers lashes out and your production has the budget. If inanimate objects are going to fly, ensure that there are no actors (or audience) in the direction the objects are travelling. This should look chaotic, but always be controlled.

Jenn Remke as Lady Macbeth and Seth Duerr as Macbeth. (*The York Shakespeare Company, 2010*)

> *La.* You lacke the season of all Natures, sleepe.
> *Macb.* Come, wee'l to sleepe: My strange & self-abuse
> Is the initiate feare, that wants hard vse:
> We are yet but yong indeed.

*[SD: I mentioned earlier that I avoided touching Jenn for the duration of the third act, as well as the reasons why. This moment was the exception. I had noticed she was getting antsy about the lack of physical contact, even though I didn't know her exact backstory at the time. So I added another secret to my arsenal, which Jenn can read about now in print. Hi, Jenn! The concept of an actor-manager has been common for centuries, but is bizarre by today's standards.] [JK: Because it's a terrible idea!] [SD: Not more so than the job title of director, which did not exist in theatre for thousands of years. But that's a conversation for another book. It's important to me that my actors feel like I'm fully in a scene with them as a partner, rather than just gauging their performance. When I can adjust a moment through action in a scene, instead of offering suggestions in a notes session afterwards, I usually will. And this was one of the most important moments of the production – it is the last time the Macbeths appear together, as well as the cue for the interval. I had three goals in mind: first, as with Chapter 1 – King Lear (3.7), I wanted the audience to be haunted into silence when the scene ends, rather than just skipping ahead to polite applause so they could start queuing for the toilets; second, I felt that the earlier question of whether killing Duncan would save the Macbeths' marriage needed to be answered for them both here; third, I wanted to make clear that the Macbeths had completely switched places from their first scene – now she was the one apprehensive about murder, and I was the one to take charge. I could have shared each of those directorial objectives with Jenn, but there was a simpler way to go about all of this, allowing her to keep her secrets whilst preserving mine. I lifted the embargo on physical contact and took her hand. But in the emptiest possible way – imagine being consoled by only the shell of a person, and you can see it disintegrating in front of you. I wagered that this simple and silent approach would elicit*

*a series of reactions from Jenn, which would address each of the open questions, and thereby gut-punch the audience. Happy to report that it worked – when the lights went to black, you could hear a pin drop. This anecdote isn't for self-aggrandisement because, let's be honest, I'll obviously pat my own back whether or not you're reading. Rather, this is a testament to Jenn. Hire the right actors. Provide a safe environment in which everyone can collaborate. Trust them to do the rest. (Except Jared.)]*

## Act 3  Scene 5

*See Glossary – Grabs (maybe); Strikes (maybe).*

We're not fans of this moment in the play (or most instances in the canon where deities appear). It's usually cut or, if kept, used as an excuse to have some scantily clad young women pout like children whilst being spanked by their mother-mistress. If you include the scene, and decide Hecate does get violent, take a cue from her legend and go for some sorcery if you have the budget/patience. We're not going to waste our word count on this scene, since we think (like Geoffrey Tennant does of the entire play) it is 'extraordinarily difficult to stage effectively'.

## Act 4  Scene 2

*See Glossary – Blood; Blood Packs; Grabs (maybe); Intimacy (maybe); Strikes (maybe).*

*[JK: When this scene is later reported to Macduff, it is explained how all of his children and the household staff have been murdered. Whilst only Lady Macduff and one son are written into the scene, feel free to fill the castle – other children in and out of the room, servants tending to chores, etc.] [SD: It would be a jarring start if you can pull this off in a major set change, as it might feel like the audience have been dropped into a different play for a moment – the emptier you can make Lady M feel in her dreary castle in 1.5, the better this scene will pay off if the Macduff family is a goddamned nursery full of light and joy and other nonsense I personally despise but 'humans' apparently enjoy.] [JK: Can you tell which one of us has kids? Technically, some of what he just said was useful. Especially if you carry this concept through with the murderers. For example, if all the murderers come into the room together (many productions add Macbeth in disguise as an additional murderer, and I'll save Seth the time of chiming in to say he thinks this is also stupid), have one murderer leave the stage whilst the first murderer is talking to Lady Macduff. When the offstage murderer returns, and his hands or face are bloody with no explanation, this will heighten the tension. Something I often do with this scene is add a crying baby. If you put a bassinet on stage, and place a speaker inside, it can be terrifying to kill the baby first. I have the second murderer cross to the bassinet, pull out a dagger, and stab downward. This cues the sound operator running the speaker to cut it off mid-cry. There is a cup of fake blood in the bassinet so that the dagger, as it is being drawn upward, is dripping with blood. You will get gasps from your audience each night.] [SD: And put the audience in Lady Macduff's headspace.*

*Which brings us to the main question – how does your Lady Macduff react to all of this, and what is she willing to do to save her family? Much as Jenn's Lady Macbeth informed many of my choices in playing Macbeth, you can consider not only what is on the page regarding Lady Macduff, but also think about the type of person Macduff would marry.] [JK: I can speak for both of us when I say that we do not anticipate a paralysed Lady Macduff; we think she would fight to the death to save her family, and make some serious headway. For example, in one production I did, we had an axe next to the fireplace for chopping wood. Lady Macduff grabbed it and cut one of the murderers (feel free to kill one), but was disarmed in the fight. She kept fighting anyway. One murderer grabbed her from behind, then she clawed his face, stomped on his foot, and it even seemed like she might get away. Of course, she did not. Fun fight, but we didn't get to use any blood. I have yet to see a production with a full-on bloodbath, but encourage one if you can afford it. (If you opt for claw marks, have furniture nearby with a lip under which some thick blood can be stashed. Lady Macduff can dip her fingerprints in the blood before making contact with the murderer's face.)] [SD: Would love to have done this with you in 2010, but we were already waaaaaaaay over budget.] [JK: When Macduff breaks down later upon hearing the news, the audience should have flashbacks. You could play some of the audio from that scene again. Whatever you can do to increase the audience's empathy with him. What the scene does not need is gratuitous violence. One production chose to have Lady Macduff lifted up, have her legs spread, and be penetrated with the pommel of a sword. There is no reason to sexually harm her in this scene.]*

## Act 5  Scene 1

Just a quick note to say your Lady M should avoid two things: (1) wringing or rubbing her hands to the point where she starts bleeding; (2) setting herself on fire with the taper.

## Act 5  Scene 2

*See Glossary – Ensemble Readiness.*

*[JK: Not every word of Shakespeare must be heard.] [SD: *walks into ocean*] [JK: Too often this is done centrestage, as a report to the audience. No one even remembers who Donalbane is.] [SD: The actor's family does. And he has dozens of relatives. All of them potential ticketbuyers.] [JK: Fair enough. Create a battlefield presence by having soldiers come and go – bring reports, tie on armour, etc. Be in a state of preparation and readiness. If you are doing a more modern version, you could have a war room with radios or whatever technology is relevant. Or you could cut the scene. The actors who get these lines have not spoken much until now, and often drag out the lines because they are the stars of their own little plays. If you keep this section, make sure your actors reflect a sense of urgency – the battle could start at any moment.]*

## Act 5  Scene 3

*See Glossary – Grabs (maybe); Strikes (maybe).*

By this point, the massacre in Fife would be known by all. Everyone already thinks Macbeth is a tyrant, so why bother pretending otherwise? He can manhandle anyone who gets in his way. The 'cream-fac'd Loone' and his horrible news would certainly not be welcome here. [*SD: Now I get to ask you the question I've always wanted to, Jared – wanna throw in something quick about a pants-rig so this dude can piss himself?*] [*JK: Sure! See Glossary – Blood Packs, under the section on advanced blood delivery devices, but use water instead of blood. Unless there's blood in his urine, which is a whole other conversation.*]

The doctor might avoid a beating since he is still of use to Macbeth, but this presumes a level of sanity he may no longer have. Find what works best for the chemistry of your actors and production.

Seyton then arrives, and gets lippy about the timing for putting on armour. Mackers might lash out at Seyton, or any others who assist Macbeth in dressing for battle, especially since he keeps changing his mind about whether or not he should.

## Act 5  Scene 4

*Drum and Colours. Enter Malcolme, Seyward, Macduffe, Seywards Sonne,*
*Menteth, Cathnes, Angus, and Soldiers Marching.*

The goal of the marching is to convey the depth and breadth of the army coming to Dunsinane. Be wary of community-theatre clomping. For more on drums and colours, see Chapter 5 – *All's Well That Ends Well* (3.5).

## Act 5  Scene 5

You could have Mackers beat the messenger here, but you'd be playing the same beat twice and this play deserves better. [*SD: I played the messenger in the 2006 production at Shakespeare in the Park in New York City and had great fun here with Liev Schreiber, who did indeed opt for his Macbeth to be violent towards the help in his prior scene. He was about to make similar mincemeat out of me on 'Lyar, and Slaue', until I delivered my version of what followed along the brazen lines of 'I don't care if you're king … go ahead and beat the shit out of me, pal … THE WOODS ARE MOVING!!!'*]

## Act 5  Scene 7

*See Glossary – Blood Packs.*

[*JK: This is a good time to add some moments of battle. Have the two sides clash as Macduff and Malcolm throw down their Birnam branches, so the audience can see their fighting skills, and then they can chase some bad guys off stage. Bring in another pair of fighters for a quick clash, to help set the stage before we see Macbeth in all his battle armour facing young Seyward.*]

*Enter Macbeth.*

*Macb.* They haue tied me to a stake, I cannot flye,
But Beare-like I must fight the course. What's he
That was not borne of Woman? Such a one
Am I to feare, or none.

*Enter young Seyward.*

*Y. Sey.* What is thy name?
*Macb.* Thou'lt be affraid to heare it.

[*SD: Is this a two-metrical-foot pause before young Seyward asks, or does he share the prior line and Mackers takes a pause before answering young Seyward just to mess with him?*]

*Y. Sey.* No: though thou call'st thy selfe a hoter name
Then any is in hell.
*Macb.*              My name's *Macbeth*.
*Y. Sey.* The diuell himselfe could not pronounce a Title
More hatefull to mine eare.
*Macb.*                    No: nor more fearefull.
*Y. Sey.* Thou lyest abhorred Tyrant, with my Sword
Ile proue the lye thou speakst.

*Fight, and young Seyward slaine.*

*Macb.* Thou was't borne of woman;
But Swords I smile at, Weapons laugh to scorne,
Brandish'd by man that's of a Woman borne.

[*JK: This would be more aptly named 'the murder of young Seyward'. As Seth mentioned at the top of the chapter, in our 2010 production he opted to make this the first moment Macbeth is seen in battle. If there was any doubt about whether his long-celebrated physical prowess might be weakened by psychological decay, that was put to rest with the five seconds it took to stop young Seward's attack and cut his throat. We utilised a blood pack to increase the visceral impact, particularly excellent one evening when the blood spray hit Seth square in the face and he didn't flinch.*]

Clifton Dunn as young Seyward. (*The York Shakespeare Company, 2010*)

[*JK: As I'll keep saying, once the battle begins, it should not stop. See Chapter 2 – Cymbeline (5.2). Macduff should be fighting his way onto stage, killing someone upon entering. Macduff can turn to look around, start his lines, and then run into another adversary. With the battle raging in the background, the stakes will remain high. Macduff can get near the end of this speech when another opponent comes in for a quick clash, gets killed, and Macduff can then start another fight that carries him off stage, whilst Malcolm and Seyward come on fighting other enemies.*]

  *Macb.* Why should I play the Roman Foole, and dye
On mine owne sword? whiles I see liues, the gashes
Do better vpon them.

        *Enter Macduffe.*

  *Macd.*     Turne Hell-hound, turne.

[*SD: This is a shared line. As we discussed in Chapter 1 –* King Lear *(5.3) and Chapter 3 –* Hamlet *(5.2), do not let the audience get ahead of you. Macduff's entrance should stun the audience as much as it does Macbeth.*]

*Macb.* Of all men else I haue auoyded thee:
But get thee backe, my soule is too much charg'd
With blood of thine already.
   *Macd.*                      I haue no words,          (*possible springboard line*)
My voice is in my Sword, thou bloodier Villaine
Then tearmes can giue thee out.


                     *Fight. Alarum.*


   *Macb.*                          Thou loosest labour
As easie may'st thou the intrenchant Ayre
With thy keene Sword impresse, as make me bleed:
Let fall thy blade on vulnerable Crests,
I beare a charmed Life, which must not yeeld
To one of woman borne.
   *Macd.*                    Dispaire thy Charme,
And let the Angell whom thou still hast seru'd
Tell thee, *Macduffe* was from his Mothers womb
Vntimely ript.
   *Macb.* Accursed be that tongue that tels mee so;
For it hath Cow'd my better part of man:
And be these Iugling Fiends no more beleeu'd,
That palter with vs in a double sence,
That keepe the word of promise to our eare,
And breake it to our hope. Ile not fight with thee.
   *Macd.* Then yeeld thee Coward,
And liue to be the shew, and gaze o'th'time.
Wee'l haue thee, as our rarer Monsters are
Painted vpon a pole, and vnder-writ,
Heere may you see the Tyrant.
   *Macb.*                       I will not yeeld          (*another possible springboard*)
To kisse the ground before young *Malcolmes* feet,
And to be baited with the Rabbles curse.
Though Byrnane wood be come to Dunsinane,
And thou oppos'd, being of no woman borne,
Yet I will try the last. Before my body,
I throw my warlike Shield: Lay on *Macduffe*,
And damn'd be him, that first cries hold, enough.


                  *Exeunt fighting. Alarums.*

[*JK: Not once in my life have we ever begun this fight by exiting. I cannot think of a more anti-climactic choice. Clearly, someone did early on and it's written down. If I could delete anything from the canon, it would be this. (And I would add more people being chased by bears, but that's just me.) The biggest question I have for each production – why does Macbeth lose? Is it fate or the witches actually controlling the world in a way where this is the only outcome, or is this something that Macbeth manifests out of his own fears of the witches' story being true? I need to know this information so that the choreography matches the intention of the production. The latter example seems the strongest and likeliest option. It would result in Macbeth beating the crap out of Macduff at the beginning, like the young Seward fight but longer. Then, just when all seems lost for Macduff, Macbeth is informed of Macduff's caesarean birth. This information disables Macbeth, and he loses. If you opt for a more Calvinist approach, the fight could be fair right from the top. Macbeth would start to wonder why this is such hard work and then, when Macduff reveals he was 'untimely ripped', it's more of an 'ah … that makes sense' moment for Macbeth. The fight will stay equal, but Macduff will win. Productions tend to go with the more theatrical choice of letting Macbeth be his own downfall, but clarity on this point is necessary for me to craft the fight.*]

### Enter Fighting, and Macbeth slaine.

[*JK: If you choose to follow the stage directions, continue the battle and have a small skirmish amongst others occur to break up the Macbeth/Macduff fights.*]

### Enter Macduffe, with Macbeths head.

[*JK: If you choose to stage the decapitation, one way to do this is to get the body partially off stage (head first), and swing a sword or axe above Macbeth's head into a piece of wood. Have someone off stage with a syringe or turkey baster (depending on the volume you prefer) full of blood to spray Macduff when the audience hear the thud. As we'll discuss at length during the history plays, you have two basic options for the head: you can get a realistic-looking replica made of the actor playing Macbeth, but this tends to be expensive (don't bother with a half-assed attempt that will just pull your audience out of the show); or you can have Macduff enter carrying a sack with a watermelon or similarly sized object (before coming on, dip the bottom of the bag in some stage blood so it drips throughout the scene). Technically, there is a third option, which contradicts the stage direction and otherwise is stupid – have Macduff point off stage or back of house on 'Behold where stands / Th'Vsurpers cursed head'.*]

  *Mal.* We shall not spend a large expence of time,
Before we reckon with your seuerall loues,
And make vs euen with you. My Thanes and Kinsmen
Henceforth be Earles, the first that euer Scotland
In such an Honor nam'd: What's more to do,
Which would be planted newly with the time,

As calling home our exil'd Friends abroad,
That fled the Snares of watchfull Tyranny,
Producing forth the cruell Ministers
Of this dead Butcher, and his Fiend-like Queene;
Who (as 'tis thought) by selfe and violent hands,
Tooke off her life. This, and what needfull else
That call's vpon vs, by the Grace of Grace,
We will performe in measure, time, and place:

[JK: This is a fencing reference – you want to be in control of the measure, time, and place. If you control all three, you will strike your adversary whilst remaining safe. The perfect hit.]

So thankes to all at once, and to each one,
Whom we inuite, to see vs Crown'd at Scone.

(I cut this couplet in production because it sounds ridiculous.)

# *from Bill Homewood*

Macbeth, *with Peter Woodward as Macbeth, Nichola McAuliffe as Lady Macbeth, Bill Homewood as Banquo. Regent's Park Open Air Theatre, 1991.*

*After the Banquo's ghost scene, I used to shower off all the blood and brains and dress up for the 'walkdown' at the end of the show, when Nichola and I would strut out in our finery for bows and applause. We used to wait behind the curtain and listen to the ringing swords of the final fight between Macbeth and Macduff.*

*On the night in question, just after 'Macduffe was from his Mothers womb / Vntimely ript', there was sudden silence. Not a word, not a sound. Then a long, bad scream from somewhere up in the audience.*

*I knew there had been a terrible accident and rushed on stage – to find Macduff kneeling, gazing incredulously at the bladeless hilt of his sword, and Peter, our Macbeth, staring down at a woman who had been sitting twenty feet away in the front row but was now on the ground. The blade of Macduff's épée had passed right through her face and was lodged there, the point actually pinning her to the ground. The sword had lost a rivet in a violent clash, the blade had flown through the air, and passed through both her cheeks.*

*There were several doctors in the house that night, one of whom was a distinguished Harley Street maxillofacial surgeon. I learned this very surgeon later performed several quite major surgical procedures to repair her horrible injury. I also heard the young woman, a model, received substantial compensation and unlimited free seats for the rest of the repertory season. I cannot imagine she will have chosen a front-row seat, if she came back at all.*

Part 3

# French Follies

*Helena and Count Bertram before the King of France.* Francis Wheatley, 1793. (*Folger Shakespeare Library*)

# Chapter 5

# All's Well That Ends Well

*'O you leaden messengers, / That ride upon the violent speed of fire'* – Helena (3.2)

Let's talk about anal fistulas!

A fistula is an abnormal connection between two parts inside the body. Whilst it can occur in many locations, the most common is the anal fistula – a tunnel running from inside the anus to somewhere in the surrounding skin. This was a common problem of the time, but was particularly thought to plague the knightly class as a result of long, wet, and cold hours in the saddle, weighed down with armour. If the patient's condition was severe enough to require an operation, there would have been cold comfort in the knowledge that it was one of the deadliest procedures in medieval surgery.

This, of all possible places, is where Shakespeare begins the action of the play.

## Act 1  Scene 1[1]

The exposition now dispatched, bear in mind your production will have to make decisions about the progress of the king's disease.

Something else in the opening of the play to track in your rehearsal process (and more in line with the subject matter of this book) is the purported fighting style of Parolles; whether it lives up to his claims, and how that (im)balance will inform his behaviour in subsequent scenes. He proclaims himself born under the Roman god of war, but it is quickly pointed out how often Parolles retreats from battle, a claim he does not deny but rather spins to sound strategic.

## Act 1  Scene 3

*See Glossary – Knees.*

You will have to decide how much time Helena spends on her knee(s) in this scene. If the costume allows, we highly recommend providing knee pads for the actress. This will allow her to safely explore not just stationary positions, but also crawling after the countess should the latter initially resist the former's entreaties.

## Act 2  Scene 1

*See Glossary – Carries; Ensemble Readiness.*

Whilst the king may have endured his initial scene with the assistance of a cane or leaning on an assistant, the fistula has worsened to such a degree that the king can no longer stand. The 'diuers yong Lords' should assist him. If your production's king wants to maintain some dignity and/or cover it up in pomp, you could employ a formal litter with a lord at each corner to carry the king. Along with our general commentary on safe carries, you might want to consider a safety rig – if one lord's hands slip, the litter is still maintained by the rig. If you have a smaller budget (or a humbler king), perhaps a modified wheelchair/throne hybrid. [*SD: WheelThrone™!*] Note that the king's pain levels are not just to be considered by the actor playing him, but also in how his subjects react.

> *King.* Giue me some helpe heere hoa, if thou proceed,
> As high as word, my deed shall match thy deed.

*Florish. Exit.*

The king will need assistance leaving as well – possibly with the same staged grandeur, but a monarch physically unable to live up to it. The greater you push the ailment, the more miraculous is Helena's cure later on. #spoilers

## Act 2  Scene 3

*See Glossary – Ensemble Readiness; Grabs (maybe); Strikes (maybe).*

The king is better thanks to Helena's intervention, so make sure the recovery matches the story you want to tell. If the king comes in completely healed, rejuvenated, and full of energy, then it wasn't medicine but a magic potion; if he's on the mend and walking with some light assistance, you're taking a more realistic route.

Explore how he expects his subjects to react as opposed to how they actually do. When Bertram gets lippy, this is not something the king saw in the cards. How does your king react? Is he strong enough to physically threaten Bertram? Does the king actually do it? Each decision reveals character. If he is a monarch who rules by fear, then he could push/slap/grab Bertram. How will this affect the king's convalescence? If he harms himself in the process, he may very well add that to Bertram's list of sins.

A reminder to continue tracking Parolles' valour/cowardice – this time, left alone with Lafew, who practically begs Parolles for a beating but never gets one due to one pathetic excuse after another.

## Act 2  Scene 5

*See Glossary – Falls (maybe); Strikes (maybe).*

Whilst we generally do not look for moments to randomly add violence, the crux of this play is Helena's unrequited love for someone of a higher station, who has imminent war on his mind, and otherwise is an entitled brat. The stakes are very high for Helena here, and there is an opportunity for physicality to reveal character – Helena, worried Bertram may never come back from the war alive, might go for a kiss at the end of the scene, with Bertram pushing her away out of disgust. This could inadvertently knock her down. Would Bertram help her up apologetically, or avoid touching her and gesture it was an accident? Does Helena fall into a clichéd heap or get up, dust herself off, and move along? The decisions you make can advance the characters – your production's Bertram should take the time to make choices about why he feels no love for Helena, and your Helena will have to decide her tolerance levels for the resulting pain and shame and how these thresholds modulate throughout the play.

## Act 3  Scene 4

*See Glossary – Strikes (maybe).*

How does the countess vent her frustrations? Does she admonish Reynaldo? Is it only verbal, or is there a physical dimension? It's doubtful she tears him to shreds, but this is not an all-or-nothing prospect – a light beating, shoving him around, or thrusting the pen in his hand are some possibilities. Remember not to add violence gratuitously – it must be specific to the actors in these roles.

## Act 3  Scene 5

*Drumme and Colours. Enter Count Rossillion, Parrolles, and the whole Armie.*

Drums and colours are referenced throughout Shakespeare's battle scenes. Here, they play a pivotal part of the plot – Parolles leaves his regiment's drum on the battlefield; if found out, he would be dishonoured. Drums were commonly used to signal advances, halts, and retreats for infantry whilst trumpets were used for cavalry.

Colours refer to the military standards – the largest of the flags. These flags bore the personal insignia of the nobility in charge of those troops, making it easier to tell which soldiers were marching for which noble. During the battle, standards were a way to separate friend from foe. And, if soldiers got separated from their ranks, they would try to get back to rally around the standard.

In the sixteenth century, Jacques Chantareau noted in his book on military arms and training footmen that there should be two drummers near the standard – one drummer to keep a consistent rhythm, the other to announce specific commands. Moving back in the ranks, there would be more drummers to convey the sound of the marching route.

*Fahnenträger und Trommler*. Hans Sebald Beham, 1544. Kupferstich auf Bütten. (*Public domain*)

*A standard bearer.* Albrecht Durer, 1503. (*Public domain*)

*Uniform Standard Bearer of Modena, Italy 1740.* Hendrik Jacobus Vinkhuijzen, 1910. (*Public domain*)

*Standard Bearer for the Canton of Bern.* Urs Graf I, 1521. (*Pepita Milmore Memorial Fund*)

*Die fünf Landsknechte*. Radierung von Daniel Hopfer, 1530. (*Public domain*)

## Act 4  Scene 1

*See Glossary – Arrests; Binds; Draws.*

Parolles' cowardice continues. How much is up to you. Upon being ambushed, he might assume the foetal position, or some variation thereof, leaving the soldiers surprised at how easy he is to capture. Notwithstanding, they should still bind and bag him. If you are covering his head completely, be sure to use a hood that will allow the actor to breathe. We also advise you to bind the actor with his hands in front, so he can remove the hood should anything go wrong.

Unlike Edmund's self-harm in Chapter 1 – *King Lear* (2.1), it is doubtful that Parolles can go through with injuring himself. But it will still be fun to watch him try. He should draw his knife on 'I must giue my selfe some hurts', and start to plan where he will place it. Just a quick glance at his arms, maybe his side, or a superficial leg cut, before quickly realising that 'slight ones will not carrie it'. He could then engage the audience – pointing the knife at his lower abdomen, the middle of his leg, upper arm, *etc.* – to see where they think is best. He finally gives up because he's too scared to harm himself, doubling down on his 'Tongue' having to do the work.

> *Int. Boskos vauvado* I vnderstand thee, & can speake
> thy tongue: *Kerelybonto* sir, betake thee to thy faith, for
> seuenteene ponyards are at thy bosome.

What are the 'seuenteene ponyards' (seventeen daggers)? Parolles is blindfolded, so they might use sticks to poke him. Or their fingers. [*SD: Or.........*] [*JK: No, Seth. No! Bad Seth.*]

## Act 4  Scene 3

*See Glossary – Arrests; Binds; Grabs (maybe); Strikes (maybe).*

[*JK: Most interrogation scenes will call for specific violence, but it's difficult to find the need here when the suspect has diarrhoea of the mouth. This is a technical term I learned from my mother-in-law.*] [*SD: I'd prefer she had taught you the actual word – logorrhoea.*] Parolles will only need to be guided in, gently pushed, and then placed in a chair. Or bound to a tree. Or just let him stand there. Or whatever you fancy because, really, where is he going to go?

How has he been treated? Note that the condition he is in is a direct reflection on his captors. If your Parolles is terrified enough during the interrogation, feel free to use the pee-rig we mentioned in Chapter 4 – *Macbeth* (5.3).

## Act 4  Scene 5

From where does Bertram's facial scar derive? If wearing an open-faced helmet in battle, it is most likely the blows could have hit his helmet and came down into his face from there. Facial lacerations were very common battle injuries. [*SD: Or he contracted syphilis.*] [*JK: I won't ask why your mind went there, but both primary and secondary syphilis symptoms can present on the face.*]

## Act 5  Scene 2

*See Glossary – Strikes (maybe).*

What kind of transformation has Parolles undergone? He says he'll just embrace being a fool, but has he? His physicality with the clowne and Lafew can answer these questions. Does Parolles try to get physical with the clowne to get him to take the letter? If so, does the clowne push Parolles away, and how would he react? Then, with Lafew, does Parolles try the same tactic he used on the clowne? Are the results the same? Or does Parolles try something new?

## Act 5  Scene 3

*See Glossary – Arrests; Draws (maybe); Ensemble Readiness; Grabs (maybe); Strikes (maybe).*

The king is back in full health, and thoughts of fistulas can be put aside. We won't mention fistulas again. Other than just now. What may still be at the forefront of the king's mind is Bertram's abandonment of Helena. Having to deal with Bertram's insolence again might be grounds for execution. The king could strike Bertram, pull his hair/ear when speaking to him, or anything else that makes sense with your particular cast. The mere specificity of desiring to do Bertram harm, but holding back, will flesh out your king's character. At the very least, a backhand is warranted when Bertram doesn't know to keep his mouth shut ('If you shall proue / This Ring was euer hers'). If your king would not bother to perform violent acts himself, he might command a guard to smack Bertram and drag him out, so he has to scream out the rest of his line whilst exiting.

If your king is willing to abuse Bertram and send him back and forth to prison, you can explore the same here with Diana since the king is equally frustrated with her. If the king did not lay hands on Bertram, it would be bizarre for him to do so to Diana. Unless your character choice for the king is that he hates women and enjoys beating them. (There is a possibility the king doesn't hit Bertram since he is a count, but feels fine striking Diana since she is only the daughter of a widow innkeeper who burst into court with a bunch of accusations and zero interest in kissing the king's ass. But this likely would not come across, and the audience would presume misogyny was the cause.) [*JK: I did notice there is no queen in this play.*] [*SD: I noticed that, too. Glad we're done with this chapter. Nothing left to say.*]

(Fistulas!)

*Before the Duke's Palace – Rosalind, Celia, Orlando, the Duke & Attendants.* William Satchwell Leney (after John Downman), 4 June 1800. (*Gertrude and Thomas Jefferson Mumford Collection, Gift of Dorothy Quick Mayer, 1942*)

# Chapter 6

# As You Like It

*'There was never any thing so sudden but the fight'* – Rosalind (5.2)

## Act 1  Scene 1

*See Glossary – Grabs; Strikes (maybe).*

If the audience are not already on Orlando's side, either from hearing about the hideous treatment he has received under Oliver, or because of the latter's current haughtiness, you could have Oliver initiate the violence with a slap or strike, so it doesn't appear that Orlando has chosen to strangle Oliver out of nowhere. This doesn't have to happen right away – there can be a struggle during the lines before the choke begins. Because there is dialogue, we do not recommend a rear-naked choke (sleeper chokehold) or other method that would constrict the character's airway. Oliver can keep a hand in between his throat and Orlando's arm, so it's clear the choke isn't yet successfully applied. *See Appendix – Bursting the Bubble.* If you choose instead to pin Oliver against the wall/ ground, there is more opportunity to apply the choke in specific moments and lay off a bit so Oliver can deliver his lines. [*JK: You may have limitations from the actors. I received a note in one production that said 'Oliver is being played by a middle-aged woman who may not be able to do extremely demanding combat.' We made sure in this case to minimise the struggle between the brothers and focused on a pin that could become a choke. Both performers were comfortable with this and it looked great.*]

Whilst there is no direction for Adam to intervene, always consider the equity you have in any given scene – here, there is an old man who, if harmed, can add to the visceral reactions in your audience. It would be natural for Adam to attempt to restore the peace in accordance with his lines, and it can make Oliver seem that much crueller if Adam is injured in the fray.

## Act 1  Scene 2

[*JK: Ensure the wrestling style is appropriate to the period in which you set your production. You can have a modern-day mixed martial arts fight. If Victorian, savate or bartitsu. The performers will need to understand the martial mechanics behind the moves they execute; since we are dealing with constraints/restraints, it is easy to hurt someone if you are not careful. For example, you can put a character in an armbar. In real life, this would be done by applying equal and opposite force above the elbow and below the wrist. For the stage, we want the victim in control at all times, so the aggressor will need to place their palm below the victim's elbow (making it impossible to actually lock the elbow joint). The aggressor would place their fingers slightly above the victim's elbow, so it appears like a proper armbar.]*

*Cha.* Marry doe I sir: and I came to acquaint you
with a matter: I am giuen sir secretly to vnderstand, that
your yonger brother *Orlando* hath a disposition to come
in disguis'd against mee to try a fall:

Please coordinate with your costume designer when choosing Orlando's disguise; you don't want something that will make the wrestling more difficult or even dangerous.

*See Glossary – Ensemble Readiness.*

### *Wrastle.*

*[JK: Remember that a fight must tell a complete story. Charles is known for always winning wrestling matches, but Orlando will somehow be the victor. The first couple of passes should show Charles almost achieving finishing moves on Orlando, which will get increasingly frustrating for him. This frustration makes Orlando angry and, as we saw in the earlier scene with Oliver, when Orlando gets angry, he sees red. This is a perfect time to show that again. If Charles is 'playing by the rules', Orlando can go ballistic and catch Charles off guard. Almost berserker crazy, since the text suggests Orlando goes too far and has to be ordered to stop by the duke. Keep in mind that Charles himself has said that anyone who 'escapes me without some broken limbe, shall acquit him well', so this is no high school sport wrestling match (unless you have set this play in a high school, I guess). There is also a brief mention in 3.2 that Orlando 'tript vp the Wrastlers heeles'. You can choose to take this literally by having Orlando move in for a tackle; Charles can counter so that Orlando moves down to grab both of Charles' ankles to pull them out from under him. Charles would do a breakfall, and roll out of it to start the next pass.*
*Charles 'cannot speake' after the match, so Orlando's finishing move should be something that takes Charles' breath away. One way is for Charles to get body slammed, knocking all the wind out of him. Another option, and the one with the most poetic justice, is for Orlando to break Charles' ribs. If you require something simpler, Orlando could choke Charles, who then passes out. If Orlando chokes Charles for too long after unconsciousness, he would die. This gives the duke a strong catalyst to stop the match.]*

## Act 1  Scene 3

*See Glossary – Ensemble Readiness; Grabs (maybe); Strikes (maybe).*

Does Duke Frederick physically threaten Rosalind? Or Celia, when she tries to intervene? There is no scripted call for either scenario, but you should consider whether they suit your production.

## Act 2  Scene 2

*See Glossary – Ensemble Readiness; Grabs (maybe); Strikes (maybe).*

Again, how violent is Duke Frederick? Maybe he goes to the first lord and grabs his jacket/shirt, forcing him to spit these lines out in order to save his skin. Maybe your duke shoves around the second lord. Keep tracking throughout tablework and blocking – what kind of ruler is your duke and what are his methods? Given that he stole his title (à la Claudius in Chapter 3 – *Hamlet* and Antonio in Volume Two – *The Tempest*), is he suspicious of his own courtiers?

## Act 2  Scene 6

The human body can go without water for three to eight days, but people have lived for more than seventy days without food. During the first stage of starvation, the focus for fuelling the body is glucose. In the second phase, fats are utilised as a source of energy. The third phase starts when fat reserves are emptied and there is a switch to proteins, which leads to muscle depletion. Actable choices of starvation include listlessness, itchy skin, and difficulty moving appendages.

> *Orl.* Why how now *Adam*? No greater heart in thee:
> Liue a little, comfort a little, cheere thy selfe a little.
> If this vncouth Forrest yeeld any thing sauage,
> I wil either be food for it, or bring it for foode to thee:
> Thy conceite is neerer death, then thy powers.
> For my sake be comfortable, hold death a while
> At the armes end: I wil heere be with thee presently,
> And if I bring thee not something to eate,
> I wil giue thee leaue to die: but if thou diest
> Before I come, thou art a mocker of my labor.
> Wel said, thou look'st cheerely,
> And Ile be with thee quickly: yet thou liest
> In the bleake aire. Come, I wil beare thee
> To some shelter, and thou shalt not die
> For lacke of a dinner,
> If there liue any thing in this Desert.
> Cheerely good *Adam*.

*See Glossary – Carries.*

## Act 2  Scene 7

*See Glossary – Draws; Ensemble Readiness.*

Duke Senior's followers are banished, roaming woods they do not know, left to harsh elements and lawlessness, and then a random stranger like Orlando swings by and his opening gambit is a threat. Is it just verbal, or does he have a weapon? How might they react (or overreact), and how will those decisions affect the comedy/drama desired in any given scene?

   The woods are scary at night, even when you know what you are doing. These characters don't, so every snap of a tree branch, sound of an owl, or squirrel scampering might signal a fatal encounter with a wild animal or other humans. Relaxation would not be a natural state for the duke and his disciples in this location. Whilst they should be scared by Orlando's arrival, any fear of him seems to dissipate rapidly as he is discovered to be 'in-land bred'. You're in a comedy (theoretically), so use the situation to your production's advantage. [*JK: I worked on a production in which Jaques heard a noise from stage right, prompting 'But who comes here?' Orlando ran up behind Jaques from stage left, and held a knife to the back of his neck. When Jaques felt the knife, his posture changed before the reveal of Orlando on 'Forbeare'.*]

## Act 3  Scene 1

*See Glossary – Ensemble Readiness.*

If Duke Frederick resorted to physical violence in 1.3 or 2.2 (or considered it), what escalation might now take place? And is there any involvement on the part of the lords and/or officers? [*SD: I've seen a production go so far as to hang Oliver upside down from chains in a torture chamber, and play the scene as an interrogation. This made for a thrilling moment, a great opportunity for the duke since this is his final scene, and one of several catalysts that will send Oliver on the road towards eventual reconciliation with his brother.*]

## Act 3  Scene 5

*See Glossary – Knees.*

There may be temptation for your production's Phebe to beat Silvius. This is an example of where the author is expressly against it. The dialogue is clear that the only harm Phebe can do is with her eyes. She might want to hurt Silvius, but has to settle for 'if mine eyes can wound, now let them kill thee'.

   Silvius, conversely, might be on his knees, crawling around, latching onto Phebe's leg as she drags him around. It's important to protect the actor's knees and elbows, so get your Silvius padded up if the costume allows. Otherwise, eight shows per week might kill him and then you end up in court and it's a whole … ya know … thing.

## Act 4  Scene 3

We hear an amazing account of Orlando's offstage bravery in defeating a lioness – the lioness had torn some flesh away, causing Orlando to faint from blood loss. When he next appears, be specific about the injuries sustained. We learn in 5.2 that Orlando's arm was damaged enough that it must be in a sling. Otherwise Rosalind can't think Orlando wears 'his heart in a scarfe'. It's also highly unlikely that this is his only injury – the lioness could have inflicted damage to Orlando's upper back or legs. This might result in blood loss sufficient enough for him to faint without warranting a limp or an unusable arm for the rest of the show.

*See Glossary – Ensemble Readiness; Faints.*

Rosalind is one of four lucky winners who get to faint on stage in this volume. Your actor should know exactly what triggers her collapse. Is it the sight of the bloody cloth in Oliver's hand? Or does she take the cloth from Oliver and become overwhelmed by the feel of the wet (or dried) blood? Either way, Oliver is probably near Rosalind, so he can help catch her if your actor is apprehensive about the safety of dropping to the floor.

## Act 5  Scene 2

We each have different thresholds for pain. Just because someone can tolerate a certain kind, doesn't mean all pains are endured easily. If Orlando is a wrestler, joint manipulations, headlocks, *etc.* are types of pain with which he might be familiar, more so than being sliced open by an animal's claws and teeth. Explore some possibilities in rehearsals – is Orlando a wimp about the pain whilst being bandaged? Is he trying to make it seem more bearable than it is and succeeding, or failing? Does he use the pain to impress Rosalind? This is a two-way street of comedy – is Rosalind genuinely trying to help, but just terrible at it? Does she injure Orlando further?

Part 4

# Plethora of Plantagenets
# (and a Tudor or two)

# Chapter 7

# King John

*'O, I am scalded with my violent motion'* – Philip (5.7)

## Act 1  Scene 1

*See Glossary – Ensemble Readiness.*

This is the first in a bottomless barrel of formal parleys we will encounter for the next 100 plus pages, rife with royals (often related) on the edge of violence. Get used to exploring the myriad avenues that may develop in your staging based on any given character's objectives and moods.

John's temper is always up for discussion. It's bad enough he spends the entire first act having to hear about his dead brother, Richard, the war hero. John will also have to face a claim to the throne from the line of his other dead brother, Geoffrey. On top of this, both historically and theatrically, no one likes John. This must be tiring over the course of a lifetime.

Notwithstanding, the ambassador is probably safe from John's ire here since ambassadors were merely mouthpieces for their kings and were to be treated diplomatically. Violence towards an enemy was reserved for the battlefield.

*See Glossary – Strikes (maybe).*

Whilst it is possible the brothers Faulconbridge may have a temptation to get physical (and your guards should be visibly prepared for this), we don't detect violence breaking out here; the brothers are more likely to be in utter shock by the grandeur of the setting and a desire to impress the king, not anger him. If you decide that the brothers should engage physically, a potential moment is when Philip interrupts his brother with, 'Well, sir, by this you cannot get my land; / Your tale must be how he employ'd my mother'. Robert could smack Philip on the arm or the back of the head to prevent him interrupting further.

When Philip denies his name, he could also get a smack from Lady Faulconbridge. Though it might be reflexive and surprising to them both.

## Act 2  Scene 1

*See Glossary – Ensemble Readiness.*

Bearing in mind the most famous thing about John is that his nobles forced him to sign the Magna Carta at the end of his reign, you can reverse-engineer the portrayal to build realistically towards this result. A king is only king because the nobles agree – they can cease to do so at any time. Don't let the endless verse here, or in Chapter 9 – *Richard 2*, fool you – danger should buzz in the air in these kinds of scenes.

In 1.1, John only had to deal with a pesky ambassador. Here, insolence is coming from all sides. A parley is already strenuous enough without having to worry whether your own people will pull the rug out from under you. How might John's frustration/ paranoia manifest in moments like these? And how much is his behaviour regarded with seriousness by those around him?

Besides tracking John's moods on any given day, you have some other wildcards who might upend normal protocols – Constance (generally thought to be borderline insane and getting worse throughout the play) and Philip (possibly unaware of the rules of parley entirely).

In formal parley, whilst actually attacking someone on the other side is a big no-no, there are many ways to channel the rage any of them may feel – slamming a fist down on a table (if you have one), kicking inanimate objects, wringing hands, *etc.* One or more of these would-be combatants may even have to be restrained by their own people. Each of these examples illustrate characters on the edge of violence, and will help to lend this scene the electricity it needs.

> *Heere after excursions, Enter the Herald of France with Trumpets to the gates.*

Excursions signify troops coming out from a defensive position to make an attack. For our purposes, an excursion can simply mean activity in the context of battle. We're intentionally keeping this broad, allowing you to consider the given circumstances of your scene, what you hope to achieve, and how it might be accomplished with your production budget. Excursions can be small frays, ending in chasing one or more characters off stage; characters running onto stage to rescue troops and take them off stage; a commander barking orders of retreat or advance; or soldiers in chase who simply pass over the stage without stopping to fight, to name just a few examples. Excursions may be brief, or go on for several minutes. Each time we encounter the term, we will offer you some options to consider.

Here, there is clearly a battle between the English and French. It is for you to decide whether the battle takes place, in whole or in part, on your stage. We will not always agree on whether or not a specific set of excursions should be staged. [*JK: This moment is a great opportunity to grab your audience with an onstage battle, moving the life-and-death stakes from the linguistic to the visceral.*] [*SD: I would keep the battle off stage, but won't tell you why until 3.2.*]

You also have to decide if the heralds are describing real-time swings in the battle, or if they are lying about the winning party at any given moment in an attempt to fool Angiers. There is some comedy to be mined in the latter, particularly if you stage the battle and it is abundantly clear there is no victor yet. Either way, these heralds can both speak whilst the battle continues. After they are denied by Hubert, you can sound the trumpets for a formal parley, have the respective sides retreat, and the kings then enter. [*JK: This is also a good time to mention that, once you establish your production's approach to violence, you should be consistent. One production I saw had an artistic dance to symbolise the fight here. Whilst that would not be my choice, it turned out to be effective and interesting. But, at the end of the play, there was actual combat. This made no sense, as it did not match with the earlier* (terpsichorean) *choice.*]

We need to get you used to the concept of shifting loyalties. This is a constant fear in the history plays and, therefore, a crucial element to add to your ensemble readiness – suspicion. When Angiers refuses to decide whether France or England is the rightful ruler, both temporarily stop fighting with each other to destroy the everloving shit out of Angiers and figure out the rest at a later date – an idea supplied by Philip, who conveniently has spent most of his life as an outsider and has creativity to spare.

Also showing some ingenuity is Hubert, who clearly wants to get the hell outta Angiers, coming up with a plan that will make the kings happy by marrying Blanche to the dauphin. Anglo-French marriages of convenience will litter the entire cycle of Plantagenet plays, so be on the lookout as it could make for a decent drinking game. [*SD: We'll point out several from which you can choose. The ultimate is knocking back your poison each time you see a stage direction for* **excursions***. This is the first scene of the volume in which it occurs, but you'll end up in hospital long before the final iteration in Chapter 17 –* Richard 3 *(5.4).*]

## Act 2  Scene 2

*See Glossary – Strikes (maybe).*

There is a potential push/slap. It may not be appropriate for your production's Constance, but punctuating 'a most vgly man' with physical violence can make Salisbury's next line more poignant. It will also serve to illustrate Constance's continued unravelling.

## Act 3  Scene 1

*See Glossary – Ensemble Readiness; Knees.*

Does Constance go beyond mere cursing? Does anyone attempt to contain her? How would certain characters react here based on their (dis)belief that her son is the true heir to the throne?

*Enter Pandulph.*

One of the rare moments of potential humour in the play occurs here – this powerful assembly loses their last remaining shred of any decorum just as Cardinal Pandulph arrives on behalf of the Pope. If you held off full physical manifestation of any violence until this point, the threat of a fight *about* to become physical will provide a better comedic pay-off (*e.g.* Constance leaping towards someone, about to scratch their eyes out) if deployed in tandem with the cardinal's entrance. And that's not just for a laugh – a theme we'll keep coming back to in these plays is that all the pomp and circumstance is ultimately meaningless. These are human beings, usually related, and they're as dysfunctional as we are. Just as Philip was the audience's outside eye into seeing the larger picture for the first two acts, Pandulph now assumes that position. This moment can work as a reset button – any subjectivity we've gathered for the last hour implodes, leaving an objective view (Pandulph's, as a stranger) of how-the-hell-are-these-people-allowed-to-govern? The concept of 'perspectives' will be brought up repeatedly throughout the history plays. Play with these changing viewpoints and shifting alliances in your rehearsal room to find a production unique to your creative team's sensibilities. [*SD: Think of how your family behaves privately. How dramatically does that dynamic shift if a neighbour comes over to borrow some sugar, or whatever it is that humans do? I don't know. Neighbours know not to knock on my door, and my only remaining family are stuffed animals.*]

Is there any physical fallout from the excommunication of a monarch? Former friends flee and declare war again. There is also a festival of begging, so ensure your actors have access to kneepads.

## Act 3  Scene 2

*Allarums, Excursions*: *Enter Bastard with Austria's head.*

[*JK: There should be more fights here before Philip enters with Austria's head. This is a great opportunity to highlight the fighting abilities of key characters on stage, revealing more about them through violence. Philip just exited the prior scene – if he comes right in with Austria's head, after only being gone for eight lines of text, it will seem comical.*] [*SD: It's supposed to be funny, so this may suit your production. We still don't know you very well.*] [*JK: Philip would have to be quite lucky to have found and decapitated Austria this quickly.*] [*SD: If I were staging this play, I would have a bunch of noises off stage … maybe some silence for a bit … and then this guy storms on with a king's severed head. This approach would also further the comedic gag we established in 2.1: there, the joke was flat-out lying to Angiers and the audience; here, the setup could be wondering what on earth is going on off stage, then Philip charges on with a dripping-wet head. To me, this is funny. Because I am broken inside.*] [*JK: Or, consider having Philip participate in fights prior to the directed entrance. His fighting style could mirror his personality – instead of facing combatants head on, Philip can surprise his adversaries with unorthodox strikes. For example, an enemy moves to split Philip in two, but Philip slips to the side and stabs his adversary in the foot. Whilst he screams in pain, Philip slices his throat. We can even see Philip fighting Austria, before chasing him*] *off stage. The skirmishes could continue until Philip's formal entrance.*] [*SD: Note yet another head being used as a prop. Also a great drinking game to help you through this book. But still not the best choice for true professionals, which continues now – time for excursions!*]

 *Bast.* Now by my life, this day grows wondrous hot,
Some ayery Deuill houers in the skie,
And pour's downe mischiefe. *Austrias* head lye there,

*Enter Iohn, Arthur, Hubert.*

While *Philip* breathes.
 *Iohn. Hubert*, keepe this boy: *Philip* make vp,
My Mother is assayled in our Tent,
And tane I feare.
 *Bast.*   My Lord I rescued her,
Her Highnesse is in safety, feare you not:
But on my Liege, for very little paines
Will bring this labor to an happy end.

*Exit. Alarums, excursions, Retreat.*
*Enter Iohn, Eleanor, Arthur, Bastard, Hubert, Lords.*

The battle can continue throughout the scene, making 'Alarums, excursions' a swelling of the fights, to fill the time between the exit and re-entrance. Consider bringing on a few adversaries near Philip's 'happy end' [*JK: don't even think about it, Seth*], so he and the rest can fight their way (or be chased) off stage. For the excursions, have more troops clash on stage to keep the battle raging and the energy high. Or, you can scrap all of that and try this instead: ignore the stage direction to exit; Philip could say his lines as he sees the remaining enemies approach; then have Philip single-handedly fight through them as John, Arthur, and Hubert watch. [*SD: If you followed my recommendation – no onstage fighting of any kind until this point – you can get the audience on the edge of their seats for this first battle.*] Once Philip has neutralised the threat, the retreat can be sounded, and some random lords could bring on Eleanor. You should also explore what John might do in this scenario. Would he try to fight? If so, does he need to be saved by Philip? Is there a moment where John thinks about using Arthur as a human shield? Stage something the audience would catch, and maybe Hubert, but no one else.

 *Iohn.* Doe not I know thou wouldst?
Good *Hubert, Hubert, Hubert* throw thine eye
On yon young boy: Ile tell thee what my friend,
He is a very serpent in my way,
And wheresoere this foot of mine doth tread,

He lies before me: dost thou vnderstand me?
Thou art his keeper.
    *Hub.*               And Ile keepe him so,
That he shall not offend your Maiesty.
    *Iohn.* Death.
    *Hub.* My Lord.
    *Iohn.*        A Graue.                      (<---*coolest shared line in the canon*)
    *Hub.*                  He shall not liue.
    *Iohn.*                       Enough.

*[SD: Here's another possible drinking game to get you through this Shakespearean spelunking – Plantagenet kings plotting the deaths of little kids with claims to the throne.]*

*See Glossary – Arrests.*

Whilst not addressed specifically, you will need to bring on additional soldiers in order to capture/guard Arthur when John commands. Or just use some of the onstage lords. It seems a rather eventless escort. And consider what happens to Austria's head when Philip exits. Does he take it with him? Is it just sitting on stage staring at someone? Does Philip give it to John, so he has it under his arm the whole time?

## Act 3  Scene 3

*See Glossary – Ensemble Readiness.*

Constance's self-harm in this scene can be as simple as hair torn out (implied by the text) or more brutal. Run a web search for 'hair ripped out of scalp' if you need inspiration. This scene is the next step in the long game we've been tracking of Constance's mental unrest. How long has she been harming herself? Is she merely scratched? Scabbed? Open wounds? She could be swollen and red in some areas (to indicate fresh, blunt-force trauma), and already bruised in other areas (injuries from days prior). Whatever you decide, the effect should be deeply unsettling for the audience, and the other characters on stage, who should be constantly gauging whether she poses further danger to herself or others and adjust accordingly.

*I saw a smith stand with his hammer thus…* Richard Houston (after Edward Penny), January 1771. (*Harris Brisbane Dick Fund, 1953*)

## Act 4  Scene 1

*See Glossary – Arrests; Binds (maybe); Strikes (maybe).*

This scene should be so terrifying that the audience have to peek through their fingers. The physical violence may be minimal, or even nonexistent, but the *threat* of violence is what will put the audience on the edge of their seats. The actual danger is completely dependent on whether Arthur can get through to Hubert, and whether Hubert's conscience will outweigh his loyalty to the king.

The irons are cold when Hubert brings them in, but you should rig them so they get red hot. If you pull the irons out of the fire and they are not red, your audience will be knocked out of the play and it may prove impossible to get them to once again suspend their disbelief. Your props department should be able to rig the irons with a button that will light up the ends. This will let you retrieve the irons during the scene and heighten the tension. The fire burns out by the end of the scene, so the irons will be cold again.

This is an amazing scene for the violence (or threat of it) to express character and advance the story: it begins with hesitation on the part of Hubert and the executioners; then changes with Arthur's desperation not to be bound by the executioners; they, in turn, will have to struggle with an unwilling prisoner and their own consciences.

Continue searching for shades in the scene (*e.g.* fighting the urge to use 'Giue me the Iron I say, and binde him heere' forcefully, but more as a barely utterable plea to the executioners, so Hubert can get this over with and forget he ever was involved) and make it as difficult as possible for all participants.

Note that the script does not specify if Arthur is bound when Hubert sends the executioners away. They may have succeeded in binding Arthur, leaving Hubert comfortable enough for a private discussion, but a stronger choice is to leave Arthur unbound.

## Act 4  Scene 2

*See Glossary – Arrests.*

You can reveal some of Peter's character through his arrest. Is he the kind of soothsayer who humbly keeps his chin high, knowing he will die and accepting it gracefully? Or is he a fake? If your Peter struggles [*JK: don't you dare, Seth*], then whomever conducts the arrest may need to drag Peter by the hair/ear, yank him by the arm or back of the head, use a wristlock, put him in an armbar, or some other pain-compliance action in order to remove him. If he is incredibly desperate, the officers may have to render Peter unconscious and drag his body out.

*See Glossary – Strikes (maybe).*

Later in the scene, many a king would harm Hubert – a push, a smack, something – but John is famously the wimp in a family full of war heroes. Your production will have to make a decision, based on everything that has come before, whether or not John is capable of physical violence. [*SD: A capable John is the opposite of a struggling Peter.*] [*JK: WHAT DID I JUST SAY?!*]

## Act 4  Scene 3

*See Glossary – Falls.*

And, now, a rousing performance of *Spider-Man: Turn on the Life Insurance.*

*Enter Arthur on the walles.*

> *Ar.* The Wall is high, and yet will I leape downe.
> Good ground be pittifull, and hurt me not:
> There's few or none do know me, if they did,
> This Ship-boyes semblance hath disguis'd me quite.
> I am afraide, and yet Ile venture it.
> If I get downe, and do not breake my limbes,
> Ile finde a thousand shifts to get away;
> As good to dye, and go; as dye, and stay.
> Oh me, my Vnckles spirit is in these stones,
> Heauen take my soule, and England keep my bones.

*Dies.*

Your production's budget, stage dimensions, and sense of taste will dictate how you stage Arthur's leap. You hopefully have some space through which the actor can safely jump and disappear. If you have an orchestra pit, that would work. If not, you should be in discussions with your set designer very early on to construct something from which Arthur can leap and fall behind. A second level or, if you're outdoors, an upstage ledge. [*JK: The key to doing this safely is minimising the actual distance Arthur falls. Something around four feet would be ideal, so Arthur can jump down and lay flat whilst continuing to scream. Note you will also need a localised 'splat' sound effect to sell this. I encourage a small crash pad for the jump and/or pads for the performer's knees/elbows. If you have an actor with the training to do a higher fall, it would be stunning to watch Arthur jump from fifteen-to-twenty feet. This requires a stunt professional to stage. And you will need an appropriate crash pad, which retails for a few thousand. Neither of us has seen a production commit that much of their budget to this one moment, but please invite us if you do!*]

*See Glossary – Draws.*

Later, the lords discover the dead boy and threaten to kill Hubert. Philip convinces them to withhold, but his heart ain't in it that much. [*JK: One of my fondest memories of working on this production was when the director requested that I work with the actors to ensure the stakes were high in this scene – that, at any moment, someone may die. He is one of the only directors (besides Seth, of course) who thought to put their fight director to work this way. I accomplish this by having the actors (only if their lines are memorised) play an unarmed game of tag. If what is happening in the scene gives them an opportunity to tag Hubert in the back, then they must. This helps the actors feel the intent to hit Hubert, and makes Hubert always on guard from being attacked. Once they have that energy in the scene, we can arm the actors and try to keep the intensity (but, now, no one can actually hit Hubert). I once had a cast who wanted to go even further, so I brought protective eyewear and rubber training knives. This really solidified the potency of the scene for these actors, but I do not recommend this unless you are an expert knife instructor who can control this training scenario.*]

*See Glossary – Grabs (maybe); Strikes (maybe).*

Hubert isn't out of the woods just because the other lords depart. Philip wants answers and is not shy to violence – he might threaten, or even employ it, to drive home his point. [*JK: Maybe a choke from behind, slamming Hubert into a wall and pinning him, yanking his hair from behind whilst speaking the lines right into Hubert's ear.*] [*SD: \*pauses to take cold shower\**]

*See Glossary – Carries.*

> *Bast.*        Beare away that childe,
> And follow me with speed: Ile to the King:
> A thousand businesses are briefe in hand,
> And heauen it selfe doth frowne vpon the Land.

## Act 5  Scene 3

See Chapter 2 – *Cymbeline* and Chapter 3 – *Hamlet* for discussions of the need to be specific with your characters' physical ailments. John was poisoned by a monk but lives for several scenes. He complains of a fever, heartache, weakness, and being faint. What slow-acting drug might this be, and how would it result in these symptoms? This is important because the actor playing John will know exactly how he is dying and play it accurately. A poison which attacks the nervous system is radically different from one corrupting the respiratory system.

The most powerful and quickest poisons tend to be obvious via smell and/or taste; subtler draughts will take longer to kill the victim. Only in Hollywood can someone drink something, not know they are poisoned, and die five seconds later. Also, the poison used should be in line with the concept of your production – it does no good to use a sixteenth-century European poison if you are staging this in feudal Japan, as they had a variety of poisons all to themselves.

## Act 5  Scene 4

*See Glossary – Blood.*

*Enter Meloon wounded.*

Meloon enters fatally wounded but then speaks in mostly stable iambic pentameter. As one does.

As we covered in Chapter 4 – *Macbeth*, there are many places to wound Meloon that would allow him to live long enough to speak but make it clear he will soon die. If you're really looking to jolt your audience awake, a small evisceration would allow Meloon to enter with some intestines hanging out, which he is attempting to shove back in. This is, unsurprisingly, quite painful and irreparable at this point in medical history. Another choice could be a wound that nicks both the stomach and descending aorta. Blood from the descending aorta would quickly fill the chest cavity, whilst stomach acid spills into the same admixture. Meloon would have to fight against immense chest pains, finding it harder and harder to breathe as he spits out these lines, along with some nasty liquids for a lucky stagehand to remove between scenes.

*See Glossary – Carries.*

> *Sal*. My arme shall giue thee helpe to beare thee hence,
> For I do see the cruell pangs of death
> Right in thine eye. Away, my friends, new flight,
> And happie newnesse, that intends old right.

## Act 5  Scene 6

Due to the cover of night, Hubert is unable to immediately ascertain Philip's identity. Hubert threatens to shoot if Philip does not reveal himself. It's possible that Hubert is bluffing, and is not armed with a projectile weapon. If you choose to arm him, select either a crossbow or a bow and arrow, both of which were common. (Guns had not arrived in Europe by 1216.) You could also choose a spear, but it's unlikely and unwise – if you hurl a spear and miss, your enemy can use it. However Hubert is armed, Philip will take the threat seriously at first. This moment doesn't really go anywhere, as both men quickly discover each other's identities.

## Act 5  Scene 7

*See Glossary – Carries.*

*Iohn brought in.*

We are told in 5.6 that the poisoner was a monk, acting also as the king's food taster who, after poisoning both himself and the king, had his 'Bowels sodainly burst out'. This gives you an idea where John will have to go by the end of this scene, and he does indeed mention that his 'bowels crumble vp to dust'. The monk may have consumed more than John, so as to die more quickly and not be held to account, which could be why John is taking several scenes longer to expire.

# Chapter 8

# Edward 3[1]

*'What need we fight, and sweat, and keep a coil'* – Prince Edward (4.6)

We're not going to spend much time on this play, as we have no idea how much of it Shakespeare authored. [*JK: Why are we spending any?*] [*SD: Because then we'd only be covering thirty-nine plays.*] [*JK: I don't follow. What's wrong with thirty-nine?*] [*SD: It makes me twitch.*] [*JK: And forty doesn't?*] [*SD: I'll make it fifty if you keep asking questions.*] [*JK: .........*]

The play opens with an endless discussion of lineage, something you should get used to for the rest of this volume. Thankfully, it is not in our purview to walk you through the tedious ancestral mapping, nor do we have the room.

We'll pause whilst you complete your homework on this portion of the Plantagenet family tree.

Edward III of England, Order of the Garter. William Bruges, circa 1430-1440. (*British Library*)

## Act 1  Scene 1

*Enter King Edward, Derby, Prince Edward, Audely and Artoys.*

*King.* Robert of Artoys banisht though thou be,
From Fraunce thy natiue Country, yet with vs,
Thou shalt retayne as great a Seigniorie:
For we create thee Earle of Richmond heere,

We shouldn't have to tell you this, but please be careful when your kings perform knightings – chopping off an actor's ear is usually ill-advised.

We do not detect any violations of parley protocol in the opening scene until King Edward draws on Lorraine. You may disagree. If you're one of the few companies on the planet ever to produce this play, please invite us to attend.

*See Glossary – Draws; Ensemble Readiness.*

> *Art.* The soundest counsell I can giue his grace,
> Is to surrender ere he be constraynd.
> A voluntarie mischiefe hath lesse scorne,
> Then when reproch with violence is borne,
>     *Lor.* Regenerate Traytor, viper to the place,
> Where thou was fostred in thine infancy:
> Bearest thou a part in this conspiracy?

> *He drawes his Sword.*

>     *K. Ed.* Lorraine behold the sharpnes of this steele:
> Feruent desire that sits against my heart,
> Is farre more thornie pricking than this blade.
> That with the nightingale *I* shall be scard:
> As oft as I dispose my selfe to rest,
> Vntill my collours be displaide in Fraunce:
> This is thy finall Answere, so be gone.

It is an alarming breach of etiquette when Edward draws. As mentioned in Chapter 7 – *King John* (1.1), ambassadors sent to parley were seen as an extension of their monarch. Edward drawing on Lorraine is tantamount to drawing on the King of France himself. (Note that the text makes it clear Edward draws, but the stage direction merely says 'He', and the placement suggests it's Lorraine. Whilst Lorraine could draw first, either on the newly dubbed earl or the king, it likely would result in death.) Once Edward draws, you'll have to decide how the room reacts.

>     *Lor.* It is not that nor any English braue,
> Afflicts me so, as doth his poysoned view,
> That is most false, should most of all be true.
>     *K. Ed.* Now Lord our fleeting Barke is vnder sayle:
> Our gage is throwne, and warre is soone begun,
> But not so quickely brought vnto an end.

The gage is thrown figuratively, not literally. The latter would initiate a duel; here, the king is making it clear he has no other choice but to wage war.

## Act 2  Scene 1

*See Glossary – Draws; Intimacy; Kneels.*

The Plantagenets are crap at wooing. Edward 4 has a single shot at keeping Elizabeth's attention in Chapter 16 – *Henry 6 Part 3* (3.2). Richard forces two of the slimiest exchanges of Chapter 17 – *Richard 3* on Anne (1.2) and Elizabeth (4.3). Not to be outdone, this play spends three full scenes on the king gettin' all thirsty for the countess.

Have your intimacy consultant and fight director on hand for these encounters. And some knee pads, since the countess kneels several times during these scenes. Does the king get handsy? Does the countess play along, or reject these advances?

## Act 2  Scene 2

Things begin politely enough, but it soon becomes clear to the countess that she will have a difficult time getting out of this. She floats the idea that she and the king should slaughter their spouses, in the hope it will be absurd enough for the king to come to his senses. No such luck. The king is so deluded by this point that he is willing to pursue the double murder. The countess, left with no other choice, threatens suicide if Edward says another word on the matter.

*See Glossary – Blood (maybe).*

If the king isn't buying the ultimatum, your countess could start cutting her wrists here, or put the wedding knife to her throat. The king relents, switching focus to battle. And foodstuffs.

## Act 3  Scene 1

 *Ph.* I say my Lord, clayme Edward what he can,
And bring he nere so playne a pedegree,
Tis you are in possession of the Crowne,
And thats the surest poynt of all the Law:
But were it not, yet ere he should preuaile,
Ile make a Conduit of my dearest blood,
Or chase those stragling vpstarts home againe,
 *King.* Well said young Phillip, call for bread and Wine,
That we may cheere our stomacks with repast,

The battell hard a farre off.

To looke our foes more sternely in the face.
Now is begun the heauie day at Sea,
Fight Frenchmen, fight, be like the fielde of Beares,
When they defend their younglings in their Caues:
Stir angry Nemesis the happie helme,
That with the sulphur battels of your rage,
The English Fleete may be disperst and sunke,
 *Ph.* O Father how this eckoing Cannon shot.

*Shot.*

Like sweete hermonie disgests my cates.
   *King.* Now boy thou hearest what thundring terror tis,
To buckle for a kingdomes souerentie,
The earth with giddie trembling when it shakes,
Or when the exalations of the aire,
Breakes in extremitie of lightning flash,
Affrights not more then kings when they dispose,
To shew the rancor of their high swolne harts,
Retreate is sounded, one side hath the worse,

*Retreate.*

The comedy in this play continues to be bizarre. You could lean into the absurdity by having some of the fighting occur on stage whilst the royals nonchalantly enjoy their snacks. The French are often treated as oblivious/ridiculous/incompetent throughout the history plays, so you'll have to decide how far you want to take this – a general could bark commands; a bloody messenger could stumble in and just die somewhere; all sorts of mayhem could happen upstage whilst the king and his kids have wine and cheese.

## Act 3  Scenes 3, 4, and 5

*Alarum. Enter a many French men flying.*
*After them Prince Edward runing.*
*Then enter King Iohn and Duke of Loraine.*

If you're bored thus far [*JK: yes*], here is an opportunity not only to wake your audience but also to advance Prince Edward's story by exhibiting his fighting prowess à la *Coriolanus* or *Macbeth*. The king isn't sending anyone to save the prince, and his skill should make it apparent why this is. If you are producing multiple plays in the cycle, the buildup of the prince here will make references to his death all the more upsetting to his son in Chapter 9 – *Richard 2* (2.1) (similar to the guilt trips Henry 6 endures after his war-hero pappy dies young, leaving a child on the throne).

Artois asks the king to send rescue for the prince. Then Derby asks. Then Audley asks. Each time, the king declines. There is no need for the king to bring the prince into this particular battle, but the king has decided that his boy is ready to prove himself in battle. Depending on the king's belief in his son and/or 'God' [*SD: *vomits**], this course of action makes sense. Newly knighted, it's important that the prince prove his worth ('laboring for a knighthood'). Make sure your actor playing the king is specific about why he has such faith. Otherwise, his lack of intervention will come off as senseless or cruel.

[*JK: This may be an allusion to the real Battle of Crécy, in which Prince Edward (only 16 at the time) went down in battle and may have been briefly seized. He was then rescued by Sir Richard FitzSimon and Sir Thomas Daniel. Then, Sir Thomas Norwich was sent to seek help from the king. Once he knew the prince was not wounded, the king sent Norwich back without assistance, saying 'My son must have a chance to win his spurs.' After the battle, Edward said to his son 'You are worthy to be a king.'*]

*See Glossary – Carries; Kneels.*

*Enter Prince Edward in tryumph, bearing in his hande his shiuered Launce, and the King of Boheme, borne before, wrapt in the Coullours: They runne and imbrace him.*

*Aud.* O ioyfull sight, victorious Edward liues.
*Der.* Welcome braue Prince.
*Ki.* Welcome Plantagenet.

*Kneele and kisse his fathers hand.*

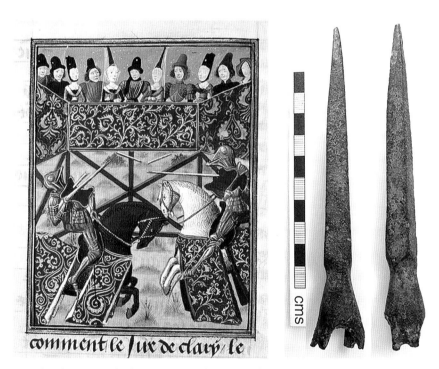

Left: French knights, Pierre de Courtenay and the Sire de Clary, jousting. Jean Froissart, circa 1470-1475. (*British Library*) Right: A post medieval - modern iron incomplete lance head (sixteenth-seventeenth century). (*Jordan Galentine, Museum of London*) (The Portable Antiquities Scheme (PAS) is a voluntary programme run by the British Government to record the increasing numbers of small finds of archaeological interest found by members of the public. The scheme started in 1997 and now covers most of England and Wales. Finds are published at www.finds.org.uk)

A lance is a long polearm, utilised by mounted warriors during the charge. It can also be used to trip a horse, batter an adversary, or parry attacks. The prince enters with a broken lance and the dead King of Bohemia. This might mean the prince bested Bohemia with the lance in a charge, but it could have been more complicated. At a minimum, we know the prince was, at some point, mounted during battle.

Bohemia has been wrapped in his own colours (see Chapter 5 – *All's Well that Ends Well* (3.5)) and bound atop Prince Edward's horse. We presume you do not have the budget for a horse to come in from off stage. If this is the case, Bohemia's body can be carried in by some of the prince's soldiers, and then handed to the prince (once he puts down the shivered lance). Or you can ignore the lance altogether and have the corpse carried in by the prince, who might drop it at his father's feet. Again, this will come down to the tone you've set; if you've been opting for some broad comedic strokes, you could have a fake pony and/or a cadaver toss.

## Act 4  Scene 1

*See Glossary – Arrests.*

Moving along to the imprisonment of Villiers, he's apparently worth at least 100,000 francs but is being held for a better occasion. There seems to be no reason to believe he has been mistreated; he enters without any guard appointed in the stage direction, and is allowed 'horse and post from hence' merely if he 'sweare by … faith' he'll come back prisoner. The scene revolves around the fact Villiers has acted and been treated as a gentleman. See the section about honour in Chapter 9 – *Richard 2*.

## Act 4  Scene 5

*Another noise, Salisbury brought in by a French Captaine.*

In contrast, the French captain can get a bit rough with Salisbury. He might fight against this treatment, and pull away from the captain upon reaching the king and Charles. *See Appendix – Bursting the Bubble.*

## Act 4  Scene 8

*See Glossary – Carries.*

*Enter Audley wounded, & rescued by two squirs.*

Next up is the rescue of Audley. [*JK: Given his uncertainty about how lethal his wound may be, I'd go with the abdominal area above the intestines, as it is an area that is only sometimes fatal. Perhaps an arrow through his right side that just missed the liver.*] [*SD: \*ferociously chugs emotional-support scotch\**] [*JK: Or a sword cut into the same area deep enough for Audley to question whether he will recover. Make sure the squires support Audley on the* *opposite side of his wound. Once muscles are ripped or cut, separating them is painful. The pain of raising the right arm would be unbearable if the injury is to the right side. Audley would have that hand over his wound anyway, trying to stop the bleeding.]*

## Act 4  Scene 9

*See Glossary – Arrests; Binds (maybe); Carries; Strikes (maybe).*

King John and the Duke of Normandy are brought in as prisoners to King Edward. Then Artois brings Philip in as prisoner.

    Whilst all the prisoners need to be brought in, the way in which this is conducted will reflect on the character of the prince. One of two competing theories to explain his moniker – the Black Prince – was his treatment of the French, the other his shield and armour colour. Does he abuse his prisoners physically, or just rhetorically? The latter may be the stronger choice since the prince need not make further exhibition of his prowess. If, however, you choose the corporeal, then be crystal clear on what you are trying to reveal about the prince's character in this moment. (This would be further contrasted by his treatment of the wounded Audley, who is offered reward and physical assistance by the prince.)

## Act 5  Scene 1

*See Glossary – Arrests.*

      *Enter six Citizens in their Shirts, bare foote, with halters about their necks.*

If characters are being brought in barefoot, it's important that a safety sweep of the area is done before they enter. This will have the added benefit of keeping your stagehands from falling asleep during the interval. As for the halters about the citizens' necks, it is safest to rig them as breakaway nooses – they will look complete, but the circle around the neck would be cut and held together with a loose stitch. The citizens come in holding the halters themselves, so there is no safety issue if they are untouched by others. Notwithstanding, the king does order the citizens to be hanged. In the time it takes for the queen to plead for the citizens' lives, it is possible that a guard or two grabbed the halters to take the citizens away. Each actor can hook their fingers around the rope to ensure it doesn't actually harm their throat. [*JK: Note that a halter is a headpiece of rope, whereas a noose is an adjustable loop of rope. This could signify that the citizens are prisoners, but not necessarily ready for the gallows.*]

*See Glossary – Arrests.*

Finally, John Copland brings in King David as prisoner, and then is knighted for it.

    As we discussed at length in this play alone, the prisoners should be treated in a manner that reveals the character of their captors. (And, again, ensure the knighting does not result in the accidental removal of the actor's ears.)

# Chapter 9

# Richard 2

*'For violent fires soon put out themselves'* – Gaunt (2.1)

Imagine yourself at age 10. Now picture the delightful little child you would be if you were handed the crown of one of the most powerful kingdoms on earth. We're not sure exactly what you were like as a kid but, odds are, it would have been a recipe for disaster. This is the situation in which Richard of Bordeaux finds himself. His grandfather, Edward 3, has just died. The practice of primogeniture in England places Richard's father next in line. But he's dead, too. So it keeps going down the line. The result of this idiotic system is the installation of a child on the throne.

Incredibly wealthy barons continually fight tooth and nail for more power, ruled by a king many of them despise and few respect. They are the most powerful people in England and their consensus is required for the king to be the king. (See Chapter 7 – *King John*.) Such agreement was generally intact as

A watercolour of Richard II in prison at Pomfret Castle. J. Coghlan, early nineteenth century. (*Folger Shakespeare Library*)

a matter of course – divine right dictated the king's legitimate placement on the throne. Throughout this play, however, supporters of Richard's alleged rights reduce in number. Exponentially.

Claims regarding which of Edward 3's children are the most legitimate, along with Richard 2's abuse of his kingdom's coffers and his subjects' patience, will lead the entire Plantagenet dynasty to destroy itself over the course of a century. This destruction is particularly terrifying since most of the key players in the histories are not just powerful enemies but also family – procreating within one's own gene pool being yet another hallmark of the British monarchy's genius.

You must commit the time to researching and understanding how these people are related, and their history with one another prior to the events of the play. This is the only way an otherwise-dense oratory will come to life – comprehending the forces that drive these royals each step of the way.

It isn't our charge to do your basic homework for you, so we'll wait whilst you research the events leading up to this play.

Still waiting.

Are you finished yet?

Okay.

You've most likely discovered some amusing factoids about the people in the room. Bolingbroke's dad, old John of Gaunt (Duke of Lancaster), was in charge of the kingdom during Richard's younger years and built up massive reserves of power. Their relationship has always been strained, though never as badly as the one between Richard and the majority of the Lords Appellant – the name for the folks who brought the suit against Mowbray and several other of Richard's favourites – led by the Duke of Gloucester. Richard has Gloucester, his uncle, killed. Before the play even starts. [*SD: Prince Hamlet should take a bloody hint.*] Bolingbroke, Richard's cousin, is now the *de facto* leader of the Lords Appellant.

The inciting question of the play is: who killed the Duke of Gloucester? Richard very likely paid off his other cousin, Thomas Mowbray (Duke of Norfolk), to do the deed. Whilst never stated outright, much of Shakespeare's audience would have been aware of this working theory. And it's implied multiple times throughout the play to be factual. But facts are curious things.

If one nobleman felt wronged by another during the Middle Ages, a challenge to trial by combat was possible. The foundations of this practice are often traced back to the Lombard Laws, compiled by King Rothair in 643. The laws consisted of 388 chapters, which were later augmented by his successors. See Katherine Fischer's *The Lombard Laws*.

The fundamental premise of trial by combat (also called judicial duel) was that one man could fight another in a 'trial of truth', and 'God' would make certain the right man prevailed. This could be used to settle a legal matter deemed worthy but only when evidence was lacking, there were no witnesses, or if an issue was hard to prove. Germanic fencing master Hans Talhoffer, arguably the most prolific of the fifteenth century, makes trial by combat the subject of several books. In his 1459 manuscript, he lists seven offences considered grave enough to warrant a judicial duel: murder, treason, heresy, desertion of one's lord, 'imprisonment' (possibly in the sense of abduction), perjury/fraud, and rape. We will continue to discuss these concepts because a thousand years of judicial duel were foundational to the personal duel seen in so many of Shakespeare's works. For more on the jurisprudence of the personal duel, see Chapter 13 – *Henry 5* (4.8). [*JK: You can also check out Shakespeare contemporary Vincentio Saviolo in* A Gentleman's Guide to Duelling, *edited by Jared Kirby.*] [*SD: You seriously just plugged your own book?*] [*JK: Have you bought a copy yet?*] [*SD: … … …*]

## Act 1 Scene 1

*See Glossary – Ensemble Readiness.*

It's clear Bolingbroke has just cause to challenge Mowbray to a judicial duel. There is, however, no justification for Richard to hide it from the public eye save that, having ordered Gloucester's death, Richard knows Mowbray is in the wrong. [*SD: Richard has to wonder whether 'God' might end the duel in Mowbray's death, thereby revealing his guilt and Richard's. Or will Richard's invisible friend strike down Bolingbroke as some sort of early birthday present? If Richard had not already begun to doubt his special relationship with the supernatural old fart upstairs, these proceedings would have moved forward. Richard has spent the last thirty years of his life convinced he is second only to a deity, and that they are besties. Shakespeare wisely ignores the last few decades and focuses on the final three years of Richard's reign, placing the inciting action of Gloucester's murder just before the play begins. Along with a seed of doubt in Richard who will – after five acts of having the religious delusions knocked out of him – realise that a king, like any other human, is nothing.*] Knowing what we know of Richard's part in the murder, note he has postponed a formal hearing until this moment:

> *King Richard.* Old *John of Gaunt,* time honoured Lancaster,
> Hast thou according to thy oath and band
> Brought hither *Henry* Herford thy bold son:
> Heere to make good the boistrous late appeale,
> Which then our leysure would not let us heare,
> Against the Duke of Norfolke, *Thomas Mowbray?*
>    *Gaunt.* I have my Liege.

He's somewhat prejudicial, labelling Bolingbroke 'bold' before the court, which has a pejorative ring. [*SD: If this were a normal day, Richard might immediately complete the remaining metric feet of the line Gaunt commenced. Instead, Richard deploys three metrical feet of silence before moving forward – either not to seem overeager, or to genuinely proceed with caution. (It is entirely possible that the six syllables of quiet occur before Gaunt's line because he's so feeble that it takes him time to step forward and answer. Since comedy doesn't leap off the page for most of the play, you could go this route if you keep it from devolving into a hackneyed Polonius gag. Do it right and weakness here could make Gaunt's strength in 2.1 utterly terrifying.)*] But Richard can't delay proceedings any further without arousing significant suspicion, so he kills two birds with one stone – questioning the credibility of the accusation (and the accuser) whilst simultaneously reminding everyone present they are subordinates. It's useful to remember that if you have to demand respect or remind people of your power, you probably possess little of either.

*King.* Tell me moreover, hast thou sounded him,
If he appeale the Duke on ancient malice,
Or worthily as a good subject should
On some knowne ground of treacherie in him.
   *Gaunt.* As neere as I could sift him on that argument,
On some apparant danger seene in him,
Aym'd at your Highnesse, no inveterate malice.

Gaunt gives Richard nothing to work with here, so this hearing will have to move forward. Each member of your ensemble should have opinions on this matter at the top of the scene. Court drama was the soap opera of their time, and every noble was hooked. They would have extensive knowledge of what is going on and murmur about it – from light mirth to outright rage – depending on their individual allegiances. [*SD: As director of multiple productions in which I've played Richard, I always encourage the Lords Appellant to exhibit suspicion of anything that comes out of my mouth and mark things that seem strange – the postponement of the proceedings, the questions on credibility, and Richard's predilection to rhyme when he is nervous.*]

   *Kin.* Then call them to our presence face to face,
And frowning brow to brow, our selves will heare
Th'accuser, and the accused, freely speake;
High stomackd are they both, and full of ire,
In rage, deafe as the sea; hastie as fire.

*Enter Bullingbrooke and Mowbray.*

   *Bul.* Many yeares of happy dayes befall
My gracious Soveraigne, my most loving Liege.
   *Mow.* Each day still better others happinesse,
Untill the heavens envying earths good hap,
Adde an immortall title to your Crowne.
   *King.* We thanke you both, yet one but flatters us,
As well appeareth by the cause you come,
Namely, to appeale each other of high treason.
Coosin of Hereford, what dost thou object
Against the Duke of Norfolke, *Thomas Mowbray*?
   *Bul.* First, heaven be the record to my speech,
In the devotion of a subjects love,
Tendering the precious safetie of my Prince,
And free from other misbegotten hate,
Come I appealant to this Princely presence.
Now *Thomas Mowbray* do I turne to thee,

And marke my greeting well: for what I speake,
My body shall make good upon this earth,
Or my divine soule answer it in heaven.
Thou art a Traitor, and a Miscreant;
Too good to be so, and too bad to live,
Since the more faire and christall is the skie,
The uglier seeme the cloudes that in it flye:
Once more, the more to aggravate the note,
With a foule Traitors name stuffe I thy throte,
And wish (so please my Soveraigne) ere I move,                    (you wanker)
What my tong speaks, my right drawn sword may prove.

Whilst 'Traitor' and 'Miscreant' may seem similarly insulting, the worse offence was 'Traitor' – indeed, few charges were graver. Not only due to the legal and emotional challenges presented, but also because of the potential ramifications to a gentleman's honour. It may be difficult for us today to understand the historical importance of this. More than just street cred, honour was also about an individual's fiscal stability. In an era where everything was done on credit, if people thought you were dishonourable, they would cease doing business with you. You would not be able to procure food, clothes, transportation, *etc.* Defending one's honour was crucial to having a good life. In this scene, Mowbray will tell us 'Mine Honor is my life; both grow in one.' Dishonouring someone – such as calling them a traitor – could have horrible repercussions. Even if the accuser doesn't have proof, the allegation alone is enough to tarnish a reputation. Imagine if your credit score appeared on your forehead, in flashing neon lights, and that it could be affected instantly by gossip. Being called a traitor is discussed in almost all of the duelling codes, and is the most common example Saviolo uses throughout his book (see Saviolo's *A Gentleman's Guide to Duelling*). [*JK: Edited by Jared Kirby. Did I mention this already?*] [*SD: Traitor!*]

Labelling Mowbray a traitor also makes the issue much more pressing to the king: this is not a private quarrel between two random citizens; calling out a traitor is an issue of the state, and one of the most powerful accusations a subject can allege to get his king's attention. Bolingbroke knows exactly what he is doing in this case. The actor playing him can use this charge to demonstrate his absolute faith before the court (whether or not he actually possesses any), and/or manipulate the king into exposing his part in it. This is one of many examples in Shakespeare in which a deeper understanding of honour and duelling will open up more acting possibilities, raising stakes more clearly and dramatically. And it's just the start of the psychological chess match Bolingbroke will force Richard to play for the next few acts.

*See Glossary – Draws (maybe).*

'My right drawn sword may prove' does not need to be taken literally here. If it is, Bolingbroke ought to be very careful about brandishing. Drawing a weapon in front of a king could get you killed, and Bolingbroke is no fool. (If your Bolingbroke feels a strong desire to draw, he should do so with his non-dominant hand – slowly – and set the point in the ground immediately whilst kneeling in genuflection.) A more politic choice for Bolingbroke would be to motion to the weapon at his side, implying he is willing to duel over this issue and prove his truth by the sword.

Once the charge has been levied, it is the other party's responsibility to accept the statement as truth or plead it is a falsehood.

> *Mow.* Let not my cold words heere accuse my zeale:
> 'Tis not the triall of a Womans warre,
> The bitter clamour of two eager tongues,
> Can arbitrate this cause betwixt us twaine:
> The blood is hot that must be cool'd for this.
> Yet can I not of such tame patience boast,
> As to be husht, and nought at all to say.
> First the faire reverence of your Highnesse curbes mee,
> From giving reines and spurres to my free speech,
> Which else would post, untill it had return'd
> These tearmes of treason, doubly downe his throat.
> Setting aside his high bloods royalty,
> And let him be no Kinsman to my Liege,
> I do defie him, and I spit at him,
> Call him a slanderous Coward, and a Villaine:
> Which to maintaine, I would allow him oddes,
> And meete him, were I tide to runne afoote,
> Even to the frozen ridges of the Alpes,
> Or any other ground inhabitable,
> Where ever Englishman durst set his foote.
> Meane time, let this defend my loyaltie,
> By all my hopes most falsely doth he lie.

The mention of blood being cooled is an important aspect of duelling: it was not considered a duel if you got into an argument and went out into the street to fight about it; a duel was always premeditated. Ergo, in cold blood. One of the fundamental beliefs during Shakespeare's time was that the only thing separating man and beast – a comparison mentioned throughout the play – was reason. Coldly reasoning your grievances would prove you better than a beast.

Mowbray has answered Bolingbroke, which solidifies both their desires for a trial by combat. By going through the proper procedures leading up to a judicial duel, this puts further pressure on the king. If he declines to grant the request for a judicial duel, his cousins would be honourbound to settle their dispute privately in a personal duel. But personal duelling was illegal. If caught, Richard would need to execute them. Even if the duel was over, and one participant dead, the winner would be killed (assuming it was proved he was part of a personal duel).

> *Bul.* Pale trembling Coward, there I throw my gage,
> Disclaiming heere the kindred of a King,
> And lay aside my high bloods Royalty,
> Which feare, not reverence makes thee to except.
> If guilty dread hath left thee so much strength,
> As to take up mine Honors pawne, then stoope.
> By that, and all the rites of Knight-hood else,
> Will I make good against thee arme to arme,
> What I have spoken, or thou canst devise.
> *Mow.* I take it up, and by that sword I sweare,
> Which gently laid my Knight-hood on my shoulder,
> IIe answer thee in any faire degree,
> Or Chivalrous designe of knightly triall:
> And when I mount, alive may I not light,
> If I be Traitor, or unjustly fight.

In legal matters, a gage was used as security against a pledge or obligation. According to Ariella Elema in her doctoral thesis *Trial by Battle in France and England*, the earliest reference to the use of a gauntlet as gage comes from the eleventh-century poem *The Song of Roland*. Pinabel gives his right glove to the king as a gage, with a promise to fight Thierry. Other articles of clothing (*e.g.* caps) were sometimes used, but gauntlets were especially suited to the purpose – they came in unique matching pairs, making it easier to identify the owner.

> *King.* What doth our Cosin lay to *Mowbraies* charge?
> It must be great that can inherite us,
> So much as of a thought of ill in him.
> *Bul.* Looke what I said, my life shall prove it true,
> That *Mowbray* hath receiv'd eight thousand Nobles,
> In name of lendings for your Highnesse Soldiers,
> The which he hath detain'd for lewd employments,
> Like a false Traitor, and injurious Villaine.
> Besides I say, and will in battaile prove,
> Or heere, or elsewhere to the furthest Verge
> That ever was survey'd by English eye,
> That all the Treasons for these eighteene yeeres
> Complotted, and contrived in this Land,
> Fetch'd from false *Mowbray* their first head and spring.

Further I say, and further will maintaine
Upon his bad life, to make all this good.
That he did plot the Duke of Glousters death,
Suggest his soone beleeving adversaries,
And consequently, like a Traitor Coward,
Sluc'd out his innocent soule through streames of blood:
Which blood, like sacrificing *Abels* cries,
(Even from the toonglesse cavernes of the earth)
To me for justice, and rough chasticement:
And by the glorious worth of my discent,
This arme shall do it, or this life be spent.

Bolingbroke compares Gloucester's death to the first murder in Judeo-Christian scripture. Bolingbroke may genuinely believe this evocation reasonable – religion is on his mind over the course of three full plays – but he would not be unaware of its added benefits. Bolingbroke shocks the room and continues to corner Richard by raising the stakes. [*SD: Bolingbroke also hands Richard an out by claiming Mowbray was a hired gun, without hazarding any guess as to the identity of his employer. Richard cannot be completely sure of the details to which Bolingbroke is privy, or who he thinks really is to blame, so it is encouraging that he seems to be fine with placing all of the blame on Mowbray and leaving Richard out of it. A new problem presents itself, however, as there is no way to gauge how loose a cannon Mowbray is starting to become, or how far he will go. It is worth exploring in your tablework what conversation, if any, Richard had with Mowbray after the murder of Gloucester but prior to this encounter. Was there a script that Mowbray now ignores, or was Richard merely sloppy? Either way, Richard does not want this to get out of hand. He attempts to pour some cold water on Bolingbroke's Bible class, whilst simultaneously giving a hint (reminder?) to Mowbray on how to proceed.*]

  *King.* How high a pitch his resolution soares:
*Thomas* of Norfolke, what sayest thou to this?
  *Mow.* Oh let my Soveraigne turne away his face,
And bid his eares a little while be deafe,
Till I have told this slander of his blood,
How God, and good men, hate so foule a lyar.
  *King. Mowbray,* impartiall are our eyes and eares,
Were he my brother, nay our kingdomes heyre,
As he is but my fathers brothers sonne;
Now by my Scepters awe, I make a vow,
Such neighbour-neerenesse to our sacred blood,
Should nothing priviledge him, nor partialize
The un-stooping firmenesse of my upright soule.
He is our subject (*Mowbray*) so art thou,
Free speech, and fearelesse, I to thee allow.

York and Gaunt are likely to be dead by the time Richard's crown is passed along and, at the moment, he is childless. Furthermore, he is painfully aware that Bolingbroke is powerful, revered, and favoured by lineage in any ensuing claims to the throne. Richard cleverly declares none of this will sway his decision-making process in a specific message to the entire court, but also a coded message to Mowbray that he won't be thrown under the bus.

> *Mow.* Then *Bullingbrooke,* as low as to thy heart.
> Through the false passage of thy throat; thou lyest:
> Three parts of that receipt I had for Callice,
> Disburst I to his Highnesse souldiers;
> The other part reserv'd I by consent,
> For that my Soveraigne Liege was in my debt,
> Upon remainder of a deere Accompt,
> Since last I went to France to fetch his Queene:
> Now swallow downe that Lye. For Glousters death,
> I slew him not; but (to mine owne disgrace)
> Neglected my sworne duty in that case:
> For you my noble Lord of *Lancaster,*
> The honourable Father to my foe,
> Once I did lay an ambush for your life,     (*holiday gatherings must be a delight*)
> A trespasse that doth vex my greeved soule:
> But ere I last receiv'd the Sacrament,
> I did confesse it, and exactly begg'd
> Your Graces pardon, and I hope I had it.
> This is my fault: as for the rest appeal'd,
> It issues from the rancour of a Villaine,
> A recreant, and most degenerate Traitor,
> Which in my selfe I boldly will defend,
> And interchangeably hurle downe my gage
> Upon this over-weening Traitors foote,
> To prove my selfe a loyall Gentleman,
> Even in the best blood chamber'd in his bosome.
> In hast whereof, most heartily I pray
> Your Highnesse to assigne our Triall day.

Richard lets these bozos go back and forth as a stalling tactic, more for show than prologue to an actual altercation. Much to Richard and Gaunt's surprise, neither of the would-be combatants backs down. If this continues, any further delay on Richard's part will make him appear guilty. Richard's nervous rhyming resumes.

*King.* Wrath-kindled Gentlemen be rul'd by me:
Let's purge this choller without letting blood:
This we prescribe, though no Physition,
Deepe malice makes too deepe incision.
Forget, forgive, conclude, and be agreed,
Our Doctors say, This is no time to bleed.
Good Unckle, let this end where it begun,
Wee'l calme the Duke of Norfolke; you, your son.
    *Gaunt.* To be a make-peace shall become my age,
Throw downe (my sonne) the Duke of Norfolkes gage.
    *King.* And Norfolke, throw downe his.
    *Gaunt.* When *Harrie* when? Obedience bids,
Obedience bids I should not bid agen.
    *King.* Norfolke, throw downe, we bidde; there is no boote.
    *Mow.* My selfe I throw (dread Soveraigne) at thy foot.
My life thou shalt command, but not my shame,
The one my dutie owes, but my faire name
Despight of death, that liues upon my grave
To darke dishonours use, thou shalt not have.
I am disgrac'd, impeach'd, and baffel'd heere,
Pierc'd to the soule with slanders venom'd speare:
The which no balme can cure, but his heart blood
Which breath'd this poyson.
    *King.*                              Rage must be withstood:
Give me his gage: Lyons make Leopards tame.

Remember the top of the scene when Richard chose not to take a shared line with Gaunt? There is no such delay here – Richard immediately follows Mowbray with the command 'Rage must be withstood'. This clearly gets to Richard and illustrates how little self-control he actually has. Making matters worse, Mowbray drives more nails into his own coffin. Explaining to someone with Richard's sociopathy how honour functions, in front of his most powerful subjects, is a terrible idea. But screw it. Mowbray powers ahead like a first-draft Iago (see Volume Two – *Othello* (3.3)).

    *Mo.* Yea, but not change his spots: take but my shame,
And I resigne my gage. My deere, deere Lord,
The purest treasure mortall times afford
Is spotlesse reputation: that away,
Men are but gilded loame, or painted clay.
A Jewell in a ten times barr'd up Chest,
Is a bold spirit, in a loyall brest.
Mine Honor is my life; both grow in one:

Take Honor from me, and my life is done.
Then (deere my Liege) mine Honor let me trie,
In that I live; and for that will I die.

Realising Mowbray has permanently turned wildcard, Richard tries his luck with Bolingbroke. Richard breaks up a line, in an attempt to exert control:

*King.* Coosin, throw downe your gage,
Do you begin.
*Bul.* Oh heaven defend my soule from such foule sin.
Shall I seeme Crest-falne in my fathers sight,
Or with pale beggar-feare impeach my hight
Before this out-dar'd dastard? Ere my toong,
Shall wound mine honor with such feeble wrong;
Or sound so base a parle: my teeth shall teare
The slavish motive of recanting feare,
And spit it bleeding in his high disgrace,
Where shame doth harbour, even in *Mowbrayes* face.

*Exit Gaunt.*

Richard is left with no other choice but to grant the judicial duel, which he does, after buying himself one final postponement.

## Act 1  Scene 3

*See Glossary – Draws (maybe); Ensemble Readiness; Grabs (maybe).*

Richard's latest recess now complete, the day has arrived for the outdoor battle at Coventry. Lances were mentioned at the close of 1.1 and, accordingly, the duel will be in the form of mounted combat. This appears to have been based on *The Ordenaunce and Fourme of Fightyng within Lists* by Thomas of Woodstock. No, your eyes are not deceiving you. Thomas of Woodstock, Duke of Gloucester, whom Richard just had Mowbray slaughter.

*Bul.* Lord Marshall, let me kisse my Soveraigns hand,
And bow my knee before his Majestie:
For *Mowbray* and my selfe are like two men,
That vow a long and weary pilgrimage,
Then let us take a ceremonious leave
And loving farwell of our severall friends.

*Mar.* The Appealant in all duty greets your Highnes,
And craves to kisse your hand, and take his leave.
    *Rich.* We will descend, and fold him in our armes.
Cosin of Herford, as thy cause is just,
So be thy fortune in this Royall fight:
Farewell, my blood, which if to day thou shead,
Lament we may, but not revenge thee dead.

[*SD: I played the first three lines of Richard's response so the entire court could hear. For the last two lines, I took the Claudius route from Chapter 1 –* Hamlet *(1.2): a private threat. And I thought I could pull it off without any immediate repercussions, given that Bolingbroke is far tamer and more predictable at the top of this play than the Danish prince is in his. In each of my prior productions as Richard, the actors playing Bolingbroke let me score the private point. Until 2010. Gentle giant Jeffrey Evan Thomas was almost a full foot taller than me, but was on his knee (along with Mowbray) during this bit. After whispering in Bolingbroke's ear that I wouldn't do a bloody thing if he ended up losing the fight, Jeffrey stood up, towered above me, and grasped my forearm. This was enough to scare the living daylights out of me, and assert his authority in front of the peers of the realm. His first few lines were for my sake, but the rest were declaimed to the full court as I scurried back to my safe-space throne.*]

    *Bull.* Oh let no noble eye prophane a teare
For me, if I be gor'd with *Mowbrayes* speare:
As confident, as is the Falcons flight
Against a bird, do I with *Mowbray* fight.
My loving Lord, I take my leave of you,
Of you (my Noble Cosin) Lord *Aumerle*;
Not sicke, although I have to do with death,
But lustie, yong, and cheerely drawing breath.

As the scene progresses, it becomes clear to Richard that he cannot allow the duel to take place. He cuts a deal with some of the elders, choosing banishment over judicial duel. Bolingbroke has too many friends in the room, and gets off with a temporary vacation abroad. Having alienated Richard, Mowbray now only has enemies and is exiled for life. It is possible he makes some move towards the king or Bolingbroke, though the verbal assault is harsh enough. Whether or not it will actually occur, all members of the court should be at the ready for unsanctioned violence.

## Act 2  Scene 1

*See Glossary – Draws (maybe); Ensemble Readiness; Grabs (maybe); Strikes (maybe).*

This kind of conversation is a dangerous one. There are countless occasions throughout history when someone presumed to be too familiar with the ruler and ended up dead.

Gaunt must be aware of this fact, yet chooses to proceed. He either hopes that Richard will be considerate of age – unlikely since Richard opens the play by calling Gaunt 'old' and 'time honoured' – or Gaunt's nearness to the grave prompts him to spend his final breaths as truth to power. If the former, then any kind of physical violence is unlikely to accompany the verbal assault; if the latter, it depends what story your production is interested in telling. Gaunt might have a cane, or simply a hand, with which he can strike Richard. Does it land? Does Richard flinch? Does he react in kind, or up the ante? Furthermore, Gaunt (like York later in the scene) mentions Richard's father (the Black Prince from Chapter 8 – *Edward 3*). This emotional manipulation, particularly in Gaunt's hands, may be worse than actual violence. [*SD: In 2001, my first Gaunt, already near me, collapsed at the peak of his pique, leaving me to decide whether or not to catch him or let him fall to the floor. You surely know which I chose. A few years later, to prevent the possibility of getting any ancient skin cells near my person, I stood far enough away that Gaunt had to charge at me, only to be restrained by York, Northumberland, etc. Like me, my Richard had been social distancing for over thirty years. This had a big payoff by contrast in the prison scene (5.5) – I dusted off the floor for the groom, inviting him to sit with me. This simple action spoke volumes about how far Richard had come in his fall from demigod to commoner. I generally do not play the end of the story at the beginning. Nor should you.*]

## Act 2  Scene 2

*See Glossary – Grabs (maybe); Strikes (maybe).*

How truthful is Bolingbroke's assertion in 3.1 that the king's favourites have disrupted the royal marriage? And do they get drunk on any of this power? The scene could be amongst friends, but that isn't particularly interesting. If the favourites are indeed intimidating the queen, does she fight back? Does she use York as a shield? This approach may not fit your production, but give it more rehearsal time than it initially may seem to require.

## Act 3  Scene 1

*See Glossary – Arrests; Binds (maybe); Grabs (maybe); Strikes (maybe).*

> *Enter Bullingbrooke, Yorke, Northumberland, Rosse, Percie, Willoughby,*
> *with Bushie and Greene Prisoners.*

Nobility would normally be treated well in captivity, but this is no typical imprisonment. A banished cousin of the king has illegally returned from exile, and taken hold of the king's favourites. How Bolingbroke feels about Bushie and Greene will be reflected in their bondage. Have they had regular meals? Were they allowed to bathe and retain access to their finery? Or are they malnourished, dehydrated, bleeding, bruised, and – most disturbing of all – forced to wear plain clothes?

If you choose to have the guards manhandle Bushie and Greene on the way in (*see Appendix – Bursting the Bubble*), they should throw themselves around whilst the guards follow this action to make it appear they are controlling it.

If you choose to bind the victims' arms, front is safer than behind since, if the actors trip, it will be more difficult for them to protect themselves. Either way, the actors should *never* be bound for real.

The removal of the prisoners offers an opportunity to reveal Northumberland's character: this could be done respectfully, showing he is a consummate soldier performing his duty; conversely, he could wait until the stage has cleared, and just kill them right there and then. This would show either that Bolingbroke and crew are wasting no time getting everything changed over, or that Bolingbroke ordered a noble execution but, when he isn't looking, Northumberland does things his own way. This foreshadowing is a good way to start portraying their relationship, which ends with Northumberland's ego eventually forcing him to part with Bolingbroke in the next play.

## Act 4  Scene 1

*See Glossary – Draws (maybe); Ensemble Readiness; Grabs (maybe); Strikes (maybe).*

This is similar to our discussion in 1.1 – Richard has been swapped out for Bolingbroke, but the same combination of hotheadedness and weaponry remains. What changes is that Bolingbroke handles the situation even more poorly than his predecessor, with virtually everyone throwing down a gauntlet. Bolingbroke opts for postponement of yet another duel that will never actually take place.

## Act 5  Scene 2

*See Glossary – Grabs (maybe); Strikes (maybe).*

This scene and the next will function as much-needed comic relief. With this in mind, how physical are the Yorks? The patriarch seems quite a gentle soul up until this scene, but people act differently at home when outsiders aren't watching. See Chapter 7 – *King John* (3.1). Furthermore, Aumerle isn't helping matters with his secret coup. And both of these gentlemen will have to answer to the matriarch. She encourages Aumerle to hit his father. If Aumerle doesn't, does the duchess? You should also consider whether the household staff get caught up in the Yorkist crossfire.

*[JK: When York snatches the letter, there is an opportunity for violence. See Chapter 1 – King Lear (1.2). If York grabs the letter quickly, and Aumerle goes after York to retrieve it, he could threaten violence to make Aumerle stop. Another option is to have a struggle here. York gets his hands on the letter, and Aumerle stops York from pulling it out. They fight a little, but York wins, which may require him to punch Aumerle in the stomach or face. If you choose to extend York's brutality beyond the dispute with the letter, he can backhand the duchess whilst calling her a fool, then start beating Aumerle on 'Boy, let me see the Writing'. If Aumerle's response is to curl up into a foetal position, the audience know this kind of abuse is normalised. Explore in production whether this is a one-off, or if York is a serial abuser in private.]*

*The Duke of York discovering his son Aumerle's treachery.*
William Hamilton, late 1790s. (*Folger Shakespeare Library*)

## Act 5  Scene 3

*See Glossary – Draws; Ensemble Readiness; Grabs (maybe); Knees; Strikes (maybe).*

As Aumerle bursts through the door, the guards (and possibly the king) draw their weapons. Given how Bolingbroke came by the crown, he can't be too careful. Everyone present should have specific reactions, especially any of Aumerle's fellow conspirators.

Bolingbroke must at least threaten violence after York proclaims Aumerle a traitor. Does Bolingbroke draw or even strike Aumerle before he says 'Stay thy reuengefull hand'? Explore violence between York and Aumerle as well, but make sure it is in accordance with what you established in 5.2.

## Act 5  Scene 5

*See Glossary – Blood (maybe); Blood Packs (maybe); Draws; Falls, Grabs (maybe); Strikes*

> *Keep.* My Lord, wilt please you to fall too?
> *Rich.* Taste of it first, as thou wer't wont to doo.
> *Keep.* My Lord I dare not: Sir *Pierce* of Exton,

Who lately came from th' King, commands the contrary.
   *Rich.* The divell take *Henrie* of Lancaster, and thee;
Patience is stale, and I am weary of it.
   *Keep.* Helpe, helpe, helpe.

Something must happen to make the keeper yell for help. Since Richard is confident the food is poisoned, he could throw the dish to the floor or across the room. Even better, at the keeper. (Given the ensuing fight, be careful no one is in danger of tripping on random foodstuffs.)

*Enter Exton and Servants.*

   *Ri.* How now? what meanes Death in this rude assalt?
Villaine, thine owne hand yeelds thy deaths instrument,
Go thou and fill another roome in hell.

*Exton strikes him downe.*

[JK: *My favourite version of this fight to date was with The York Shakespeare Company in 2010. It happened to star Seth, with fights by me.*] [SD: *Cheque's in the mail, broseph.*] [JK: *Richard usually just rolls over and dies. No one expects a poet to know how to fight, so Exton and his men overpower Richard and that's that. In our production, Richard fights for his life. Everyone worked with me on what it is like to be attacked with a knife, and how hard it is to defend. That said, we made sure Richard took on Exton and his servants, so they were not leaving unscathed. It adds a little excitement at the end.*] [SD: *I'll add that the text is a bit vague. 'Villaine, thine owne hand yeelds thy deaths instrument' is generally taken to mean Richard either gets a weapon out of one servant's hands, or grabs hold of the servant's arm and forces him to stab himself. 'Go thou and fill another roome in hell' could be a second servant Richard somehow manages to wound fatally, or the prelude in an attempt to kill Exton. In my production with Jared, I was well on my way to surviving the servants' onslaught until Exton – whom neither I nor the audience had seen enter – stabbed me in the back. We've highlighted in earlier chapters the power of staying ahead of your audience. They should not have time to anticipate Cordelia's corpse, Claudius' death, or Macduff's entrance to the final battle. Similarly, any expectation on the audience's part of what Richard would be like in a fight should be flipped on its head, thereby making his eventual loss more upsetting.*] [JK: *This doesn't mean Richard suddenly becomes a superhero-level fighter. An unskilled person might still find success in some combination of adrenaline, luck, and the new-found high of seeing the world through human eyeballs.*]

*Falstaff choosing his recruits.* John Cawse, 1818. (*Folger Shakespeare Library*)

# Chapter 10

# Henry 4 Part 1

*'Thou art violently carried away from grace'* – Hal (2.5)

[*JK: As with Chapter 4 – Macbeth, there is an opportunity to start your show off with a battle. The Battle of Homildon Hill was the skirmish between the Douglasses and the Percies that took place on 14 September 1402. This is what is being reported to Henry by Westmoreland in 1.1. The advantage of staging this battle is that the audience get to see Hotspur's fighting prowess firsthand. This approach was very successful at the Hudson Warehouse Theatre in 2015. It was a great idea by the director, Nicholas Martin-Smith, and this production was the Shakespearean debut of Steve Guttenberg (a blast to work with). And you also have the audience's attention with this big fight, so maybe they'll stay awake as Henry opens with a boring speech.*] [*SD: I will, again, completely disagree with this approach. I want Hotspur's martial skill, like Macbeth's, built up verbally so much that it cannot possibly be believed. When we finally see it in action hours later, we will experience it from Hal's perspective and have a collective fightgasm. The play's opening speech is only boring if the actor you cast as Henry is a moron. Don't cast morons.*]

We start with the elevation of solemnity and verse in this first scene, which is immediately undercut by the baseness and prose of the second.

*See Glossary – Ensemble Readiness (roughhousing and such, which could incorporate other Glossary entries such as Grabs, Strikes, etc. – just assume this for these next few plays, we won't keep mentioning it).*

Much has been written about the Hal/Falstaff relationship. We will not discuss it here. Whether it's father/son, best friends, or frenemies, be particular about how physical they are with one another. If you open up their corporeal dynamics here, you will have more options available throughout the coming scenes. Explore arm punches, noogies, smacks upside the head ('Thou art so fat-witted'), belly smacks, and other juvenile nonsense (more to come in Volume Two – *Romeo and Juliet*). We can see them have fun one-upping each other in deeds as well as words. This is not an invitation to improvise. Your actors must have consent from each other and, for safety, these hijinks will need to be choreographed. Poins, Francis, *et al.* need to function within this construct as well. Are they part of the roughhousing? Do any consider themselves above it and choose not to participate? This could make them targets for the others. We're going to be amongst the tavern folk for the next few plays. Dedicate rehearsal time to building a specific, engaging ensemble. Or just issue your audience refunds and go home.

## Act 1  Scene 3

*See Glossary – Ensemble Readiness; Falls (maybe); Grabs (maybe); Strikes (maybe).*

The verbal tensions are already severe enough between King Henry and Hotspur that physical violence would be counterproductive. But this scene does give you an opportunity to reveal more about the relationship between Hotspur and his father. Hotspur is enraged. If he chases after King Henry when he leaves, it would most certainly cost Hotspur his life. Northumberland could physically prevent Hotspur from this pursuit. This might be as minor as Northumberland blocking Hotspur's way, but could also be grabbing him by the ear, backhanding him, or pushing him hard enough that he falls to the ground. You then reveal more of their dynamic in how Hotspur counters. Does Hotspur cower in submission, or get right in Daddy's face? Any subsequent action is interrupted by Worcester's entrance.

> *Hot.* And if the diuell come and roare for them
> I will not send them. I will after straight
> And tell him so: for I will ease my heart,
> Although it be with hazard of my head.
> *Nor.* What? drunke with choller? stay & pause awhile,
> Heere comes your Vnckle.

If the father/son relationship here is particularly physical in your production, Northumberland might resume the beatings when Worcester leaves.

## Act 2  Scene 2

*See Glossary – Binds; Ensemble Readiness; Strikes (maybe).*

*Heere they rob them, and binde them.*

Continue tracking and building the physical dynamics established in 1.2. Here, the comedy lies in the distance between how each character envisions themselves versus their actual ability to intimidate. This probably isn't the first robbing rodeo for this crew. Even if Falstaff is all bark and no bite, this is often enough to terrify most people. But, if he does need to make an example, he might land a stomach punch on the plumpest of the 'gorbellied knaves'. Maybe your production's Bardolph is the strong/silent type who commits violent acts and has to be pulled off a traveller by Gadshill? Again, this depends on your cast; we encourage you to explore each permutation that strikes your fancy, and even a few that do not.

*As they are sharing, the* Prince *and* Poynes *set vpon them.*
*They all run away, leauing the booty behind them.*

There is no need to add gratuitous violence; if a good scaring does the trick (there is nothing beyond 'the Prince and Poynes set vpon them'), then leave it at that. Whatever physical violence took place earlier in the scene will underline the utter lack of it here.

## Act 2  Scene 3

*Enter Hotspurre solus, reading a Letter.*

[*SD: The best version of this speech I've seen was by Stephen Cavanagh when we were students. He treated the letter as a surrogate for its author, proceeding to beat the everloving bejeezus out of it. I cannot remember if he sustained a paper cut, or if that thought came to me years later. We'll say it was his idea because I am known for my humility.*] [*JK: This is a great idea and easy to sell – just suck on the injured finger and shake it after. If you're doing a student matinee performance, it could be the little finger referenced later in the scene. Lady Percy can tend to the pinky, and then threaten to break it. For the adult performances, she's probably threatening the other kind of little finger.*]

*See Glossary – Grabs (maybe); Intimacy; Strikes (maybe).*

    *La.* How so farre?
    *Hot.* Not an inch further. But harke you *Kate*,         *(completion of dick threat?)*
Whither I go, thither shall you go too:
To day will I set forth, to morrow you.
Will this content you *Kate*?
    *La.*                        It must of force.

We need to invest in their relationship quickly here, so that it will pay off in later scenes of this play and the next. How does Lady Percy elicit information? Beating her husband senseless? Self-harm like Portia in Volume Two – *Julius Caesar* (2.1)? Seduction as a disguise for the eventual grab-and-squeeze of his 'little finger'? And how might he respond to any of these?

## Act 2  Scene 4

*See Glossary – Ensemble Readiness; Falls (maybe); Strikes (maybe).*

*Heere they both call him, the Drawer stands amazed, not knowing which way to go.*

Francis is being pulled in multiple directions, so you can add a pratfall here if you're that type of monster. And Poins might throw things at Francis to get his attention. If so, make sure they are soft objects or, if real/hard, they are aimed to miss.

*Enter Vintner.*

 *Vint.* What, stand'st thou still, and hear'st such a calling? Looke to the Guests within: My Lord, olde Sir
*Iohn* with halfe a dozen more, are at the doore: shall I let
them in?

Whilst it's a short moment, the vintner might chase Francis off stage, or even smack him with a towel to spur his exit.

 *Fal.* A plague of all Cowards I say, and a Vengeance
too, marry and Amen. Giue me a cup of Sacke Boy. Ere
I leade this life long, Ile sowe nether stockes, and mend
them too. A plague of all cowards. Giue me a Cup of
Sacke, Rogue. Is there no Vertue extant?
 *Prin.* Didst thou neuer see Titan kisse a dish of Butter,
pittifull hearted Titan that melted at the sweete Tale of
the Sunne? If thou didst, then behold that compound.
 *Fal.* You Rogue, heere's Lime in this Sacke too: there
is nothing but Roguery to be found in Villanous man; yet
a Coward is worse then a Cup of Sack with lime.

Falstaff may be the kind of fellow who wants to vent his frustrations on others but, being a coward, only has the nerve to beat the helpless. This would make Francis a perfect target.

## Act 3  Scene 3

*See Glossary – Ensemble Readiness; Grabs (maybe); Intimacy (maybe); Strikes (maybe).*

How flirty is the dynamic between Mistress Quickly and Falstaff? We'd point out that a pub in the early fifteenth century would be replete with men who get handsy, but not much has changed. We know Falstaff fools around with Doll Tearsheet in Chapter 11 – *Henry 4 Part 2*. It's up to your production to determine if Falstaff is into the hostess as well. Time to bring your intimacy consultant back into the rehearsal room. If you're headed down the road of slaps, grabs, or gropes (playful and/or admonishing), you'll need to bring in the fight director as well.

 And don't forget the other miscreants. You've had a few scenes to establish a baseline of how the men deal with one another. Do any of these dynamics shift when the women are around?

 *Prin.* O, if it should. how would thy guttes fall about
thy knees.

Does Prince Hal juggle Falstaff's boobs/guts? This is another moment to explore with the help of your intimacy consultant and fight director. Yes, we're being paid for these lines of inquiry.

## Act 5  Scene 2

*[JK: The Battle of Shrewsbury begins. Shakespeare's version varies from history. Shocking, I know! On 21 July 1403, the king met Hotspur and his army. This was the first recorded battle in which English archers fought each other. The battle ended when Hotspur was killed (supposedly shot in the face when he opened his visor). The king had Hotspur quartered; his head was impaled in York, and the rest displayed in various corners of the country. Historical details can offer interesting moments you might want to incorporate – you could include the archers in your battle, or Hotspur could die by being stabbed in the face.]*

> *They embrace, the trumpets sound, the King entereth with his power,*
> *alarum vnto the battell. Then enter Dowglas, and Sir Walter Blunt.*

*Blu.* What is thy name, that in battel thus thou crossest me?
What honor dost thou seeke vpon my head?
　*Dow.* Know then my name is *Dowglas,*
And I do haunt thee in the battell thus,
Because some tell me, that thou art a King.
　*Blunt.* They tell thee true.
　*Dow.* The Lord of Stafford deere to day hath bought
Thy likenesse: for insted of thee King *Harry,*
This Sword hath ended him, so shall it thee,
Vnlesse thou yeeld thee as a Prisoner.
　*Blu.* I was not borne to yeeld, thou haughty Scot,
And thou shalt finde a King that will reuenge
Lords Staffords death.

> *Fight, Blunt is slaine, then enters Hotspur.*

*Hot.* O *Dowglas,* hadst thou fought at Holmedon thus
I neuer had triumphed o're a Scot.
　*Dow.* All's done, all's won, here breathles lies the king
　*Hot.* Where?
　*Dow.* Heere.
　*Hot.* This *Dowglas?* No, I know this face full well:
A gallant Knight he was, his name was *Blunt,*
Semblably furnish'd like the King himselfe.
　*Dow.* Ah foole: go with thy soule whether it goes,

A borrowed Title hast thou bought too deere.
Why didst thou tell me, that thou wer't a King?
    *Hot.* The King hath many marching in his Coats.
    *Dow.* Now by my Sword, I will kill all his Coates,
Ile murder all his Wardrobe peece by peece,
Vntill I meet the King.

[*JK: Start the battle off properly, with troops lined up and an initial charge from both sides. There will be many individual fights coming, but they need to feel like part of the battle and not random, unrelated vignettes. The king enters, as the stage directions call for, and he can fight a bit to show the audience his level of skill. Then the king exits and Blunt comes on, as does Douglas. They can enter already fighting, which will help the audience believe it's still the king. Keep the battle raging all around the stage as Douglas and Blunt move downstage to speak. Douglas and Blunt are probably highly trained swordsmen, so the fight should reflect this. Once Blunt falls, the audience should believe it was the king and that the war is over. This offers more suspense (and more disappointment) for Douglas and Hotspur when they discover Blunt is not the king.*] [*SD: I would avoid giving away anything about the king's fighting ability until the next scene. And I also would not have other fights taking place upstage during Douglas and Blunt because those would … ya know … upstage.*]

## Act 5  Scene 3

*See Glossary – Carries (almost).*

There is an alarum and excursions before Hal's entrance. He was somewhere else in the previous scene, but enters here. To make sense of this, see Chapter 7 – *King John* (3.2). Hal has an injury bad enough to make his father question whether continuing is wise. Consider a laceration on the crown of Hal's head. This will produce a sufficient quantity of blood to freak out everyone. [*SD: In real life, Hal was also hit in the face with an arrow (and survived surgery).*] [*JK: Wow, Shakespeare lined up with history for once! Keep the battle going during this scene. Have fights behind Henry, Hal, Lancaster, and Westmoreland. Bring adversaries in so one of them has to fight during the dialogue. You can reveal more about characters in these small frays whilst keeping the stakes of the scene high. The characters should never feel safe enough to just chat with each other. When crafting the fight choreography, remember that it should be a story in and of itself. There are many ways to choreograph this, but I recommend having the king win the opening phase since he will ultimately lose the fight. Douglas can turn the tables in the middle phase, whether through skill or a trick (decide with the actor what will reveal more about their version of the character). The climax can be a big injury to the king that makes it look like he is nearly vanquished. For example, in the 2015 Hudson Warehouse production, I had Douglas hit the king's shield so hard that his arm broke. The battle lingered around Douglas and the king. Hal entered fighting, won, and then saw the king in peril.*]

*They fight, the K. being in danger. Enter Prince.*

    *Prin.* Hold vp they head vile Scot, or thou art like
Neuer to hold it vp againe: the Spirits
Of valiant *Sherly, Stafford, Blunt*, are in my Armes;
It is the Prince of Wales that threatens thee,
Who neuer promiseth, but he meanes to pay.

*[JK: Explore Hal and Douglas having very different fighting styles. If Douglas is bigger, he can use strength to his advantage whilst Hal, being smaller, can focus on dodges, ducks, and weaves. (Humans have perpetually been enthralled by contests between a big, strong brute and a light, quick pipsqueak.) Another option is to have an emotionally driven Douglas, whilst Hal is a more mindful, calculating fighter, focused on tactical manoeuvering.]*

*They Fight, Dowglas flyeth.*

Why does Douglas fly? There could be a bevy of English storming the stage as Hal is winning, so Douglas realises fleeing is the best option. It's also possible that Hal disarms Douglas. It could be both. Hal could start to chase Douglas, even almost catch him, but decide to turn back and take care of the king. This choice would reveal Hal's nobility and lead right into 'Cheerely My Lord: how fare's your Grace'.

    The battle has continued, and it would be wise to bring Douglas back on stage. We're told in Chapter 11 – *Henry 4 Part 2 (1.1)* that Douglas had at least 'three times slaine th'appearance of the King'. Let Douglas fight one more person dressed as the king as the campaign continues.

*Fight.*

Next, the moment everyone knows is coming. Hal and Hotspur should have the most epic fight. We are nearing the end of the battle, so you can clear most of the stage for it. *[JK: You may want to bring one or two brief fights on stage, so no one (including Hal and Hotspur) forgets there is a full battle still going. This will also make Falstaff's entrance more organic.]* *[SD: I politely, insofar as I am able, disagree. Complete focus should be on the massive Hal/Hotspur set piece. Foreshadowing will dilute their fight, and deflate Falstaff's entrance.]*

*[JK: When creating this fight choreography, do you want to mirror the Hal/Douglas dynamic chosen earlier, or do you want Hal and Hotspur to have similar fighting styles? These boys grew up together, and were probably trained by the same swordmaster. If so, the choreography can almost immediately move into feints/attacks and second-intention strategy, which will make for much more complex choreography.]*

*Enter Dowglas, he fights with Falstaffe, who fals down as if he were dead.*

This fight should be ridiculous. It can be more of a chase than a fight, in order to make sense of how long Falstaff can stand up to Douglas. *[JK: I staged this with Hal/ Hotspur fighting centrestage. Falstaff would run a complete circle around them, then run into the audience. Douglas will finally catch Falstaff, and deliver a blow that a seasoned warrior would believe could kill someone (e.g. a pommel to the face, or an attack to the shield that knocks Falstaff to the ground). It would be wise to have a couple of soldiers enter at this point, to chase Douglas off stage before he can check on Falstaff, or turn to help Hotspur fight Hal.]*

### *The Prince killeth Percie.*

Finally, Hal kills Hotspur. From Falstaff's report upon waking, we know that Hotspur was disembowelled. [*JK: Removal of the stomach, gastrointestinal tract, and bowels. It might seem disembowelment would result in immediate death, but it can take a while if no major arteries have been severed in the process.*]

Falstaff stabs Hotspur at least once, but maybe a few times. [*JK: One small cut is funnier.*] The safest way to do this is to have Falstaff place his blade on Hotspur's thigh and draw a cut across it. If you prefer to make it a thrust, aim a little upstage of the body and have Falstaff stab the ground.

*See Glossary – Carries.*

### *Takes Hotspurre on his backe.*

And now back to some much-needed comedy. Play with the different ways Falstaff can try to take the body away and fail. Remember the amount of blood, intestines, and other internal organs strewn about. Falstaff can certainly try to scoop up the body à la Lear/Cordelia but, as soon as the blood and guts get near him, he can almost vomit. You'll probably end up needing to drag Hotspur off, so have Falstaff scoop up the corpse under the arms, and keep it's torso near his chest whilst lifting with the legs. This will create a safe drag off, and Falstaff can play with making it look awkward. Falstaff's exit is interrupted and he drops Hotspur. Hotspur can slide down Falstaff's legs so Hotspur's head is safe as it gets down to Falstaff's feet. Then, Hotspur can create a little tension in his neck so his head doesn't actually fall on the ground whilst Falstaff removes his feet. This will make it look like Falstaff dropped Hotspur, but the actor playing Hotspur is in control of getting his head to the ground whilst making it look like it dropped.

## Act 5  Scene 4

*See Glossary – Arrests; Binds (probably); Strikes (maybe).*

> *The Trumpets sound. Enter the King, Prince of Wales, Lord Iohn of Lancaster, Earle of Westmerland, with Worcester & Vernon Prisoners.*

The treatment of prisoners is always a reflection on the captors. Does Henry treat them with civility, despite the deep betrayal he feels? Or does he finally lose his trademark cool and beat the traitors?

# *from Steve Guttenberg*

*One of the most fascinating endeavours of stage play is the fight. These encounters can either be fraught with mistakes and punches that land rather than whiz by your noggin'. And an expert like Jared makes sure that all on the wooden boards are safe, and the blows, punches and swordplay that look oh so certain from the groundlings' view, are actually strictly composed choreography that sings like Renée Fleming.*

*We were doing Henry 4 a few years ago for our beloved Hudson Warehouse in the perpetually oxygen-filled Stage on the Hudson River. Jared had multiple engagements happening on stage, and I was amongst many that gave the audiences gasps of fright and delight. There is nothing like a Shakespearean army fighting to save their glory. And I was one of Jared's students during that summer. I learned how to be ferocious upstage whilst not hurting a fly, or my castmates. Stage fighting is an art, and I worked with the Michelangelo of the craft.*

*Thank you, Jared, for teaching me how to appear like a barbarian, whilst having dinner with my foe immediately after on Central Park West. Bravo Maestro!*

# Chapter 11

# Henry 4 Part 2

*'Where hateful death put on his ugliest mask'* – Morton (1.1)

## Act 1  Scene 3

Another openin' … another medical discussion.

Gout is a form of arthritis, usually in the joint at the base of the big toe. It is a sudden and severe pain, swelling, and tenderness. It feels like your big toe is on fire and anything coming in contact with it will be intolerable. Falstaff starts the play with gout. Since the self-discipline required to change his diet is likely non-existent, his gout could worsen and give you added options in staging.

## Act 2  Scene 1

*See Glossary – Arrests; Draws; Ensemble Readiness; Intimacy (maybe).*

This attempted arrest of Falstaff could be staged as a Mexican standoff. [*SD: That's not PC, hermano.*] [*JK: Let's try again.*]

This attempted arrest of Falstaff could be staged as a confrontation wherein no party can claim success, but there is no way for either to withdraw without a loss. You could opt for a simpler staging, but you will miss out on a solid comedic fight in a play that should take any opportunity it can to keep the audience awake. (*Part 1* is an excellent standalone piece; *Part 2* … not so much.)

Is Quickly using seduction to get her way in this scene? Innuendos include 'entred the Action', 'lusty yeoman', and 'he stabd me'. What happens if Fang or Snare accidentally kicks Falstaff's gout-ridden toe? And what if your hostess gets enraged and is strangling Falstaff, so Fang and Snare have to pull her off Falstaff in order to complete the arrest? You have all sorts of options in this setting – chasing amongst food, goblets, cutlery, plates, *etc.* Again, take the time in rehearsals to explore these possibilities with your actors. [*JK: In one production, I had someone beaten with a lobster.*] Note this is an opportunity for anyone who missed *Part 1,* or somehow has never heard of Falstaff, to get a quick sense of his cowardice. You also need to continue tracking the Falstaff/Mistress Quickly dynamic. What is her objective here? This sounds like more than just an argument about the bill. And it is contradictory with her description of Falstaff in 2.4, when she has to stop herself from gushing at his departure – 'Well, fare thee well:

I haue knowne thee these twentie nine yeeres, come Pescod-time: but an honester, and truer-hearted man – Well, fare thee well.'

> *Falst.* Away Varlets, draw *Bardolfe:* Cut me off the
> Villaines head: throw the Queane in the Channel.

If you've chosen to keep the fighting minimal, you'll have all these strong words with no one actually willing to draw their weapon. Fang can threaten, Bardolfe can hesitate on his draw, then Fang and Snare can try to pull Falstaff out of the chair. Bardolfe would pull Fang and Snare off Falstaff. Quickly can move in, to tussle with Falstaff, whilst Bardolfe continues wrestling with Fang and Snare. By the time the chief justice enters, everyone can be in a pile.

If you chose to have a sword fight, then we applaud you. Fang would draw his weapon timidly, proclaim the arrest, and put Falstaff on point. Falstaff would see right through Fang's false bravado, and ignore the sword.

> *Host.* Throw me in the channell? Ile throw thee there.
> Wilt thou? wilt thou? thou bastardly rogue. Murder, mur-
> der, O thou Hony-suckle villaine, wilt thou kill Gods of-
> ficers, and the Kings? O thou hony-seed Rogue, thou art
> a honyseed, a Man-queller, and a woman-queller.
> *Falst.* Keep them off, *Bardolfe.*

Bardolfe can draw, and beat Fang's blade away. This would be a catalyst for Snare to draw, aiding Fang so the three of them can square off. With this two-on-one fight, Quickly can go after Falstaff and start attacking him. She may be unarmed, but explore the comedic options of her having a rolling pin, towel, or cup in hand. Falstaff's page needs to be added or excluded from the fight. It's funny to have the page cowering in the corner during the fight, but he could be assisting Falstaff fight Quickly.

Another option would be having Falstaff as part of the sword fight, but not the type to do his own dirty work if others will. You'll find more comedy in him just trying to stay seated.

> *Fang.* A rescu, a rescu.
> *Host.* Good people bring a rescu. Thou wilt not? thou
> wilt not? Do, do thou Rogue: Do thou Hempseed.

The two-on-one fight can be going well for Fang and Snare, when Fang suddenly notices the hostess and Falstaff fighting, so Fang yells to rescue the hostess. Alternatively, you could have Bardolfe beating the crap out of Fang and Snare, so that Fang's line is a desperate plea to help himself.

*Page.* Away you Scullion, you Rampallian, you Fustil-
lirian: Ile tucke your Catastrophe.

*Enter. Ch. Iustice.*

If you have kept Quickly and Falstaff fighting, have Quickly get the upper hand to
incite the page to go after her. She could slam Falstaff's head into the table and stand
up in triumph, which would be a great catalyst for the page to start attacking wildly.

*Iust.* What's the matter? Keepe the Peace here, hoa.
*Host.* Good my Lord be good to mee. I beseech you
stand to me.
*Ch. Iust.* How now sir *Iohn*? What are you brauling here?
Doth this become your place, your time, and businesse?
You should haue bene well on your way to Yorke.
Stand from him Fellow; wherefore hang'st vpon him?
*Host.* Oh my most worshipfull Lord, and't please your
Grace, I am a poore widdow of Eastcheap, and he is arre-
sted at my suit.

The success or failure of the chief justice to stop the fight will reveal a lot about his
place in this world. If he yells 'Keepe the Peace here' and all the characters stop fighting
immediately, we know the chief justice commands respect. If he has great martial ability,
he can sweep the room and stop each fight efficiently to show the audience he's a badass.
Maybe he enters with several officers who do the dirty work.

## Act 2  Scene 4

*See Glossary – Intimacy; Strikes (maybe).*

Time to track another physical dynamic, this one between Falstaff and Doll Tearsheet,
in terms of violence and/or SexyTimez™. Bring in your intimacy consultant and fight
director as there is plenty to explore. The tavern has a very different feel from the court
– ass-smacking, lap-dancing, neck-and/or-ear-nibbling, *etc.* Other given circumstances
to play with – Falstaff's gout may be getting worse and Doll is already drunk, burping,
and violent from the top. Have fun, folks.

*Pist.* 'Saue you, Sir *Iohn*.
*Falst.* Welcome Ancient *Pistol*. Here (*Pistol*) I charge
you with a Cup of Sacke: doe you discharge vpon mine
Hostesse.
*Pist.* I will discharge vpon her (Sir *Iohn*) with two

Bullets.

*Falst.* She is Pistoll-proofe (Sir) you shall hardly offend her.

*Host.* Come, Ile drinke no Proofes, nor no Bullets: I
will drinke no more then will doe me good, for no mans
pleasure, I.

You also have the possibility for a running gag – if Pistol has a pistol and issues controlling
his discharge. If you use a blank-firing gun, it's important to have an armourer on staff.
See Chapter 12 – *The Merry Wives of Windsor* (1.1) and Chapter 13 – *Henry 5* (2.1). For
a list of general safety measures when handling firearms, refer to your theatrical union's
guidelines. If you don't have a union, or you'd just like a more thorough understanding,
we recommend *The Theatrical Firearms Handbook* by Kevin Inouye.

*See Glossary – Draws; Ensemble Readiness; Grabs (maybe); Strikes; ALL SORTS OF
THINGS!!!*

Doll is an equal-opportunity fighter and her next victim is Pistol. The tavern folk may
all be rather incestuous; just as there is a Falstaff/hostess/Pistol triangle, there may
be a Falstaff/Doll/Pistol one. Has Pistol scorned Doll in the past? Maybe she had a
husband, a brother, or a lover (all three being the same individual if your production
is set in West Virginia) die in battle, which earned him the title of captain. This could
explain why she so roundly detests Pistol's unearned adoption of the title. Go as light or
dark as you like since everyone in this play has war stories, but Doll clearly has a bone
to pick with him. She goes after Pistol, so this is another chance to have a small chase/
fight. Doll could attack him with a hand towel, smack him, maybe even choke him with
it. More use of the tavern items can ensue. Does she already have a knife on her person?
If not, she could find one in that moment, then turn to go after him. This would escalate
matters. More people might get involved to prevent bloodshed. Or not. The clearer you
are about everyone's shared pasts, the more specific the violence will be.

Bardolph has to repeat himself because Pistol is not listening. At first, Bardolph
might try to usher Pistol out gently, then with slightly more force, and then very harshly.
Or maybe Bardolph only asks nicely once, then immediately draws on Pistol. This would
give Pistol a good reason to draw. Or maybe Bardolph is worried about his place in all
this, so Pistol draws on Bardolph and he ends up drawing in reply. Until you have the
actors in the room, and explore their characters' relationships in your production, it will
be hard to solidify the order of escalation.

But weapons must come out. Falstaff jumps in as well. Whilst he asks for his rapier,
it's not clear if he draws. Doll repeatedly asks him not to do so. Does he listen or, lacking
any restraint by this point, does the weapon come out? Either choice can be supported,
so long as you're clear on what it would express to the audience. With Bardolph and
Pistol drawn, Quickly's line will make sense and Falstaff does not have to be drawn.

Either way, we have a scuffle after 'Get you downe stayres' as, once more, Pistol doesn't listen. Falstaff joins a 'turmoil' that ends with him injuring Pistol's shoulder. This can be by sword or some other method. Falstaff can avoid a punch, catch the arm, and apply an armbar that pops Pistol's shoulder out of the socket. You also have to ensure Pistol has a swipe at Falstaff's belly/crotch in plain view of Doll so her line will make sense ('me thought hee made a shrewd Thrust at your Belly').

It's highly likely others get caught in the crossfire. Bardolph might get a superficial wound and be nursing it when he returns. And what happens with the boy?

Continue tracking the physical dynamics you've built in prior scenes. When Hal reveals himself, Falstaff could go in for a hug. Does Hal push him away? Finally, keep your intimacy consultant on hand for the remaining moments between Falstaff and Doll.

## Act 4  Scene 1

*See Glossary – Arrests; Blood (maybe); Blood Packs (maybe); Carries (maybe); Draws; Ensemble Readiness; Grabs (maybe); Knees (maybe); MORE OF THE THINGS!!!*

This is one of the rare times a parley actually leads to peace in Shakespeare's works. The troops disband and there is no battle. Unfortunately, the rebels didn't think carefully about their wish after rubbing the proverbial lamp; Johnny the Genie has found a loophole. This technically is acceptable because it's the rebels' fault for not considering themselves in the negotiations.

> *Mow.* Is this proceeding iust, and honorable?
> *West.* Is your Assembly so?
> *Bish.* Will you thus breake your faith?
> *Iohn.*                              I pawn'd thee none:
> I promis'd you redresse of these same Grieuances
> Whereof you did complaine; which, by mine Honor,
> I will performe, with a most Christian care.
> But for you (Rebels) looke to taste the due
> Meet for Rebellion, and such Acts as yours.
> Most shallowly did you these Armes commence,
> Fondly brought here, and foolishly sent hence.
> Strike vp our Drummes, pursue the scatter'd stray,
> Heauen, and not wee, haue safely fought to day.
> ~~Some guard these Traitors to the Block of Death,~~
> ~~Treasons true Bed, and yeelder vp of breath.~~
>
> *Exeunt.*

[*SD*: *As director in 2004, I cut John's final couplet. Instead of an arrest, the rebels discover their drinks are poisoned. Then, John tells them they're fucked and has their throats slit before they can escape.*] [*JK: Ooh, I like that. Everyone do that!*]

> *Col.* I thinke you are Sir *Iohn Falstaffe*, & in that thought
> yeeld me.

Falstaff captures Coleville. By which we mean Coleville surrenders peaceably, because dumb luck is the only way Falstaff can win a fight. To figure out why Coleville surrenders, and since we can't cover every conceivable combination in your casting/direction, let's reverse-engineer a solution.

When Coleville is ordered by Prince John to be brought to execution, Coleville's reaction will show his true character. But first decide if he even hears the order. The command for execution may have been uttered out of his earshot. In this case, does he comply with being led away? Is there any confusion on his part about where he is being led? If John makes execution a clear pronouncement that Coleville hears, we get to see Coleville's character come through in his reaction to the news. Is he calm and resigned, or does he attempt to flee? Once you weigh up some options here, you will hopefully find a reason why Coleville yielded to Falstaff.

## Act 4  Scene 2

How has the king's sickness advanced? If your actor has been playing apoplexy, blurry vision will make sense of the line here since Clarence is right in front of his father. Gloucester says it's apoplexy in the scene. If you make a choice that contradicts this, be clear what it says about Gloucester. Is he lying on purpose, making broad assumptions, or is he just an idiot?

If you've chosen appendicitis, early symptoms take about twelve to seventy-two hours to progress to perforation. Pain would begin near the belly button, then shift to the lower, right-hand side of the abdomen. His appendix might rupture just before 'And wherefore should these goods newes make me sick.'

*See Glossary – Faints.*

*Hal with King Henry in his sickbed.* Eduard von Grützner, late nineteenth or early twentieth century. (*Folger Shakespeare Library*)

The king faints, or otherwise zones out, and this apparently is 'ordinarie'.

*See Glossary – Carries.*

> *King.* I pray you take me vp, and beare me hence
> Into some other Chamber: softly 'pray.

*See Glossary – Blood (maybe); Falls (maybe); Grabs (maybe); Strikes (maybe).*

The king's abdominal pain will increase with walking, standing, or coughing. It will be aggravated further with transport. Peritonitis will quickly spread bacteria through his bloodstream. As his body releases chemicals to fight the infection, sepsis will trigger and cause overwhelming oxygen demand, which will weaken his heart and lead to septic shock. Then, multiple organs (lungs, kidneys, liver) will quickly fail. Your actor has plenty of choices to deploy throughout the coming scene with his sticky-fingered son. Does Henry get out of bed? Does he attempt to strike his son? Does Henry fall? Does he cough blood?

Eventually, the king must die. In some cases, people feel better for a short time before actually dying. This could give the king a burst of energy here. He certainly wants to beat the shit out of his son, but you'll need to play the disease to know if Henry actually can. Just about anything the king would throw at Hal he would take – a smack, push, or even a punch here could be justified, but would only be useful if you want to show the audience that Hal desires it as some kind of *mea culpa*. [*JK: I had a few moments like that whilst writing this book.*] [*SD: *readies fists**]

*See Glossary – Carries.*

> *King.* Doth any name particular, belong
> Vnto the Lodging, where I first did swoon'd?
> *War.* 'Tis call'd *Ierusalem*, my Noble Lord.
> *King.* Laud be to heauen:
> Euen there my life must end.
> It hath beene prophesi'de to me many yeares,
> I should not dye, but in *Ierusalem*:
> Which (vainly) I suppos'd the Holy-Land.
> But beare me to that Chamber, there Ile lye:
> In that *Ierusalem*, shall *Harry* dye.

No matter what the illness, the king will need help to get off stage.

## Act 5  Scene 4

*See Glossary – Arrests; Binds (maybe); Ensemble Readiness.*

Hostess Quickly and Doll Tearsheet resist arrest. You need to decide if Quickly is literal or figurative about her shoulder being out of its socket. This would be very painful and needs to be played throughout the scene. If you decide she is exaggerating, she will lose credibility with the officer.

Next, there is the question of Doll's pregnancy. How does this impact the arrest? If the officer doesn't know how to handle Doll but keeps trying to gently arrest her, there is potential for some amusement here. Quickly and Doll could even end up self-arresting, marching themselves in the direction of the prison and beckoning the officers to come with them. This is one way to justify the repeated call of 'come' at the end of the scene.

But there is another line which stands out – 'you have haue a dozen of Cushions againe, you have but eleuen now.' [*SD: In my production, the officer didn't believe she was pregnant. The officer punched her womb, then removed a cushion from under her blouse.*] If the bump is a fake, upon being discovered, this could make the beating Doll gets even worse.

## Act 5  Scene 5

*See Glossary – Ensemble Readiness; Falls; Knees (maybe); Strikes (maybe).*

You may have a desire to have Falstaff get physical with the new king, and for him to backhand Falstaff to drive home the point they are no longer friends. Whilst this could be justified, it's the weaker choice. The crueller one is the prevention of physical contact, using the language for the kill. [*SD: LIKE HIS ALLEGEDLY BORING FATHER WHO OPENS PART 1 WITH NOTHING MORE THAN HIS VERSE, JARED?!?!?!*] [*JK: Okay, fine, he got better as the plays moved along.*] Whether Falstaff is struck physically or linguistically, it could be enough to take the legs out from under him. Maybe he falls to his knees, grovelling to no avail. Do the king's guards have to intervene? Experiment with different staging options. If the new king's back is to the audience and Falstaff is upstage, we see the scene through the king's eyes; if those positions are reversed, through Falstaff's eyes. As with the banquet in Chapter 4 – *Macbeth* (3.4), you have the possibility for two wildly different scenes, depending on what you show (or don't).

*See Glossary – Arrests.*

The way in which this arrest is conducted will reflect on the new king. If the king chose violence earlier, the guards would follow suit and be rough with Falstaff whilst arresting him. If not, the guards might err on the side of caution.

*Anne Page.* Thomas Francis Dicksee, 1862. (*Folger Shakespeare Library*)

# Chapter 12

# The Merry Wives of Windsor

*'To these violent proceedings all my neighbors shall cry aim'* – Ford (3.2)

We've mentioned that it is impossible to anticipate every possible iteration of violence. This play is a shining example. Whilst the histories and tragedies contain a majority of verse scenes with physical restraint and a minority of prose scenes with awkward fights, the comedies invert this ratio. Your fight director and intimacy consultant can help you create a specific physical universe for your actors to inhabit, allowing the horseplay to enliven the proceedings and still be safe.

## Act 1  Scene 1

*See Glossary – Ensemble Readiness; Strikes (maybe).*

There are plenty of given circumstances for you to explore, as some violence has already occurred just prior to the start of the play. Does anyone lose their self-control here? Drunkenness, tempers, lack of decorum, and insults flying left and right are all a recipe for disaster. Some examples to get you going: when Falstaff references breaking Slender's head, Falstaff can give it a good smack; when Pistol later says 'scum thou liest', Slender can slap Pistol with a glove on 'By these gloues'. The text supports an encounter here, and you should explore all the options that can express your characters physically.

Shakespeare tends to lack nuance in character names, particularly in the comedies; you may gain some traction treating the names as clues. If you are performing this in rep with other plays in which Pistol appears, and opt for the running gag of Pistol's pistol, then continue it here. See Chapter 11 – *Henry 4 Part 2* (2.4) and Chapter 13 – *Henry 5* (2.1). (If this is a standalone production, speak with your doctor to decide whether a pistol gag is right for you.) Also note that Nym has a morbid focus on 'slice' and 'bite', so he knows his way around a blade and/or is a terrifying fanboy.

## Act 1  Scene 4

*See Glossary – Ensemble Readiness; Strikes (maybe).*

As the audience meets Dr Caius for the first time, how physically he plays this scene (or not) will reveal his character. Is he a civilised fellow who loses his cool upon discovering a man hiding in his closet? Or is he a constant brute? You can begin to tell this story in how he treats the help. Whilst bragging about all the violent things he's going to do to Hugh Evans, does Caius harm Rugby as a proxy?

There is also potential for violence when Caius finds Simple. We are told by Page in 2.1 that Caius 'the French-man hath good skill / in his Rapier'. Does he employ it here? Is he rash and hotheaded? Or aloof, declining to engage with those he sees as common?

Dr Caius' command at the end to 'follow my heeles' sounds like he thinks of Rugby as a dog. The same order is given in their next scene. This could inform how you physicalise their relationship in production. [*JK: In Shakespeare's time, it was normal to view a servant like a dog. There is even an Elizabethan idiom discussed by Saviolo.*] [*SD: Yes, Jared, we remember your godforsaken book.*] [*JK: Saviolo noted that an insult to the servant was the same as insulting the master – 'According to the proverb, love me and love my dog.'*] **Whether** this is analogous to Caius' treatment of Rugby is entirely up to your production. You should also explore Rugby's perspective. Is he a happy puppy?

## Act 2  Scene 3

*See Glossary – Draws; Ensemble Readiness; Strikes (maybe).*

Continue where you left off with the Caius/Rugby relationship. If you established an abusive one, Caius can get a few more smacks in here. Again, his physical choices will convey character (*e.g.* if your Caius is all bravado, 'I vill tell you how I vill kill him' could be highlighted with a wild swing of his arm, almost accidentally hitting Rugby, who has to duck).

If we take Rugby at his word that he cannot fence, add some comedic choices here. If Rugby has a sword, it doesn't mean he possesses any skill. Furthermore, the quality of the weapon may be so poor that Caius is just making fun of Rugby (read 'Rapier' sarcastically). If you decide Rugby is unarmed, his line can be taken to mean he is unable to fence because he has no weapon. In this case, Caius may have a second one he could toss at Rugby's feet.

[*JK: You also have an opportunity to show Caius' skill (or lack thereof) when he says 'Villanie, take your Rapier'. The very next line stops Caius but, in one production, the director wanted the audience to know right there and then if Caius could fight. Here's an example of a short fight that, despite its brevity, has each phrase of choreography reveal character in a different way, and tells a story in and of itself:*

*First phrase – Caius engages and advances on Rugby. Caius backs Rugby up and, whilst he parries every attack, he has no time to riposte.*

*Second phrase – Rugby goes on the offensive with wild moves Caius easily parries and lets Rugby continue until he lunges with a thrust, but it is clearly out of distance. Caius gives a quick look down at the space between his body and Rugby's blade and, with a quick laugh, beats the sword upstage, making Rugby stumble to catch himself.*

*Third phrase – Caius decides this is a good way to pass the time, so there is slightly more equality to the moves, instead of one attacker and one defender. Caius' ripostes are more of a lesson but, in the end, Caius becomes bored – he binds Rugby's attack and expels the blade, which once again sends him unbalanced upstage but, turning around, he sees the group approaching and says 'Forbeare: heer's company.'*

*For the rest of the scene, whilst Caius walks around with his sword, he keeps gesturing with the weapon as he proclaims things with no regard for how close he is to his listeners, who do their best to avoid him.*]

Is the host's hodgepodge of fencing terminology an attempt to sound intelligent, or is he an actual swordsman? He could (in)correctly demonstrate the moves. [*JK: To 'foigne' is a term for feint. The feint is a simulated attack, meant to draw a defensive reaction, which is deceived for the actual attack. If the host moves to poke someone in the chest and they try to block it, the host can avoid the block and poke their belly. Traverse is often a diagonal step off the line of direction. Maybe a small sidestep if someone is coming after the host after being poked in the belly. Next, the host bungles Italian fencing terminology. 'Puncto' is an anglicisation of 'punto', meaning a thrust. 'Stock' is 'stoccata', an ascending thrust. 'Reverse' is 'reverso', any attack performed from your left side* (punto reverso *is a thrust from your left side). 'Distance' is … um … distance. Maybe Shakespeare couldn't recall the Italian fencing term – 'misura'. 'Montant' is a 'montante', a vertical rising cut.*] [*SD:* Non piaci a nessuno. Morirai da solo.]

## Act 3  Scene 1

*See Glossary – Draws; Ensemble Readiness; Grabs (maybe); Strikes (maybe).*

Both Caius and Evans are upset by their various and sundry perceived slights. The comedy of this confrontation comes from them remaining on the verge of drawing without doing so (since this is not the appointed place for the duel, this would technically just be a street fight). They can push each other, and even be nose to nose when the host steps in to explain what he has done. Remember that when a character wants to threaten, even just moving the hand to the hilt of the rapier will do the trick. Have your fight director explore the scene with your actors, and explore potential acts of violence that never quite occur.

If the disarmament is successful, this is a great character moment to see how each relinquishes his weapon(s). Do they just turn them over? Is there a tug-o'-war? Do they threaten the folks trying to disarm them? If Caius had multiple weapons in earlier scenes, he may take particularly long to disarm.

## Act 3  Scene 3

*See Glossary – Grabs; Intimacy; Strikes (maybe).*

Once alone with Mistress Ford, it may be difficult for Falstaff to restrain himself. There is plenty of potential comedic violence here as Falstaff tries to grab her (*e.g.* she can push him away, smack his hand, and maybe even get a slap in there).

*See Glossary – Carries.*

Later in the scene, Falstaff hides in a laundry basket and is carried off the stage. Depending on your set, the safest approach is to have a trapdoor in the back, out of which the actor playing Falstaff can crawl. If the basket is empty when the servants start to carry it, they can mimic heavy weight, lift it on their shoulders, and even drop it for gasps from the audience. A sound effect for the 'body' hitting the ground would be great. Use a speaker inside the basket, so the sound is localised.

A watercolour of Act 3, Scene 3: *Falstaff wooing Mistress Ford.* John Masey Wright (allegedly), early nineteenth century. (*Folger Shakespeare Library*)

If you cannot remove the actor from the basket, you'll need to build something that can support his bodyweight. And you may need more than two servants to lift it. To do this safely, there are several precautions that need to be taken. Start by padding the inside of the basket with a crash pad, or some kind of lining to protect the actor as much as possible. Next, the basket should never be lifted up too far from the ground. Distance creates velocity and velocity creates pain in a fall/drop. Finally, make sure the people lifting the basket are in shape, with no pre-existing conditions, and that they know how to lift with their legs and not their backs. They do not need to lift the basket onto their shoulders here. We are told by Falstaff in 3.5 that 'a couple of Fords knaues, his Hindes, were cald forth by their Mistris, to carry mee in the name of foule Cloathes to Datchet-lane: they tooke me on their shoulders', but that could have happened off stage or simply be an exaggeration by Falstaff. Whether true or not, when we see Falstaff next, he could rub his head or backside when he recalls being severely dropped.

## Act 3  Scene 4

*See Glossary – Strikes (maybe).*

Whilst George Page seems to rely on his words to deal with Fenton's offence, there is potential here for Mistress Page (depending on how your production has portrayed her thus far) to physically intimidate, push, or even strike Fenton if he makes a move towards Anne.

## Act 4  Scene 2

*See Glossary – Blood; Ensemble Readiness; Strikes.*

Ford 'buffettes himselfe on the for-head'. How your actor plays this pain will convey the depth and frequency of his self-harm. He might come on bruised and bloodied. Maybe he winces in pain when touching his head. Whichever you decide, make sure to incorporate it into the ensuing fight with Falstaff.

Concussed and at the pinnacle of his rage, Ford might opt for huge swings. Make sure to stage this so there is no need for him to pull back the energy – ducks, avoidances, near-misses, and knocking over inanimate objects. The more the entire room is dishevelled and destroyed, the better. Be specific in pairing the dialogue with each swing (*e.g.* 'you Witch', 'you Ragge', 'you Baggage', *etc.*).

Besides dealing with the given circumstance of Ford's head injuries (which he may make worse by accidentally landing punches on himself, or running into set pieces or props), there is the joy of getting to stage Falstaff having to remember to impersonate a woman. After avoiding a variety of swings, you could have Falstaff stop one with 'manly' strength by having him intercept and catch Ford's arm, so Falstaff is at the centre of the swing and not trying to stop the object being swung. Both men can pause, Ford shows confusion, then Falstaff remembers to react 'womanly'.

Falstaff is beaten out of doors by Ford (who has a cudgel) and his men (who have 'Birding-peeces'). Depending on what you use as a cudgel, you may be able to get a prop version made. If so, you can actually make impact with Falstaff. Ensure the fight director tests this out, as you should pad the performer when using foam-rubber replicas. This would give Ford freedom to swing and land a few more hits on Falstaff, before he runs off, as Ford yells 'I'll fortune-tell you!'

## Act 5  Scene 5

The children of Windsor, disguised as fairies, can pinch Falstaff simply by placing their fingers on the top of his body and twisting with aggression. As long as there is none of Falstaff's actual skin between their fingers, this will not hurt your actor and will make it easy for him to time his reactions to the pinches. [*JK: Your production will probably be using fake candles for the burning, and I recommend these to allow your actor to play the pain of being burned without it actually occurring.*] [*SD: Surely you could use real flames on closing night, no?*]

# Chapter 13

# Henry 5

*'An oath of mickle might, and fury shall abate'* – Pistol (2.1)

The chorus makes it clear from the start that the audience will have to put their imagination into overdrive. Your production has a decision to make – is this due to budget constraints, modesty (false or otherwise), or something else entirely? Whichever you choose, the battles need to match your selected scope. We advise that you allocate at least an hour of each rehearsal in your final weeks to running fights (and this is only after many hours dedicated to choreography in weeks prior).

## Act 2  Scene 1[1]

*See Glossary – Draws; Ensemble Readiness; Grabs (maybe).*

*Draw.*

The comedy here lies in Nym's bravado and desire to fight, despite knowing he would probably lose the conflict ('I dare not fight'). Conversely, Pistol is ready to fight and probably the better swordsman. His new wife, Mistress Quickly, intercedes and we watch Pistol struggle between his desire to fight and his desire to appease the missus. Which of his two heads will prevail? (A reminder that you can continue Pistol's gun gag here, if you've already been doing it in the other plays. See Chapter 11 – *Henry 4 Part 2* (2.4) and Chapter 12 – *The Merry Wives of Windsor* (1.1).)

*[JK: Nym and Pistol might never actually draw their weapons, but there are more choices if they do. They don't need to be hasty to draw; give them time to huff and puff at each other. If Nym can't handle it anymore and draws, Pistol will need to draw in self-defence. They can go into guard positions. It can look like a fight is going to happen, but then Nym jumps back in fear. He can even compose himself, going into guard again. On Pistol's part, you can have Quickly stop Pistol from drawing at one point by pinning his arm down. If he does draw and go into guard, Quickly can wrap her arms around his neck and pull him back. This should be a lot about two people wanting to fight but not actually starting.]*

If weapons are out when Bardolph draws, he can beat them away and put the quarrellers on point. This will allow them both to back down whilst saving face. If there are no weapons out, Bardolph can skip straight to the threat.

## Act 2  Scene 2

*See Glossary – Arrests; Binds; Draws; Ensemble Readiness; Grabs (maybe); Knees; Strikes (maybe).*

Scroope, Cambridge, and Gray do not know they are about to be arrested. Others in the room do. How is this tension staged? Upon arrest, the three traitors submit themselves to the king's mercy, apparently not resisting arrest. When the final judgment is handed down for them to be executed, do any of them change their mind and attempt to flee? Cambridge is the only one at the end of the guilt-trip speech who floats the idea of a pardon, not only of faults committed but also to stay the execution of his body. And he's the first to confess.

[*JK: I love this scene. Henry gives them enough rope to hang themselves. Since the other characters in the room know what is going to happen, they should be staged to cover all exits. Scroope, Cambridge, and Gray are not idiots, so make sure the exit coverage is not conspicuous; there should be other soldiers around, so it just seems like a typical day. You'll need at least three arresting officers to tie up Scroope, Cambridge, and Gray. Again, they should not be standing behind the traitors, ominously salivating. Whilst Henry is speaking, the arresting officers can casually cross into position. As the traitors will be busy reading, they will fail to notice them sneak into place. Ensure each of the reactions to the letters are different; it ain't particularly interesting if the turncoats all just fall to their knees. When I worked on this production, we had one person resigned to being arrested; one completely surprised, and tied up before he could process the information; and one who tried to flee, so we punched him in the guts and bound him. All three will be on their knees whilst Henry is talking, and the costumes will hopefully allow the actors to use knee pads. If not, the arrestors can assist the prisoners to the ground (but make it look violent). Please be careful their knees are not driven into the ground. Bone into stage is extremely dangerous and sounds like nails on a chalkboard to me.*] [*SD: Is this why you cringe whenever I do it?*] [*JK: Nah, that's just due to your terrible acting.*] [*SD: Fair.*]

It's also worth asking whether Henry ever physically loses his cool. Particularly with Scroope, given how personal a betrayal it seems to Henry. A grab? A strike? [*SD: You won't be surprised that I kept the violence strictly linguistic in this scene as Henry, a role I never had any business playing but did execute in this scene quite well. His sixty-six-line set speech is quite a roller coaster – stable iambic pentameter, then 'feminine endings' creeping in (the term to describe the final of an eleven-syllable line, which goes unstressed and warrants a less-sexist name), then mid-line starts, then trochaic attacks, then regaining self-restraint via the armour of iambic stability.*]

## Act 2  Scene 4

*See Glossary – Ensemble Readiness; Falls (maybe); Grabs (maybe); Knees (maybe); Strikes (maybe).*

[*SD: The mention here of the Black Prince is an unsettling piece of foreshadowing. Just as the Black Prince was a war hero who died too young and left his less-than-ready child – Richard 2 – to rule over England, whatever Henry accomplishes over the next few hours of stage time may be all for naught since he will follow the Black Prince's footsteps and leave an even younger child to rule – Henry 6 – plunging the country into the Wars of the Roses. Fun!*]

The French herald was treated with respect in the English court, but how is Exeter treated here amongst the French? The only real wildcard in this scene is the dauphin, who might be stupid and/or disrespectful enough to violate rules of parley, but none of his own people seem to like him, and the constable feels quite comfortable telling the dauphin to shut the hell up ('O peace'). He might try to push Exeter, knowing full well he would restrain himself from striking back. Or maybe the dauphin has one of those delightful tennis balls on hand, hurling it at Exeter on 'I did present him with the Paris balls'. Exeter could catch it, one-handed, in the blink of any eye.

If the dauphin breaks decorum, how does Charles put him back in his place? He could backhand his son, sending him to the ground. Maybe the king just grabs and shakes his son. Or grabs and gives a knee to the guts (to knock the wind out of him) or the nuts (to emasculate him), which would drop the dauphin to the floor. They clearly disagree on strategy. If the father/son dynamic is contentious (similar to Henry 4 when ill, worried about his legacy, and jealous of someone else's kid), the king might smack his son upside the head on 'Think we King *Harry* strong'.

Note that Exeter is an intimidating figure and, if anything, the dauphin probably soils himself by the end of the scene. A bellow from Exeter might be enough for the dauphin to fall to the ground and/or piss his pants. See Chapter 4 – *Macbeth* (5.3).

## Act 3  Scene 1

The Siege of Harfleur – chambers going off, ladders being climbed, speeches being speeched.

*Alarum, and Chambers goe off.*

And downe goes all before them. Still be kind,
And eech out our performance with your mind.

*Exit. Enter the King, Exeter, Bedford, and Gloucester.*
*Alarum: Scaling Ladders at Harflew.*

Even if you fall back on the audience's imagination in the staging, the directions clearly want alarms and cannons going off, so get those sound cues ready. As Henry and co enter, the troops can be tying on their last bits of armour, saying prayers, *etc*. We don't need everyone to stop and give focus to Henry. He can simultaneously rally the troops whilst moving amongst them. [*SD: I worked on low-budget versions of this play in 2002 and 2005, both in the same three-quarter space, with five aisles amongst the audience, and ladders leading to a second level. This achieved the scrappiness the chorus sets up at the start – total immersion for the audience, without having to go bankrupt in the process.*]

## Act 3  Scene 2

*See Glossary – Ensemble Readiness; Grabs (maybe); Strikes (maybe).*

Fluellen might threaten the 'Dogges' with the cudgel he later uses in the play. Or he might push them up to the breach, but they keep slipping away and have to be corralled. If you choose this route, Fluellen's trademark lack of patience could result in striking one of the pups, to keep them moving along and make an example for the others.
  [*JK: Later in the scene … put an Englishman, a Welshman, an Irishman, and a Scot all in the same location and, in this time period, a fight will quickly break out.*] [*SD: As opposed to now …?*] This could move from the verbal to the physical – maybe strikes, or some folks holding one another back. Take the rehearsal time to explore with your cast. Stylistically, you should go for a different type of comedy here than the one you pursue in the French court. Either could devolve into farce. [*SD: The playwright's never-ending predilection for making fun of foreign accents is, on its own, a war crime.*]

## Act 3  Scene 6

*See Glossary – Strikes (maybe).*

The Fluellen/Pistol friction continues building here. Pistol pleads for Fluellen to intervene and reverse Bardolph's death warrant, but is still unable to muster a physical attack, giving Fluellen only a crude hand gesture – 'The Figge of Spaine'. Fluellen may or may not have to repel Pistol physically, but this will come down to your mix of actors.
  If your production opts for spectacle rather than imagination, you could show the hanging of Bardolph. For the mechanics of this, see Chapter 18 – *Sir Thomas More* (3.1).

## Act 4  Scene 1

The low-budget premise is being floated yet again. If followed in production, what might this look like? It could be a ticket out of having to stage much of the battle – the chorus picks up half-a-dozen swords and distributes them to the actors; since the weapons are 'vile and ragged foyles', feel free to pick them up by the blade to make it clear they're fake; we'll then be conditioned to expect some pantomime version of fighting. [*SD: You can decide whether to follow through on the cheap approach, or surprise the audience with a huge-ass battle sequence. Jared mentioned in Chapter 7 – King John (2.1) that, once you have established a vocabulary for your production's universe, you should remain consistent. I agree. But, every so often, subversion of your audience's expectations will present itself. For this play, consider your chorus' claims these last few hours as a long con; keep all the fight sequences low budget, possibly to the point of silliness, so that a sudden big–budget Battle of Agincourt completely blows the doors off your production. This is a rare exception to the rule, and we won't even bother asking Jared if he likes it because, by now, you probably know.]*

*See Glossary – Ensemble Readiness; Grabs (maybe).*

The night before battle, all soldiers are on edge. If a disagreeable stranger drops by your campfire, you'd probably not suffer him gladly. The discussion between Williams and the king quickly escalates to argument, then to an official challenge. By the time Williams says it's 'a foolish saying', Henry is on his feet to make it clear he is willing to schedule a duel. They might start pushing each other, chest-bumping, or other such nonsense machismo. This allows the other people in the scene to pull Williams and the king apart, who can both speak their remaining lines whilst being physically restrained. Note that the physical interplay should not involve actual strikes. See Chapter 9 – *Richard 2* (1.1). This little bit of violence is more dynamic than just two dudes yelling at each other.

## Act 4  Scenes 4, 5, and 6

*Alarum. Excursions.*

*[JK: The Battle of Agincourt scenes should all blend together seamlessly. There is no reason to break up the fighting; the audience will feel much more satisfied by continuous action, rather than halting the battle so characters can speak. In a 2019 production for which I did the fights (directed by the brilliant Mary Lou Rosato), it all started after Henry's last line in 4.3. Whilst the chorus spoke, all the troops lined up, facing the audience. They knelt with Henry, made the sign of the cross, and began to move forward. We had a second level to the stage, so I positioned several archers above, shooting arrows down on the French as they attacked the stage (to do this, the archers don't actually need arrows; if it's dimly lit, and they go through all the motions, the people getting hit with an arrow will have it palmed, bringing it up when hit). The fight should happen all around the audience, so they never know where the danger will come from next. In this production, there were over twenty fight moments – above, behind, and in front of the audience – and the action never stopped. I find this relentlessness a more exciting approach than just piping battle sounds in through the speakers. Give your audience an immersive experience. Note that this will take extensive fight rehearsal hours, so plan accordingly (once choreographed, at least forty-five minutes to an hour at almost every rehearsal).]*

*Enter Pistoll, French Souldier, Boy.*

*[JK: As Pistol chases le Fer, the fighting can continue around them (punctuating the scene). In the 2019 production, they were displaced several times by fights spilling onto stage. Throughout this, we inserted moments that showcased Henry's battle prowess. He commanded his troops, fought back to back with two other noblemen, and later even had a 'hero fight' where Henry single-handedly defeated four Frenchmen. This may sound like you'll need a cast of forty, but we only had seven or eight actors who came on in different costumes. Even the actors playing Pistol and the boy had time to come in and get killed at the top of the fight before returning to their original characters.]*

*See Glossary – Grabs (maybe); Strikes (maybe).*

*[JK: Pistol is physical with le Fer as well. There can be an occasional punch, push, or pull as Pistol perceives the insults. 4.5 should roll right into the constable, Orleance, Bourbon, the dauphin, and Ramburs entering in disarray, tired and bloody. An English soldier or two can enter during the scene, so the French have to fight whilst speaking these lines. Towards the end of 4.5, bring in a troop of English soldiers to surround the French. The French can fight a little before running, so hack down any you'd like here. For example, in 2019, we kept the French constable for last, so he could be killed and dragged out. Just because it says 'exit' doesn't mean they have to do so alive.]*

*See Glossary – Arrests; Binds (maybe); Blood (maybe); Blood Packs (maybe).*

*Alarum. Enter the King and his trayne, with Prisoners.*

*[JK: As we move into 4.6, there should still be small frays. Henry and his men enter with their prisoners, but some English can still be fighting the fleeing French soldiers. This should feel like the culmination of a long battle winding down, not quite over. Everyone is tired, but still alert and on edge as the enemy can pop out from anywhere. Once the alarm sounds, and Henry orders the prisoners to all be killed, this should be done promptly. Dispatch the onstage prisoners by cutting their throats, or thrusts to the chest cavity.]*

You then have to decide whether to show the murdering of the children, and if the boy is discovered amongst them. Again, this depends on the story you're telling. This play has been edited/staged as anti-war, pro-war, anti-England, pro-England, *etc.* You should have chosen a course several acts ago.

*See Glossary – Arrests; Binds (maybe); Knees (maybe).*

*Alarum. Enter King Harry and Burbon with prisoners. Flourish.*

## Act 4  Scene 8

*See Glossary – Strikes.*

*Flu.* Know the Gloue? I know the Gloue is a Gloue.

*Will.* I know this, and thus I challenge it.

*Strikes him.*

Williams mentioned a 'a box on the eare' several times prior to this scene, so it may be his preferred method in striking Fluellen here. To box someone's ear is to hit them on the side of the head, or sometimes literally on the ear. *See Appendix – Bursting the Bubble.* Ensure the victim is facing the audience. The aggressor will strike the victim's *trapezius.* This has to be an ascending hit – it starts low, makes impact on the *trapezius,* then continues rising to give the illusion of striking the back of the head.

Fluellen is following the duelling code correctly. There were only two ways to start a personal duel – by word and by deed. An offence by word could be averted prior to the duel taking place; an offence by deed had to be resolved by spilling blood. For more on this, Saviolo:

> All injuries are reduced to two kinds, and are either by words or deeds. In the first, he that offers the injury ought to be the Challenger. In the later, he that is injured. For example, Caius says to Seius that he is a traitour unto which Seius answers by giving the lie. Whereupon ensues that the charge of the Combat falls on Caius, because he is to maintain what he said and therefore to challenge Seius. Now when an injury is offered by deed, then they proceed in this manner. Caius strikes Seius, gives him a box on the ear or some other way hurts him by some violent means. Wherewith Seius offended says unto Caius that he has used violence towards him, or that he has dealt injuriously with him, or that he has abused him or some such manner of saying. Whereunto Caius answers, you lie. Whereby Seius is forced to challenge Caius and compel him to fight to maintain the injury which he had offered him. The sum of all therefore in these cases of honour is that he unto whom the lie is wrongfully given ought to challenge him that offers that dishonour and by the sword prove himself no liar. – Saviolo's *A Gentleman's Guide to Duelling* [*JD: edited by …*] [*SD: yeah, we know.*]

Fluellen chooses the clearest offence by words – 'That's a Lye in thy Throat'. The wording was important, as duelling codes were quite particular about types of lies (lies in vain, false lies, *etc.*). An offence by words can be resolved with words. One could simply clarify what they said, offer an apology, and all is well. If the offence by words was in public, and the clarification happened privately, rectification was required; the injured party may demand the offender publish the details of the clarification/apology in a local newspaper to make right the public's knowledge.

Williams has chosen to strike Fluellen, making this an offence by deed, so he is obliged to answer it on the duelling ground. Of course, the fact that Fluellen was put up to this by the king can change things. [*JK: Williams' strike with a glove may be done by making contact with Fluellen's chest to create the sound effect. Fluellen should have his back to the audience. Williams is facing downstage and holds the glove high, then strikes diagonally under Fluellen's chin. This will sell as a strike to the face. I love this one so much I call it the Kirby Slap. I don't think I invented it, but I use it so often that I call it my own.] [SD: I wonder if our readers are as tired as you have just made me.]*

*See Glossary – Draws (maybe); Ensemble Readiness.*

Once Fluellen has been slapped, his response reveals character. Is Fluellen so hot-tempered that he strikes back? It's more likely that Fluellen starts to move in with a desire to attack, but Gower holds him back/steps in the way. Fluellen could also collect himself, knowing that he is on the king's business.

The reactions of Warwick, Gloucester, and Exeter are important components of this story. Would any of them try to stop Williams and Fluellen? If so, how would the king stop the nobles without giving up the game? Are any of the others in on it? Be specific so the ensemble can heighten the tension in this scene.

## Act 5  Scene 1

*See Glossary – Draws (maybe); Strikes.*

### Strikes him.

*[JK: This scene never really excited me until I worked on the 2019 production. The gentleman playing Fluellen (Mark Guerette) was hysterical, and Pistol (Patrick Hamilton) completely understood the character and was terrific. We were able to create a very physical scene, which kept the audience wondering how bad Pistol was going to get beaten. Pistol is probably armed, so Fluellen's first blow should be so devastating and surprising that Pistol doesn't have time to draw. A big uppercut or strike to Pistol's* solar plexus *with the cudgel would knock him down. With Pistol on the ground, Fluellen can pin him down (so Pistol can't get to his weapon) and comedic struggling over the leek can ensue. At some point, it can look like Pistol is going to get up, but Fluellen knees him in the face to knock him down again. This fight has to wear Pistol down since he finally caves in. After a big hit, like a knee to the face, Fluellen can pin Pistol on the ground again, and start to choke him with the cudgel. See Appendix – Bursting the Bubble. This is a great position for Fluellen to shove the leek in Pistol's face. Ultimately, Pistol takes a bite, but he can also spit it out. You'll get quite the reaction from the audience if Fluellen picks up the spat-out leek, and puts it right back in Pistol's mouth. For the most part, Gower can hang back and enjoy the show. You could add some physical comedy on Gower's line – 'Enough Captaine, you haue astonisht him'. If Gower is bigger than Fluellen, Gower can pick Fluellen up by the nape of the neck, or put him in a full nelson, thus pulling Fluellen off the pinned Pistol. This would let Fluellen deliver his reply before getting right back to it with Pistol. Gower could just resign himself to more of the show.]*

*Fluellen intimidating Pistol.* Joseph Noel Paton, 1850.

## Act 5  Scene 2

*See Glossary – Grabs (maybe); Strikes (maybe).*

You'll need to decide if Henry is calling himself ugly for Katherine's amusement or referring to scars from battle. If the latter, ensure your fight director includes the specific injuries as part of the staging in prior scenes.

Finally, consider Alice's presence in this scene, which alone might be enough to keep the king from overreaching. But, if Henry chooses to test physical limitations, Alice could intervene – slaps, smacks, beatings with a fan, whatever you like.

# *from Ian Gould*

*One of my very first gigs out of drama school was an outdoor production of* Henry 5, *a rough-and-ready project where the audience brought blankets and chairs, had a picnic, and at sunset we stormed the walls of Harfleur after spraying each other with clouds of bug repellent, occasionally visited mid-siege by a raccoon or a curious crane from the salt marsh nearby.*

*My principal role, in addition to filling out the ranks of English yeomen, was the dauphin. In rehearsal for the scenes in and around the battle of Agincourt, the director and the fight director decided to stage an incident that is lamented in the play but never seen: the French attack on the young squires guarding the English supplies. It's a war crime, and it was decided that the dauphin himself would kill the beloved boy known only as 'Boy', through whose eyes we see the ragtag English soldiers in earlier scenes.*

*I didn't even face him, I snuck up behind him and cut his throat. It gave an extra, more dangerous dimension to the dauphin: he's clearly a useless braggart and a coward, exasperating even to his fellow Frenchmen, but now he's also a murderer, and a murderer of a young person agreed to be 'off-limits' by the rules of combat.*

*None of that is expressly in the text as Shakespeare wrote it: we only hear reports that the French have killed the boys guarding the English luggage, we don't know who, or how, or why. Sometimes, though, you can add your own bits of extra-textual storytelling to Shakespeare's play, and contribute your own character details and plot twists. It's possible to make the dauphin a comic villain, no real threat to anyone, but it's also possible to make him something more threatening. The right bit of stage violence can pivot an audience's perspective in an instant and allow a character a new dimension without needing to change a word.*

*Plucking the Red and White Roses in the Old Temple Gardens.* Henry Arthur Payne, circa 1908. (*City Museums and Art Gallery*)

# Chapter 14

# Henry 6 Part 1

*'Although ye hale me to a violent death'* – Joan (5.4)

The impotency of our next monarch is highlighted by Shakespeare's decision to name three plays after Henry 6 and make him the star of none.

Whilst the groundwork has been laid over the last few chapters, the Wars of the Roses do not officially commence until this play. As such, the ensemble-readiness concept we've been pushing needs to be dialled up significantly. There is little (if any) respite within the history plays. It is imperative that everyone be on their toes at all times and that the stage be charged with palpable electricity. All hell could break loose any moment and often does. Child murders will multiply. Prisoners will not only be taken, but also tortured beyond all human recognition.

Pay attention throughout these next four plays to the increasing number of wildcards. They couldn't care less about respecting the rules of formal parley. And monitor the splintering factions amongst each play's principal characters, most of whom are related, and how often their alliances change. Your audience may not know these works intricately – use this to your advantage.

## Act 1  Scene 1[1]

*See Glossary – Ensemble Readiness.*

It is unlikely any violence breaks out here amongst the lords. This will, as usual, come down to the chemistry of your cast and the world in which you set your production. Humphrey and Winchester's men eventually fall to blows later in the play and there is, at a minimum, linguistic foreshadowing in this opening scene.

## Act 1  Scene 2

These next few plays contain loads of skirmishes. Be prepared to dedicate serious rehearsal hours to crafting the fights.

*Sound a Flourish.*
*Enter Charles, Alanson, and Reigneir, marching with Drum and Souldiers.*

You could stage the entry of this scene with a brief fray in which the English are pushed back by the French, then the text would begin with them taking a bit of a victory lap. Drunk on their capture of Talbot, the French get cocky and immediately bite off more than they can chew.

*Here Alarum, they are beaten back by the English, with great losse.*

If your space allows, have the French flee down the aisles, around the back of the house, and then return to the stage. You don't need a large cast to pull off the feeling of a large battle, just a handful of people in good shape. [*SD: You may want to feature Salisbury in the fight. He is specifically praised here as a badass and will die two scenes later. Make them worthwhile.*] [*JK: Dude, spoilers!*]

> *Reigneir. Salisbury* is a desperate Homicide,
> He fighteth as one weary of his life:
> The other Lords, like Lyons wanting foode,
> Doe rush vpon vs as their hungry prey.

[*SD: The audience may as well get conditioned to 'good guys' ending up dead in this dramatic universe. Salisbury's short arc is a preview of Talbot's fate over the course of four acts.*] [*JK: Talbot dies, too? I can't continue working with you.*] [*SD: Sure, but did you ever really start?*]

*See Glossary – Draws; Ensemble Readiness.*

Expectations and sympathies in any given fight are often toyed with long before physical contact. Use the rampant misogyny of the fifteenth century (not that things have changed) to your advantage (and Joan's). The opening position of the men here is that a woman participating in the 'manly' arts (reading, philosophy, fighting) is ludicrous. Your actors can emphasise this by laughing at the bastard's account of Joan.

But something is off about the men's presumptions. We get to discover this in real time, along with them. The first shock is Joan calling out Reigneir as an impostor. Some confusion should appear amongst the court, but subsequently dissipate as they fall back on their collective delusion that no woman is ever going to defeat a man in combat. Joan will use this paradigm repeatedly as an edge in combat.

*Here they fight, and Ioane de Puzel ouercomes.*

After the beating the French have just received, they're in need of a miracle. Or at least a laugh. All Shakespeare tells us is that the dauphin and Joan fight, and she overcomes. Make sure it's not too short; otherwise you make the dauphin look weak, which lessens the impact Joan should have on the audience and her countrymen in this first look. Joan should not simply be the victor; she must best a fighter who would normally win. She is the French counterpoint to Talbot, so the audience should see her ability at least on par with what we have heard of his. One way to accomplish this is for her fighting style to be unique and difficult to forecast. There are many ways to go about this. Is she smarter? If so, she can anticipate what the dauphin is going to do in his attacks, easily avoiding or parrying. Does she possess a litheness the men don't have? [*JK: A production I worked on gave Joan great acrobatic skills. At one point, she did a run up the wall, then flipped to avoid a cut from the dauphin.*] Or is it something else entirely that sets her apart? As always, this comes down to exploration in rehearsal with your fight director and actors.

If you opt for a long fight, you could have Joan beat the dauphin move for move: each pass they have, she is just a little better than he is; she surprises him, he makes the next phrase a little more complex, and she surprises him again; when he finally gives it his all, she moves in to disarm him, putting him on point with his own weapon.

Alternatively, the dauphin could be so cocky that Joan takes him down in the blink of an eye. It still moves the story along, but leaves in the court's/audience's mind a question mark – is she good, lucky, or both?

Whichever way you go with her fighting style, make sure the dauphin's 'heart and hands' are 'at once subdu'd'. Joan can finish the fight with a move that trips the dauphin, or otherwise takes him down. Her sword should be at his chest or threatening to cut his throat, which will prompt the dauphin's 'Stay thy hands.' If she is using a hand-and-a-half sword or longer, both hands can be on the weapon, so the plural in his statement makes sense. If the fight is with a single-handed sword, the blade would be short enough for her to grab him with one hand, and lay the blade across his collarbone to threaten him.

None of the courtiers should know whether Joan will kill the dauphin. Some of the men could offer to intervene, and the dauphin can refuse/accept in accordance with his courage.

The dauphin offers himself as Joan's 'prostrate Thrall', because she has physically put him in that position by the fight's end and/or he is proposing.

## Act 1  Scene 3

*See Glossary – Binds (attempted); Draws; Ensemble Readiness; Strikes.*

If foreign troubles were not enough for the English, they have some domestic squabbles as well.

Remember that fights reveal character. Are Humphrey and Winchester just a couple of old farts who happen to have soldiers in their employ, or do they have some fighting experience themselves? [*SD: A lord protector and a cardinal sound pretty indoorsy as professions go but the 1420s were lit, yo.*] [*JK: How did you learn the lingo of the yoot?*] [*SD: Oh, you know me. Out all night, high off my ass on MDMA, and twerkin' at da klerb.*] Whether you have them join in the skirmishes or not, the important thing is they loathe each other so completely that they're willing to fight in front of the mayor.

> *Glost.* What? am I dar'd, and bearded to my face?
> Draw men, for all this priuiledged place,
> Blew Coats to Tawny Coats. Priest, beware your Beard,
> I meane to tugge it, and to cuffe you soundly.
> Vnder my feet I stampe thy Cardinalls Hat:
> In spight of Pope, or dignities of Church,
> Here by the Cheekes Ile drag thee vp and downe.

This may be a good place to start the fight. They can scream the next few lines as things progress. Gloucester may get Winchester in some kind of a hold, justifying his call for a rope. As with Pandulph's arrival in Chapter 7 – *King John* (3.1), a complete stranger is about to walk into the middle of a shitshow, giving us the opportunity for comedic relief. The difference here is that we get a second laugh when the stranger in question is shown zero reverence – everyone just goes back to fighting.

> *Winch.* *Gloster*, thou wilt answere this before the Pope.
> *Glost.* Winchester Goose, I cry, a Rope, a Rope.
> Now beat them hence, why doe you let them stay?
> Thee Ile chase hence, thou Wolfe in Sheepes array.
> Out Tawney-Coates, out Scarlet Hypocrite.

> *Here Glosters men beat out the Cardinalls men, and enter in the hurly-burly the*
> *Maior of London, and his Officers.*

> *Maior.* Fye Lords, that you being supreme Magistrates,
> Thus contumeliously should breake the Peace.
> *Glost.* Peace Maior, thou know'st little of my wrongs:
> Here's *Beauford*, that regards nor God nor King,
> Hath here distrayn'd the Tower to his vse.
> *Winch.* Here's *Gloster*, a Foe to Citizens,
> One that still motions Warre, and neuer Peace,
> O're-charging your free Purses with large Fines;
> That seekes to ouerthrow Religion,
> Because he is Protector of the Realme;
> And would haue Armour here out of the Tower,
> To Crowne himselfe King, and suppresse the Prince.
> *Glost.* I will not answer thee with words, but blowes.

> *Here they skirmish againe.*

The second time's the charm – the mayor is finally respected. Maybe. His officers could make a far more dramatic threat this go around, if you have the budget. But, if you think the mayor asks for the proclamation to be read 'as lowd as e're thou canst' for a reason other than to chill some bones, it may be that the skirmishing has not stopped, and the poor officer has to give himself laryngitis to little or no avail. This would again increase your laugh count, if you're into that kind of thing. See Chapter 7 – *King John* (2.1).

## Act 1  Scene 4

As Talbot enters, remember to play the wounds of his battle and imprisonment. We know he was thrust in the back with a spear. He may have been beaten as well. If Salisbury greets Talbot with a big hug, he might wince in pain.

The tower is rocked by an explosion, but the stage directions are vague: the gunner has set up some insurance ordnance to maximise casualties; his boy is somewhere nearby with a linstock; and 'here they shot' is unclear. Does the boy detonate the blast, or do the English accidentally do so upon firing? You need to find a way to stage the blast and the flying bodies.

*Here they shot, and Salisbury falls downe.*

*See Glossary – Blood; Blood Packs; Falls; Knees.*

Make sure the actors know how to fall safely. Pad their knees and elbows if the costumes allow. Talbot makes it clear that Salisbury and Gargrave are killed. [*JK: The gunner's boy must be as well; due to his proximity to the cannon, there is no way he can survive the blast.*] Add a few more soldiers to the scene for wounds and deaths if you can.

Shakespeare is specific about Salisbury's wounds. Half his face is gone (whichever side was closest to the cannon/explosion) and his death seems certain. Gargrave's less so, since he was probably farther away from the eruption. Make sure to block the scene so that it makes sense Talbot wasn't killed. You can place him far from the explosion, but it would be a stronger choice to have him survive all the shrapnel as a result of Salisbury's body effectively functioning as a Meatshield™. Instead of running to Salisbury's body, Talbot can speak whilst trying to extract himself from under his half-faced friend.

[*JK: Another option is to have Gargrave survive the explosion but then, after saying his line and getting Salisbury off Talbot, get shot (arrow, bullet, whatever, based on your time period for the production) and spray blood over Talbot as well. This is a more dynamic option than just having Talbot stand there talking to corpses.*] [*SD: And it will make the messenger's day more interesting.*]

If you want onstage gore, you will need to plant all the blood, viscera, and limbs. The actor playing Salisbury could have blood packs to smear his face and pop one of the bags on his body, as your lighting and sound team deal with an explosion distracting enough to hold the audience's attention. You'll need to hire a certified pyrotechnician for this. It is also possible to have an eyeball fly somewhere across the stage.

*See Glossary – Carries.*

The messenger and/or soldiers can assist Salisbury and other injured off stage. Maybe the master gunner comes on to retrieve his boy. You can fade to black to keep things moving, but at least show the beginnings of handling the dead.

## Act 1  Scene 5

Since Talbot was the last to leave the stage, you may garner some unwanted laughter if he immediately comes back chasing the dauphin. If you prefer to avoid this, consider a brief skirmish amongst the general forces. [*JK: The French (with the dauphin) might push the English off stage left and immediately get pushed back stage right, as the English are reinforced by Talbot. Then, Talbot and the dauphin can meet on the stage's battlefield, and you can pick up the stage directions from there, with Talbot pursuing/driving off the dauphin, as the English push the French off stage right. It will really pop if you have Talbot chase the dauphin down an aisle to the back of the house. The French can then push the English back, as they are reinforced by Joan, and the French ultimately drive the English off stage left, fighting the whole time. Finally, Talbot could come back down the aisle with his lines and meet the sole French soldier remaining – Joan. If it feels like anyone can enter from anywhere at anytime, this chaos will help convey the terror of war and keep your audience from getting complacent. See Chapter 13 –* Henry 5 *(4.4).*] [*SD: I agree with that last bit, but why are you siding with the French?*] [*JK: Huh?*] [*SD: You have them entering from the sympathetic side of the stage.*] [*JK: THE WHAT?!*] [*SD: We read from left to right, so we're naturally inclined to assume heroes enter stage right (house left) and villains stage left (house right).*] [*JK: Now you're just fucking with me.*] [*SD: 'Left' in Italian is 'sinistra'.*] [*JK: Please make it stop.*] [*SD: We call it heaven and hell, not hell and heaven. The entrances of characters in Commedia dell'arte reflected this.*] [*JK: *shoots self; misses**] [*SD: Good and evil, not evil and good. Also, you never noticed in our time working on* Macbeth *that I always entered from stage left except for the very few scenes in which I merited the audience's sympathies?*] [*JK: Ohmygodjustswitchtheentrancesandexits.*] [*SD: Cool.*]

The language reveals a frustrated Talbot at the top – baffled feminine endings, and trochees in an attempt to gain control over an increasingly chaotic situation. [*SD: I noticed when playing him (and a thousand other characters for Twenty Feet Productions in 2005, under the careful watch of artistic director Marc 'Producing, Directing, and Starring in Eight Plays at Once Strikes Me as a Good Idea' Silberschatz) that Talbot's language mostly reverted to Marlowe's 'mighty line' after each bout with Joan. It struck me that she gave him more life than any of his useless soldiers, and elevated him to the poetic in order to describe her accomplishments and his own troops' failings.*] Remember to continue tracking Talbot's injuries – his back, anything the French did to him in captivity, and the damage sustained in the explosion.

The next question you have to address – how perceptive is Joan? Each production has to answer how much 'God' is speaking to Joan. Is she getting inspiration from a higher power, or is she a charlatan? Whichever you decide, she has already discerned in her first scene that Reigneir was not the dauphin, and could very well pick up on Talbot's wounds here and use them to her advantage. Your staging could include a clear punch to Talbot's wound, inflicting crippling pain. This would finish the first part of the fight, leaving Talbot to scream out in agony on 'Heauens'.

> *Here an Alarum againe, and Talbot pursueth the Dolphin, and driueth him:*
> *Then enter Ioane de Puzel, driuing Englishmen before her. Then enter Talbot.*

   *Talb.* Where is my strength, my valour, and my force?
Our English Troupes retyre, I cannot stay them,
A Woman clad in Armour chaseth them.

> *Enter Puzel.*

Here, here shee comes. Ile haue a bowt with thee:
Deuill, or Deuils Dam, Ile coniure thee:
Blood will I draw on thee, thou art a Witch,
And straightway giue thy Soule to him thou seru'st.
   *Puzel.* Come, come, 'tis onely I that must disgrace thee.

> *Here they fight.*

   *Talb.* Heauens, can you suffer Hell so to preuayle?
My brest Ile burst with straining of my courage,
And from my shoulders crack my Armes asunder,
But I will chastise this high-minded Strumpet.

> *They fight againe.*

   *Puzel. Talbot* farwell, thy houre is not yet come,
I must goe Victuall Orleance forthwith:

> *A short Alarum: then enter the Towne with Souldiers.*

O're-take me if thou canst, I scorne thy strength.
Goe, goe, cheare vp thy hungry-starued men,
Helpe *Salisbury* to make his Testament,
This Day is ours, as many more shall be.

> *Exit.*

   *Talb.* My thoughts are whirled like a Potters Wheele,
I know not where I am, nor what I doe:

A Witch by feare, not force, like *Hannibal*,
Driues back our troupes, and conquers as she lists:
So Bees with smoake, and Doues with noysome stench,
Are from their Hyues and Houses driuen away.
They call'd vs, for our fiercenesse, English Dogges,
Now like to Whelpes, we crying runne away.

*A short Alarum.*

Hearke Countreymen, eyther renew the fight,
Or teare the Lyons out of Englands Coat;
Renounce your Soyle, giue Sheepe in Lyons stead:
Sheepe run not halfe so trecherous from the Wolfe,
Or Horse or Oxen from the Leopard,       *(pronounced LEE-o-PARD, if ya nasty)*
As you flye from your oft-subdued slaues.

*Alarum. Here another Skirmish.*

This is a good time to remind the audience that Joan's besting of Talbot is the exception, not the rule – throw some French soldiers at Talbot, whom he can quickly dispatch. The more you display Talbot's skill, the more you raise Joan's status and make the audience look forward to another meeting.

## Act 2  Scene 1

*See Glossary – Ensemble Readiness; Grabs (maybe); Intimacy; Strikes (maybe).*

*The French leape ore the walles in their shirts. Enter seuerall wayes,*
*Bastard, Alanson, Reignier, halfe ready, and halfe vnready.*

The English catch the French revelling unawares, half-naked, and drunk. An intimacy consultant can assist with determining the various states of undress with which your ensemble may be comfortable, as well as Joan's attempts to pacify Charles when he blames everyone but himself for the ambush. Does he grab Joan or Alanson or one of the others, desperately seeking accountability? Does anyone push back? Charles seems to fall for Joan's enchantment rather quickly; it is entirely possible they were having a private celebration off stage, given their dual entrance well after the others have arrived.

*Alarum. Enter a Souldier, crying, a Talbot, a Talbot:*
*they flye, leauing their Clothes behind.*

## Act 2  Scene 2

*See Glossary – Carries.*

> *Talb.* Bring forth the Body of old *Salisbury*,
> And here aduance it in the Market-Place,
> The middle Centure of this cursed Towne.

## Act 2  Scene 3

*See Glossary – Arrests; Binds; Strikes (maybe).*

*[SD: And, now, our usual game show – To Stage or Not to Stage? The countess thinks she has captured Talbot, but discovers the opposite when his soldiers enter, having subdued the countess' household off stage. Ultimately, it doesn't matter, as Talbot decides to spare the countess and have a party. Jared is now going to suggest an alternate, more-violent universe because I hate parties.] [JK: When the countess announces Talbot is her prisoner, I would have her guards enter to cover all the exits. One guard can have the shackles in hand to which the countess refers. Since Talbot was prepared for this, his soldiers can pop up behind each of the French soldiers and either slit their throat, thrust behind the clavicle to sever the subclavian artery, or do a Hollywood neckbreak. Ideally, a variety of quick kills, and then render the countess helpless via a basic hold, or using those shackles introduced moments ago, or binding to a chair. Maybe all three!]*

## Act 2  Scene 4

*See Glossary – Draws (maybe); Ensemble Readiness; Strikes (unlikely).*

The lords have come out into the garden after being too loud in Temple Hall. Does any violence break out here? Whilst it would be uncouth to devolve into fisticuffs, everyone should be prepared if a lesser mind prevails. *[SD: Probably Somerset, that little shit.]* Some folks might make a motion to draw or even succeed in doing so, but the blows should generally be verbal in these initial arguments, versions of which will be played out over and over and over again for the next few plays, getting bloodier with time. The trick in these early iterations is to somehow make thrilling the constant question of how the king (and his lord protector) should behave, or even who should rightfully be king. Let the language do the work. The only blood drawn here (if any) would be if someone accidentally pricked themselves whilst plucking a rose. *[SD: Again, Somerset. Have I mentioned how much I hate him?] [JK: Yeah, dude. What's the deal?] [SD: You've been working with me for two decades at The York Shakespeare Company and never noticed the name?]*

## Act 2  Scene 5

*See Glossary – Carries.*

> *Enter Mortimer, brought in a Chayre, and Iaylors.*

## Act 3  Scene 1

*See Glossary – Blood; Draws; Ensemble Readiness; Strikes.*

> *Flourish. Enter King, Exeter, Gloster, Winchester, Warwick, Somerset,*
> *Suffolk, Richard Plantagenet. Gloster offers to put vp a Bill:*
> *Winchester snatches it, teares it.*

This is more indecorous than 2.4. The lords are now in the presence of the king, but he is a child, and everyone is vying to be puppetmaster. [*SD: Be specific with your actors. The stage directions require that Winchester snatch the bill from Gloucester but say nothing about whether the process goes smoothly. They could scuffle a bit, maybe even end up with paper cuts.*] [*JK: What's your deal with paper cuts, buddy? You already suggested this in Chapter 1 – King Lear (1.2) and Chapter 10 – Henry 4 Part 1 (2.3).*] [*SD: Because, if you're not the victim, paper cuts are hilarious.*]

> *A noyse within, Downe with the Tawny-Coats.*

> *King.* What tumult's this?
> *Warw.*                     An Vprore, I dare warrant,
> Begun through malice of the Bishops men.

> *A noyse againe, Stones, Stones. Enter Maior.*

If there is any other physical manifestation of the lords' mutual disregard, it may be an 'accidental' shouldering but nothing too crazy. Particularly since Gloucester and Winchester's men have been fighting again, this time off stage, and enter bloodied from throwing pebbles at each other.

As the mayor enters, maybe a stone flies by him before he can close the door, to set the scene for what he is going to report.

> *Enter in skirmish with bloody Pates.*

> *King.* We charge you, on allegeance to our selfe,
> To hold your slaughtring hands, and keepe the Peace:
> Pray' Vnckle *Gloster* mittigate this strife.

1. *Seruing*. Nay, if we be forbidden Stones, wee'le fall
to it with our Teeth.
2. *Seruing*. Doe what ye dare, we are as resolute.

*Skirmish againe.*

*Glost*. You of my household, leaue this peeuish broyle,
And set this vnaccustom'd fight aside.
3. *Seru*. My Lord, we know your Grace to be a man
Iust, and vpright; and for your Royall Birth,
Inferior to none, but to his Maiestie:
And ere that we will suffer such a Prince,
So kinde a Father of the Common-weale,
To be disgraced by an Inke-horne Mate,
Wee and our Wiues and Children all will fight,
And haue our bodyes slaughtred by thy foes.
1. *Seru*. I, and the very parings of our Nayles
Shall pitch a Field when we are dead.

*Begin againe.*

*Glost*. Stay, stay, I say:
And if you loue me, as you say you doe,
Let me perswade you to forbeare a while.

Humphrey and Winchester's men have been hurling stones at each other because they are 'Forbidden late to carry any Weapon'. The skirmishes can be hand to hand, but some may have leftover pebbles to deploy whilst the fighting continues. This chaos provides an opportunity for each man to react differently, revealing detail about his character. Does anyone try to curry favour with the king by guarding him? Maybe others don't care about the king and just think of themselves. Does anyone attempt to get others to stop fighting? Does anyone in a powerful position get struck by a flying pebble? If Henry gets hit accidentally, we can learn much about his character here in his first appearance. Is he saint-like, turning the other cheek? Does he attempt physically to get everyone to stop, but fail? This would make it clear he has a kind heart and is therefore the worst-equipped person to rule. There are myriad moving pieces – the most powerful people in the kingdom are all assembled in the same room. Please dedicate sufficient rehearsal time to exploring specifics in the violence.

## Act 3  Scene 2

*See Glossary – Carries.*

*An Alarum. Talbot in an Excursion.*

*Talb.* France, thou shalt rue this Treason with thy teares,
If *Talbot* but suruiue thy Trecherie.
*Pucell* that Witch, that damned Sorceresse,
Hath wrought this Hellish Mischiefe vnawares,
That hardly we escap't the Pride of France.

*Exit. An Alarum: Excursions. Bedford brought in sicke in a Chayre.*
*Enter Talbot and Burgonie without: within, Pucell, Charles, Bastard,*
*and Reigneir on the Walls.*

Joan and her cronies have the high ground now. Do they throw anything at their enemies below? Small rocks, rotten food, or pieces of wood could be used to torment Talbot (see Chapter 10 – *Henry 4 Part 1* (2.4)). This could add some humour if Talbot gets pelted whilst saying 'Dare yee come forth, and meet vs in the field?'

*Exit. An Alarum: Excursions. Enter Sir Iohn Falstaffe, and a Captaine.*

[*JK: Once again, keep the battle going throughout the scene as the Talbonites run back into the town to fight the French.*]

*Capt.* Cowardly Knight, ill fortune follow thee.

*Exit. Retreat. Excursions. Pucell, Alanson, and Charles flye.*

The tides turn as the English drive the French out of the city. Continue the fighting.

*Bedford dyes, and is carryed in by two in his Chaire.*
*An Alarum. Enter Talbot, Burgonie, and the rest.*

Raise the English flag again – to signal they are victorious and make sense of Bedford's speech.

Finally, we remind you to track any and all wounds sustained by the surviving characters and bear these injuries in mind as the play continues.

## Act 3  Scene 4

*See Glossary – Strikes.*

*Bass.* Why, what is he? as good a man as *Yorke*.
*Vern.* Hearke ye: not so: in witnesse take ye that.

*Strikes him.*

*Bass.* Villaine, thou knowest
The Law of Armes is such,
That who so drawes a Sword, 'tis present death,
Or else this Blow should broach thy dearest Bloud.

Vernon and Basset are settling a matter that was unable to be handled earlier. This scene is often played hot-blooded and physical, but the language they are using is that of duelling – their prior discussion is reiterated, and each of them is given a chance to clarify, rectify, or apologise. When the latter does not happen, Vernon invokes an offence by deed by striking Basset (see Chapter 13 – *Henry 5* (4.8)). This could be a slap, a cross, or even a punch to the guts. Basset wants to convert this spat to a judicial duel, presided over by the king, and will need the king's permission to challenge Vernon. This was the only way to obtain satisfaction legally, as personal duels were illegal. See Chapter 9 – *Richard 2* (1.1).

## Act 4  Scene 1

*See Glossary – Carries (maybe); Draws (maybe); Ensemble Readiness; Falls (maybe); Strikes (maybe).*

The Order of the Garter, established by Edward 3 in 1348, is said to have been inspired by tales of King Arthur and the Knights of the Round Table. It exists to this day, limited to approximately two dozen members. The motto for the organisation comes from an actual garter being dropped and the king putting it on. Members were granted the right to wear a dark blue garter, as well as a coat of arms that displayed a garter surrounding the flag of Saint George. The garter Talbot strips from Falstaff can be a literal garter and/or the cloak bearing the emblem.

Falstaff has fled battle twice. He no longer deserves to be a knight, let alone be in such exclusive company. Talbot is finally face to face with the cause of his capture and ridicule. Depending on your combination of actors, there is no reason Talbot can't sucker-punch Falstaff. If Falstaff has a cloak, Talbot can grab it and pull Falstaff to the ground. For safety, the actor playing Falstaff would need to grab the cord of the cloak, keep his fingers between the cord and his throat, and execute a sitfall. This will allow Talbot to drag Falstaff a bit before stopping and taking the cloak over Falstaff's head. The actual garter can be ripped away quickly since it is worn on the outside of the trousers/leggings as a status symbol. With Falstaff on the ground, it would take Talbot little effort.

The way Falstaff is removed will further reveal character. Does he put up a fight, or resign himself to banishment? You could go as far as having Falstaff move towards the king, then Talbot draws and puts Falstaff on point. Talbot or some of the guards can then march Falstaff out of the king's presence.

*Procession of the Knights of the Garter* (second sheet). Marcus Gheeraerts the Elder, 1576. (*British Museum*)

*Procession of the Knights of the Garter* (ninth sheet). Marcus Gheeraerts the Elder, 1576. (*British Museum*)

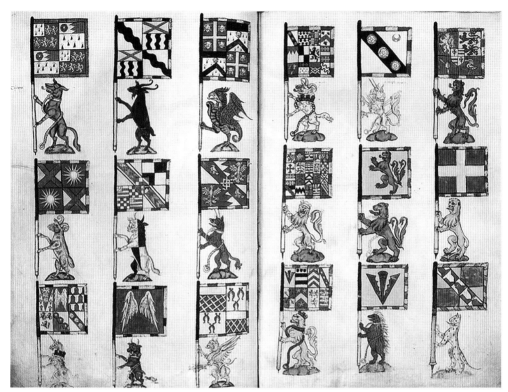

*Banners of mid-sixteenth-century Knights of the Order of the Garter supported by single beasts. (The Oxford Guide to Heraldry)*

Later in the scene, you may feel inclined to continue the fisticuffs between Vernon and Basset. We advise against this; if either gentleman were to do more than verbally argue his case before the king, it would go poorly.

*[SD: Whilst York will wait until the next play to express his ambitions for the throne, he is reminiscent of* Chapter 4 – Macbeth *(1.4) insofar as instructing a monarch on how to do his job. To my ears, York's language goes further than the Scot's subconscious selection; if someone tells me what I 'shall' do, it tends to make my blood boil. See Volume Two –* Coriolanus *(3.1).]*

> *Som.* The quarrell toucheth none but vs alone,
> Betwixt our selues let vs decide it then.
> *Yorke.* There is my pledge, accept it Somerset.

The 'pledge' could be straightforward, like the gauntlets in Chapter 9 – *Richard 2* (1.1; 4.1). But

*Knight of the Garter.* Wenceslaus Hollar, unknown date (lived 1607–1677). (*Thomas Fisher Rare Book Library*)

York might make a bolder play here and, instead of throwing down a glove, strike Somerset. If you opt for York to strike, it would constitute an offence by deed and must be resolved on the duelling ground. Somerset must answer or be dishonoured. See Chapter 13 – *Henry 5* (4.8). Shocking the court like this would have the twofold benefit of empowering York whilst humiliating Somerset. But it also comes with a potential drawback – emasculating the king. (This is our way of reverse-engineering an explanation for what happens next: Henry not only denies York's request to allow a duel, but chooses to wear a red rose. The king claims such a choice is not prejudicial, but we are fundamentally a tribal species.) Another choice would be to simply have York throw the gauntlet down, giving Somerset a choice whether or not to pick it up. This would keep York from shaming Henry, but also give Somerset more control of the situation than York might desire. Explore in rehearsals what works best with your actors' chemistry.

## Act 4  Scene 5

*See Glossary – Draws (maybe); Falls (maybe); Grabs (maybe); Knees; Strikes (maybe).*

[JK: *The scene with Talbot and his son may become quite physical, even violent. When Johnny drops to his knees and begs to stay, Talbot could pull his son up and start to drag him off stage; he could struggle and eventually break away from his father; or maybe Talbot puts Johnny in an armbar, and he can get out of it using some technique learned from his father, which might make Talbot annoyed but also a bit proud. Depending on how physical they get, you can even explore the possibility of Johnny drawing a knife during the debate. If it were me, and my boy was invested in his honour enough to threaten me, I would be delighted.*] [SD: *I forgot after closing night to ask the actor who played my son – noted rapscallion-and-Nicolas-Cage-enthusiast Mike McGuire – whether or not he felt as dumb as I did in this scene every night. I hate rhyming.*] [JK: *Volume Two –* A Midsummer Night's Dream *has lots of wonderful rhymes, Seth!*] [SD: *Go fuck yourself, Jared.*]

## Act 4  Scene 6

*Alarum: Excursions, wherein Talbots Sonne is hemm'd about,*
*and Talbot rescues him.*

[JK: *We have a change of location, so make sure the Talbots exit after the last scene or it will look like they were ambushed.*]

## Act 4  Scene 7

*See Glossary – Carries.*

*Alarum. Excursions. Enter old Talbot led.*

*[JK: You can ignore the scene breaks and make this feel like one big battle. Talbot and his son have run off stage to fight; more skirmishes should happen before Johnny comes back on, so we see him mortally wounded and rushed off stage; Talbot can enter with his own mortal wounds, possibly so hurt he can't walk on his own and is assisted by an officer. Talbot can look through bodies on stage to try and find his son.]*

*Enter with Iohn Talbot, borne.*

We suggest you allow the audience to sit for a moment in the theoretically heartbreaking tableau of dead Talbots. Then, cut it immediately by having the oncoming French slaughter Talbot's servant and soldiers. This will be jarring enough to put everyone on their toes again.

## Act 5  Scene 2

*[JK: I would swap this with 5.1 and make it a continuation of 4.7. The battle is won but not over, so there could be a few more frays as the scene is ending.] [SD: Okay, but our job is also to address the text as written. Willy probably had good reason for the relief in battle at the act break.] [JK: And we're supposed to ask him how exactly?] [SD: \*travels to Stratford-upon-Avon; exhumes and reanimates corpse\* SPILL THE BEANS, YA SONOFABITCH!!!]*

> *Pucel.* Of all base passions, Feare is most accurst.
> Command the Conquest *Charles*, it shall be thine:
> Let *Henry* fret, and all the world repine.
>   *Char.* Then on my Lords, and France be fortunate.

*Exeunt. Alarum. Excursions.*

*[JK: And … more battles. By this point, the fighting is in full force and we should see the English winning. The French are getting pushed back and, in a particularly brutal pass, Joan can run in from one side of the stage to join the fight, only for the French to run past her. This would justify her report in 5.3 that 'the Frenchmen flye'. Again, don't bother with a formal scenebreak.] [SD: I'm not against Jared's idea in theory, but it wouldn't have worked when I played Talbot unless my fat-ass cadaver actually was carried off stage. I needed this brief window of offstage time to execute a quick change and transform into Margaret – a performance most of the global population was blessedly spared.]*

## Act 5  Scene 3

*See Glossary – Blood.*

If you opt to have Joan spill her own blood, the simplest method is to have her palm a sponge of blood and use a stage knife to cut her palm. As soon as she starts to pull the knife through her hand, she will contract that hand in pain, which will simultaneously squeeze the sponge so the audience get to see blood dripping from her palm. As the scene escalates in desperation, she has a knife in hand and can threaten her wrist at 'lop a member off' or try to cut herself again to offer more blood.

*Excursions. Burgundie and Yorke fight hand to hand. French flye.*

[*JK: In these excursions, Burgundy and York can be part of the opening fray. The stage directions are explicit – this fight is unarmed. But Burgundy and York could have had weapons during the excursions and been disarmed.*]

*See Glossary – Intimacy.*

*Kisse her.*

We start tracking the Margaret/Suffolk affair here and will keep coming back to it. Bring in your intimacy consultant and fight director. Build something with sparks and kink to form a stark contrast with Margaret's eventual marriage to King Henry, that milquetoast pint of vanilla.

## Act 5  Scene 4

*See Glossary – Arrests; Binds; Ensemble Readiness; Grabs (maybe); Knees (maybe); Strikes (maybe).*

Joan deploys multiple survival tactics in this scene. How many of them are not just verbal but also physical? Set aside proper rehearsal time to explore your options. Is she struggling against the soldiers bringing her in? Does she temporarily escape their clutches? If so, would she attempt to attack York (if bound, by kicking or biting)?

And how do the others react? Does the shepherd shake Joan to try and get her to remember? Or force her to her knees after she refuses to kneel? Or slap/spit in anger? The shepherd has dynamic potential – from a seemingly harmless and distraught old man to a vicious relic calling for his own daughter's execution.

Then there are York, Warwick, and any soldiers in their employ. If they manhandle Joan, how far do they go? She suddenly claims a pregnancy. Warwick says 'we'll haue no Bastards liue' and you can determine in rehearsal whether or not there is a physical expression of this threat. See Chapter 11 – *Henry 4 Part 2* (5.4).

*The marriage of King Henry and Queen Margaret.* James Stephanoff, nineteenth century. (*Folger Shakespeare Library*)

# Chapter 15

# Henry 6 Part 2

*'They will by violence tear him from your palace'* – Salisbury (3.2)

## Act 1  Scene 3

*See Glossary – Ensemble Readiness; Grabs; Strikes (maybe).*

The first petitioner mistakes Suffolk for the lord protector. As the petitioner tries to sneak away, Suffolk should grab him. Suffolk may have hands on both petitioners by the time Margaret says '*Suffolke* let them goe'. Given Margaret will have no problem striking a noblewoman later in the scene, how might she treat commoners in her way? At a minimum, we know she tears the supplication. It's up to you to decide other ways she and Suffolk might use violence to get answers. In Margaret's case, consider the height of her violence in Chapter 16 – *Henry 6 Part 3* (1.4) and chart a course backwards from there.

*See Glossary – Intimacy.*

> I thought King *Henry* had resembled thee,
> In Courage, Courtship, and Proportion:    *(four syllables cuz Suffolk's well-endow'd)*

Continue tracking the dynamics of Suffolk and Margaret's affair with your intimacy consultant and fight director. Kinks take many forms and the scene is full of innuendo. Get the audience turned on and tuned in to these two from the get-go. (Imagine the Macbeths but with no scruples to suppress.)

*See Glossary – Draws (maybe); Ensemble Readiness; Strikes.*

> ***She giues the Duchesse a box on the eare.***

Having established that 'Strangers in Court, doe take' Eleanor for the queen, Margaret pretends to mistake Eleanor for a servant. For more about the 'box on the eare', see Chapter 13 – *Henry 5* (4.8). After being struck, Eleanor should turn to return the attack on her assailant. This immediate threat will feed Margaret's 'I cry you mercy'. Her feigned surprise will only infuriate Eleanor further. Upon realising it is the queen who hit her, and hearing the bullshit excuse, the duchess makes it abundantly clear what would happen if Margaret were not queen. Whilst Eleanor cannot exact revenge here, every bone in her body should ache to do so. She might temporarily forget her place, moving with her 'ten Commandements' outstretched towards the queen's face. If so, the guards would intercede and possibly escort Eleanor out as she's still speaking.

*See Glossary – Ensemble Readiness.*

As discussed in Chapter 14 – *Henry 6 Part 1*, there would not normally be violence in the king's presence. But this is no normal time. You have a group of extremely powerful and often violent people, and you should use your rehearsals to cultivate an an atmosphere swelling with unpredictability. We've already seen the nobles devolve into violence with each other and, whilst Humphrey has recently been taking courses in meditation and self-help, he's the exception and not the rule. Add to this some pesky commoners, and anything can happen. The lords might get in each other's faces, push/shove, *etc.*, but we don't anticipate actual draws or strikes. See Chapter 13 – *Henry 5* (4.1).

> *Armorer.* And't shall please your Maiestie, I neuer sayd
> nor thought any such matter: God is my witnesse, I am
> falsely accus'd by the Villaine.
> *Peter.* By these tenne bones, my Lords, hee did speake
> them to me in the Garret one Night, as wee were scow-
> ring my Lord of Yorkes Armor.

After Peter's lines, the armourer might attempt to strike. He should restrain himself, but it will offer an insight into the legitimacy of his apprentice's allegations, and reflect poorly enough on York that Gloucester transfers the regency of France to Somerset.

*See Glossary – Arrests.*

> *King.* Away with them to Prison: and the day of
> Combat, shall be the last of the next moneth. Come
> *Somerset*, wee'le see thee sent away.

This arrest probably does not get violent – the armourer consents and Peter is a pipsqueak.

## Act 1  Scene 4

> *Here doe the Ceremonies belonging, and make the Circle,*
> *Bullingbrooke or Southwell reads,* Coniuro te, &c.
> *It Thunders and Lightens terribly: then the Spirit Riseth.*

If you have the budget and want to conjure the spirit using a rigging system, see Chapter 18 – *Sir Thomas More* (3.1). Since these charlatans were hired to con the duchess, you can play with letting the audience in on some of the stage magic whilst keeping Eleanor in the dark.

*See Glossary – Arrests; Binds (maybe); Draws; Strikes (maybe).*

> *Enter the Duke of Yorke and the Duke of Buckingham with their Guard, and breake in.*

Witchcraft is a one-way ticket to the gallows or burning at the stake. These folks know they're screwed when the guards enter. There should be scuffles as the guards attempt capture of the conjurers – punching, dragging, and binding are all fair game. As for Eleanor, is she politely taken away? Does she hold out her hands in an offer to be arrested peaceably? Or does she go full badass? If so, have her attack a guard, force him to the ground, take the cuffs away from him, and bind herself.

## Act 2  Scene 1

*See Glossary – Ensemble Readiness.*

Again, the desire amongst the lords to cause each other physical harm must remain fervent, but consider your production's mix of actors in deciding whether this brittle decorum is broken. Gloucester and Winchester deliberately keep their plans for a duel private. Whatever happens here physically, one thing is for sure – everyone is annoying the everloving shit out of Henry, who really just wants to focus on things like birds and Jesus. Conversation of the former having been exhausted, we move now to the latter.

> *Enter one crying a Miracle.*

*See Glossary – Carries.*

> *Enter the Maior of Saint Albones, and his Brethren,*
> *bearing the man betweene two in a Chayre.*

*See Glossary – Strikes.*

*After the Beadle hath hit him once, he leapes ouer the Stoole, and runnes away:*
*and they follow, and cry, A Miracle.*

The process of whipping a character on stage requires several precautions, starting with the creation of a stage-safe whip. Replace the end of the whip with thin pieces of cloth instead of leather (which, if something went wrong, could slice open your actor's flesh). This custom whip will not make a cracking sound, so get your sound team to help sell this moment. Place the beadle far enough upstage to never actually make contact with the actor. *See Appendix – On the Bubble.*

*See Glossary – Arrests (maybe); Carries (maybe).*

The wife exits with the rest of them, but in what manner? Gloucester says 'take this Drab away', so is she formally arrested? Dragged? Beaten off of the stage?

## Act 2  Scene 3

*See Glossary – Arrests; Binds (maybe); Draws (maybe); Ensemble Readiness; Grabs (maybe); Strikes (maybe).*

*Sound Trumpets. Enter the King and State,*
*with Guard, to banish the Duchesse.*

Commoners would have been thrown in a filthy dungeon and forgotten. Depending on how many days have passed, they would be ragged, dirty, hungry, and sore from being shackled. There is a great fear of witchcraft in this era, so it's possible the prisoners' hands and feet would be chained to a wall, to prevent them from performing any kind of magic in the dungeon. They might also be blindfolded to stop them giving anyone 'the evil eye'.

The way a noble has been treated in captivity says a lot about their soverign. (And, in the case of a weak ruler, the indifference the jailors may have regarding said ruler's preferences.) The duchess, theoretically, would have the benefit of better accommodation along the lines of a house arrest. She would have been fed regularly and allowed to have time to put herself together before being brought out for trial. The jailors couldn't give a damn. If she appears as filthy and malnourished as the commoners, then we know how things went.

*Elianor.* Welcome is Banishment, welcome were my Death.

Is Eleanor in agony? Or is she saying 'SCREW YOU, GIVE ME A REAL SENTENCE!!!' As for Hume, he told us in 1.2 that he was bribed by Suffolk and Winchester to manipulate the duchess. Does he try anything once sentenced to execution? A pleading look towards his employers? An attempt to attack them before being restrained by guards? Be just as specific with the others sentenced to death. See Chapter 13 – *Henry 5* (2.2).

> *Yorke*. I neuer saw a fellow worse bestead,
>   Or more afraid to fight, then is the Appellant,
>   The seruant of this Armorer, my Lords.

> *Enter at one Doore the Armorer and his Neighbors, drinking
> to him so much, that hee is drunke; and he enters with a
> Drumme before him, and his Staffe, with a Sand-bagge
> fastened to it: and at the other Doore his Man, with a
> Drumme and Sand-bagge, and Prentices drinking to him.*

We learned in an earlier scene that, by his own admission, Peter cannot fight. York now informs us Peter is not just ill-equipped but also terrified. (The fact that Peter is surrounded and supported by other apprentices implies that the armourer, Horner, is not kind to his staff. This is another reason why we recommend the armourer start a striking motion in his prior scene.)

In this duel, Horner is using a sand flail (a sandbag attached to a pole) against Peter, who is using a sand club (a long, tubular sleeve filled with sand). These would cause great hurt and could render one unconscious, though not necessarily dead. (They could be made lethal by wetting the sand.) Sandbags had the advantage of being silent and leaving no marks. Commoners were more likely to be familiar with utilitarian tools like these rather than formal weaponry. Stage versions of these weapons can be made by using cotton instead of sand, allowing the actors to hit each other safely. The fight must still be choreographed but, where we would make hits to the bubble with regular weapons, we can make actual impact with these stage-safe versions.

> *They fight, and Peter strikes him downe.*

See Chapter 9 – *Richard 2* (1.1) for an in-depth discussion of judicial duels. Two drunken commoners will offer several options for a comedic fight. If one gets hit in the guts early on, he can almost (or successfully) vomit. An accidental groin hit can be funny. Peter is scared, so decide how you want him to win. Does he get lucky, or is Horner just that much drunker and inept?

*See Glossary – Blood; Carries.*

The king says 'For by his death we doe perceiue his guilt'. We can assume the strike was fatal and Horner has died. But remember these weapons were designed to bludgeon and not to kill; you will need a strike to land in the right place. If Horner is on the ground and receives a crushing blow to the chest, this could crack his ribs, which could perforate his lungs. He would be spitting up blood as he admits his guilt, then dies.

## Act 2  Scene 4

*See Glossary – Blood; Strikes (maybe).*

This is a story with which Shakespeare's crowd would have been familiar. On 13 November 1441, the Duchess of Gloucester was rowed to Temple Stairs off the River Thames, and had to walk barefoot to St Paul's Cathedral (just under a mile away). Bareheaded and dressed in white, she carried a two pound wax taper. People came out in droves to watch her act of public penance.

> *Enter the Duchesse in a white Sheet, and a Taper burning in her hand, with the Sherife and Officers.*

*[JK: If you're going to stage things literally, massive crowds of loud and angry commoners would throw things at Eleanor as she is paraded through the streets, and the majority of lines would have to be spoken over the sounds of the rabble.]*

## Act 3  Scene 1

*See Glossary – Arrests; Binds (maybe).*

This is one of the few instances in the cycle where a significant majority of the Plantagenets band together – to complete the dismantling of the former lord protector and any remaining sway he has over the king. Having a conscience is the surest way to get you fired or killed in the universe of this play. The vultures seize this opportunity to descend. Gloucester has likely seen this coming, but there is only so much of a fight he can offer here, as any display of fear or an attempt to evade arrest would add to apparent guilt. If you are going to handcuff him, have Gloucester extend his wrists to the guards.

*See Glossary – Draws (maybe); Strikes (maybe).*

The objective of its temporary unity achieved, the lords' alliance splinters into its former factions once the king departs. York and Somerset are in each other's faces again. You get to decide whether they come to blows, as well as how physical an intervention Margaret deploys.

## Act 3  Scene 2

Whilst not explicit in the stage directions, you have an opportunity to show the murder of Humphrey. The second murderer asks of the first 'Didst ever hear a man so penitent?' And we find out from Warwick that Humphrey appears to have been strangled. You could have one of the murderers choke Humphrey during prayer. [*SD: Since Hamlet is not available and, even if he were, too incompetent.*] A stranglehold from behind or a pillow-smothering should do the trick. Humphrey eventually ends up in a bed brought on stage. You can choose whether this is due to the murderers trying to make it look as though he died in his sleep, or if he was in bed already when praying. Holding Humphrey down, pinching his nose, and covering his mouth would be deliciously vicious if that's your thing. You're welcome to tell instead of show, but the corporeal nature of these plays is often worth exploiting to keep the stakes high and the audience awake.

*See Glossary – Faints.*

*King sounds.*

King Henry faints upon hearing of the demise of The Artist Formerly Known as the Lord Protector.

*See Glossary – Ensemble Readiness; Grabs (maybe); Knees (maybe); Strikes (maybe).*

Your interval, if you have one, is likely to be at the close of this scene or the next, and your playwright is happily up to the task of inundating the audience with one hideous event after another to keep us breathless. Tensions are high, corpses are piling up, and any idea that class might restrain these folks is about to go out the window. Reflect this chaos in your staging – guards rushing back and forth, members of court bustling in and out to handle news accordingly, and all hell eventually breaking loose when the commoners flood in.

   Henry is not the type to grab people and start throwing them around but, if he ever was going to get physical, this would be the time. One possibility is when Henry says 'Hide not thy poyson with such sugred words' and Suffolk moves to calm him. Henry could smack Suffolk's hands away, and/or grab him, and/or start shaking him, and/or push him into a wall for the next few lines, before throwing him away on 'out of my sight'.

   This approach also opens up the scene for physicality between Henry and Margaret. Margaret can get right in between Henry and Suffolk on 'Why do you rate my Lord of Suffolke thus?', or grab Henry's face with 'looke on me' after he has just turned from her, or push him into a wall (to mirror what Henry just did to Suffolk, if you chose that option). Her speech is lengthy, so you should explore the deployment of multiple tactics in rehearsal, instead of playing the same beat *ad infinitum*.

*Noyse within. Enter Warwicke, and many Commons.*

Combine the chaos of Macduff announcing Duncan's murder in Chapter 4 – *Macbeth* (2.3) with the tension from troops at the gate when Laertes comes in to avenge Polonius' murder in Chapter 3 – *Hamlet* (4.5), then submerge it in the fickle, murderous mobs of Volume Two – *Julius Caesar* [*JK: have you purchased Volume Two yet?*], and you'll have an idea of the feeling required for these next few moments. The guards must keep the commoners at bay (who are currently 'like an angry Hiue of Bees') and could make an example of one or two of them, punching their guts or face. Whatever it might take to remind them of their place, and keep them away from the king (and the queen, for whom the guards probably have more respect). This scene should boil right up to the edge of murderous rebellion, but not actually spill over until Jack Cade's hijacking of the play in the fourth act.

*See Glossary – Carries; Draws.*

*Bed put forth.*

Warwick submits evidence outlining the obvious murder of Humphrey and, of course, one of the conspirators who planned the death plays dumb. Warwick spells out the accusation for those assembled. Suffolk mentions his possession of a sword to egg on Warwick, and invites him to go elsewhere for a duel. They leave only for a moment, as the commoners of Bury immediately side with Warwick, forcing Suffolk to flee back here for safety.

*A noyse within.*

*Queene.* What noyse is this?

*Enter Suffolke and Warwicke, with their Weapons drawne.*

Being drawn in the king's presence is enough to warrant immediate execution. All hands on deck need to take note and react appropriately to what would be treated as an attempted assassination, whether or not it actually is. In particular, the king's guards need to surround him and the queen, whilst keeping Warwick and Suffolk at bay. A safe distance between the monarch(s) and combatants having been achieved, the guards will then want to put an end to the fight. It would be wise for Warwick and Suffolk to lay down their swords and step away from them, but up to you to decide if this occurs neatly.

There is a slight break in the violence whilst Salisbury declares the sentence required by the clamouring mob at the door. The king acquiesces and pronounces banishment of Suffolk, within three days on 'paine of death'. You can resume the physical dynamics amongst Suffolk, Margaret, and Henry from earlier in the scene, until Henry exits in dismay.

*See Glossary – Intimacy.*

This is the last scene in which to track the Margaret and Suffolk SexyTimez™ (whilst Suffolk is alive anyway). [*JK: Eeeeeewwwwwwwwwwwww!!!*] [*SD: Oh, please, Jared. Let him who is without necrophilic experience cast the first gravestone.*] This scene takes plenty of emotional twists and turns. We mentioned in 1.3 that you could think of these two like the Macbeths minus the morals. We did not, however, say you should avoid empathising with them. Set aside proper rehearsal time and find a way to make even these garbage bags seem human.

## Act 3  Scene 3

The cardinal makes his final confession, terrifying himself to death. Expiration by emotion may seem unlikely, but fear can trigger fatal amounts of adrenaline. The damage of severe ventricular fibrillation may cause sudden death. The actor playing Winchester can sell his final fits as a heart attack.

## Act 4  Scene 1

*See Glossary – Arrests; Binds (maybe); Draws (maybe); Knees (maybe); Strikes (maybe).*

*Alarum. Fight at Sea. Ordnance goes off.*

[*JK: If you have the budget to show an entire 'Fight at Sea', please pick up the phone and call me.*] You probably won't be staging a full-out attack but can make it clear one is taking place – cannon sounds, 'jumping aboard' from one section of the stage to another, and a skirmish or two to give the illusion of a grander battle happening off stage.

Explore in rehearsal whether things get physical during the ransom negotiations since tensions are extremely high – Whitmore just lost an eye in battle with the prisoners, and the lieutenant delivers one hell of a speech about how much the people hate Suffolk. The gentlemen might fall to their knees to plead, but Suffolk makes a point of refusing to stoop. Notwithstanding, Whitmore could force Suffolk to the ground. Just because he is imperious when faced with a death sentence, this does not mean he leaves with Whitmore quietly. There could be a struggle requiring him to punch Suffolk in the guts (or further south since everyone but the king seems to know Suffolk and Margaret were boning).

William de la Pole, 1st Duke of Suffolk, was murdered while his ship was sailing him to exile. James William Edmund Doyle, 1864. (*Public domain*)

*See Glossary – Carries.*

*Enter Walter with the body.*

*Wal.* There let his head, and liuelesse bodie lye,
Vntill the Queene his Mistris bury it.

*Exit Walter.*

1. *Gent.* O barbarous and bloudy spectacle,
His body will I beare vnto the King:
If he reuenge it not, yet will his Friends,
So will the Queene, that liuing, held him deere.

If you choose to follow history, note that it took six swings of a rusty sword to separate Suffolk's head from his body. [*SD: If you opted for the decapitation drinking game offered in Chapter 7 –* King John *(3.2), congratulations on your patience until now. This fourth act will more than make up for the delay.*] Get splashes of blood on Whitmore's face and clothes. The corpse should be dripping blood as well. You'll need to work with costumes to create something that brings Suffolk's outfit over his head so he appears decapitated, or use a fake body.

Cover the head in blood, as the severed carotid arteries would spray everywhere. Whitmore can have the body over one shoulder, and the head in his other hand. If you use a fake body, Whitmore could just drag the corpse by one foot whilst bearing the head under his arm like a football.

## Act 4  Scene 2

*See Glossary – Arrests; Binds (maybe); Carries (maybe); Draws; Ensemble Readiness; Strikes (maybe).*

Hints of a class rebellion have been a long time coming; now, it has arrived in full. Consider working with your design team and fight director to use the set as proxy for England writ large. Destruction. Havoc. Bedlam. Multiple murders and beheadings ensue. Plenty of bathos as well, in an absurd brand of comedy Shakespeare will later perfect in Volume Two – *Titus Andronicus*. Have a rollicking good time and scare the everloving shit out of the nobility.

You can start with a few random acts of violence at the top of the scene, made all the more amusing if Bevis and Holland are oblivious – *e.g.* a character running out of town with everything they own in their arms; a noble failing to escape some muggers; one person dragging another across stage by the hair; bricks being tossed at supernumeraries or set pieces, *etc.* There are endless permutations of the chaos Jack Cade and his rebels could foment. Again, work with your production team to help build items that can be pushed over, thrown, or flipped without permanently damaging them. And consider what kind of person Jack Cade is. He speaks in the royal 'We' from the get-go, which is an immediate red flag. Is he violent, or does he leave that to his subjects? Dedicate significant rehearsal time to staging this upheaval of the kingdom so it will be ripe for destruction upon York's return from Ireland.

We mentioned in 3.2 the beginnings of a feeling like that in Act 3 of *Julius Caesar*, but this will now be taken to the nth degree. The psychology of a mob still holds – whilst no individual necessarily wants to 'throw the first stone' during the ensuing interrogations, once someone does, the rest of the crowd will feel emboldened to attack.

Note that the stage direction requires Cade to enter with 'infinite numbers'. This could be horrifying (if your budget can handle 100 background actors) or hilarious (if you have cardboard cutouts or painted backdrops of crowds of violent commoners and sound effects to go with them).

The clerk enters to account for his sin of literacy, a charge which tells us much about the crowd. Does he enter of his own volition? Is he prodded with bizarre makeshift weapons? Is he dragged in and thrown to Cade's feet? How much does the clerk resist? Was he apprehended with a pleasant invitation, or ambushed with a bag over his head? We can't list every possibility in this scene, let alone the entire act. We ask you again to dedicate real rehearsal hours and explore your cast's chemistry. Since norms will be given little (if any) regard, neither the clerk nor the audience should have any idea what is to come next.

The clerk's hanging having been ordered, we're about to find out if a bump up in class will be of use to the next set of unlucky bastards who have to engage with Cade and his cronies. To even things out before the nobles enter, Cade decides to perform a knighting like no other in the canon – on himself.

As always, don't take anything for granted – is Cade an expert with a sword or a complete idiot? Maybe he almost hits another character (or himself), or does indeed land a blow, maybe even fatal. The world is upside down and you have a lot of leeway here.

> *Cade.* To equall him I will make my selfe a knight pre-
> sently; Rise vp Sir *Iohn Mortimer.* Now haue at him.

The civil norms of parley have been deteriorating for some time and this next moment can devolve even further. The Staffords' aggressive opening would normally be admirable, but here it is meaningless. Cade and his followers are drunk with the power of rebellion and have nothing to lose. Explore ways they can toy with the Staffords until they finally give in, proclaim Cade and his followers traitors, and get ready for battle.

## Act 4  Scene 3

Historically, the king marched through London to the rebel camp at Blackheath, but it was deserted. Cade moved to Sevenoaks because the road was narrow. Once the royal army was bottlenecked, the ambush began. Stafford and his brother were killed. The king fled, leaving the city undefended.

*Alarums to the fight, wherein both the Staffords are slaine.*

[JK: You can create a full battle scene or not. I find it interesting to mirror history. The rebels flank centrestage, but hide; the Staffords enter with the English troops; the rebels can pop out shooting arrows (see Chapter 13 – Henry 5 (4.4; 4.6)), and/or engage in sword fights (or weapons appropriate to the time period in which your production is set). The rebels win, so the troops can be chased off stage by Cade and a few others, allowing them to re-enter at the top of the scene. We should see the Staffords killed on stage, so that Cade can take the 'Monument of *the victory' (the body armour) off a Stafford corpse.*] [*SD: I used to have a hard time believing Cade and his followers were smart enough to pull this off, or the Staffords dumb enough to fall for it, but I saw how easily the US Congress was sieged and realised anything is possible.*]

## Act 4  Scene 4

> *Enter the King with a Supplication, and the Queene with Suffolkes head, the Duke of Buckingham, and the Lord Say.*

If you kept the head off stage earlier, you can bring in a luxurious bag with the bottom covered in dried blood. The only problem with this is that Margaret specifically mentions Suffolk's face, which is a bit clunky if she's staring into a bag. If you can, spend the time and money to create a replica of Suffolk's head.

Consider merging the end of this scene with the entirety of the next, pushing through the act, and not taking your foot off the gas until York's majestic return in 5.1. If you have anything left in your budget, feel free to show instead of just tell – stage the taking of the bridge!

## Act 4  Scene 6

The mob is in complete ecstasy; they shouldn't have had much luck earlier in battle, yet they were successful. Let the collective adrenaline rush fuel further killings.

> *Enter Iacke Cade and the rest, and strikes his staffe on London stone.*

Cade. Now is *Mortimer* Lord of this City,
And heere sitting vpon London Stone,
I charge and command, that of the Cities cost
The pissing Conduit run nothing but Clarret Wine
This first yeare of our raigne.
And now henceforward it shall be Treason for any,
That calles me other then Lord *Mortimer*.

> *Enter a Soldier running.*

Soul. Iacke Cade, Iacke Cade.
Cade. Knocke him downe there.

> *They kill him.*

The murder of this soldier need not be drawn out. As soon as ~~Cade~~ Mortimer issues the order, have one of the rebels grab the soldier, and another slit the soldier's throat (or stab below the heart to sever the descending aorta for a quick kill). This way, the body can drop and the next two lines can come quickly. Or they can just shoot him. Whichever is funniest and stays a second or two ahead of the audience's anticipation rate.

> *But*. If this Fellow be wise, hee'l neuer call yee *Iacke*
> *Cade* more, I thinke he hath a very faire warning.
>     *Dicke*. My Lord, there's an Army gathered together
> in Smithfield.
>     *Cade*. Come, then let's go fight with them:
> But first, go and set London Bridge on fire,
> And if you can, burne downe the Tower too.
> Come, let's away.

If you've already been spending the big bucks, set London Bridge on fire! Each decision you make throughout this act should leave the nation as vulnerable as possible for York's landing in 5.1. Literal scorched earth would certainly assist towards this end.

## Act 4  Scene 7

> *Alarums. Mathew Goffe is slain, and all the rest.*

Continue making this act one big battle. You can have a large force meet on stage to dispatch Goffe and 'all the rest'.

*See Glossary – Arrests; Binds (maybe); Draws (maybe); Strikes (maybe).*

If you're continuing to show some of the violence mentioned, you could have the army 'burne all the Records of the Realme' during the ensuing interrogation of Lord Say.

>     *Cade*. Giue him a box o'th' eare, and that wil make 'em
> red againe.

It's unclear if Say actually gets a box on the ear like Eleanor in 1.3 but, considering everything that has happened up to now, it's quite probable. And others may taunt and torture Say throughout, in accordance with your production's whims.

Did you mistakenly spend the entirety of your severed-head budget solely on Suffolk? Time to raise more money! Say will be taken off and beheaded. Then Cromer must be found off stage and beheaded. #cheers

*Enter one with the heads.*

Someone re-enters with each of the heads on a pole. You might be tempted to bring them in some other way, but the rebels would follow the exact instructions of 'bring them both vppon two poles hither' since we just saw a soldier killed for unwittingly calling ~~Cade~~ Mortimer by his old name. What would he do to someone disobeying a direct order? It's also in keeping with a recurring theme in our next chapter. [*SD: Heads on poles. Not the make-out session that now ensues, leading to the first (and only) homonecrophilic act in the canon.*]

> *Cade.* But is not this brauer:
> Let them kisse one another: For they lou'd well
> When they were aliue. Now part them againe,
> Least they consult about the giuing vp
> Of some more Townes in France. Soldiers,
> Deferre the spoile of the Citie vntill night:
> For with these borne before vs, in steed of Maces,
> Will we ride through the streets, & at euery Corner
> Haue them kisse. Away.

## Act 4  Scene 8

*See Glossary – Draws; Ensemble Readiness.*

KEEP. UP. THE. MAYHEM. Stalk the aisles and back of the house, bang crappy armour, destroy more set pieces, *etc.*

> *Alarum, and Retreat. Enter againe Cade, and all his rabblement.*

> *Cade.* Vp Fish-streete, downe Saint Magnes corner,
> kill and knocke downe, throw them into Thames:

> *Sound a parley.*

This parley, unlike earlier ones throughout the act, appears to remain non-violent. It is a battle for the allegiance of a mob that switches several times. They eventually desert Cade, who realises his reign is at an end. Whether the rebels are tired, or moved by the thought of Henry 5 and a pardon from his son, or this plotline has simply come to a close since the kingdom is now destabilised enough for York's purposes, all good things must end.

*Cade.* Was euer Feather so lightly blowne too & fro,
as this multitude? The name of Henry the fift, hales them
to an hundred mischiefes, and makes them leaue mee de-
solate. I see them lay their heades together to surprize
me. My sword make way for me, for heere is no staying:
in despight of the diuels and hell, haue through the verie
middest of you, and heauens and honor be witnesse, that
no want of resolution in mee, but onely my Followers
base and ignominious treasons, makes me betake mee to
my heeles.

Cade is concerned for his safety. He is drawn and ready to fight his way out if necessary
('My sword make way for me'). Do the rebels politely part as Cade flees, or does he have
to swing at a few menacing traitors to the cause?

## Act 4  Scene 9

*Enter Multitudes with Halters about their Neckes.*

See Chapter 8 – *Edward 3 (5.1).*

## Act 4  Scene 10

*Cade.* By my Valour: the most compleate Champi-
on that euer I heard. Steele, if thou turne the edge, or
cut not out the burly bon'd Clowne in chines of Beefe,
ere thou sleepe in thy Sheath, I beseech Ioue on my knees
thou mayst be turn'd to Hobnailes.

*Heere they Fight.*

O I am slaine, Famine and no other hath slaine me, let ten
thousand diuelles come against me, and giue me but the
ten meales I haue lost, and I'de defie them all. Wither
Garden, and be henceforth a burying place to all that do
dwell in this house, because the vnconquered soule of
*Cade* is fled.

This fight can be as long or short as you like in order to reveal more about the characters.
Iden has been presented as kind-hearted and fair. This should come through in his fighting
style. Depending on what choices you made regarding Cade's martial prowess up to this
point, add to his given circumstances five days of starvation and a heavy sword. Lifting,

let alone swinging, will be difficult and affect his fighting style. The harder he tries, and the less Iden does (deflecting rather than striking), will establish Iden as a good guy. [*SD: Insofar as that carries any currency in this world. Which it doesn't.*]

> *Iden.* Is't *Cade* that I haue slain, that monstrous traitor?
> Sword, I will hallow thee for this thy deede,
> And hang thee o're my Tombe, when I am dead.
> Ne're shall this blood be wiped from thy point,
> But thou shalt weare it as a Heralds coate,
> To emblaze the Honor that thy Master got.
> *Cade. Iden* farewell, and be proud of thy victory: Tell
> Kent from me, she hath lost her best man, and exhort all
> the World to be Cowards: For I that neuer feared any,
> am vanquished by Famine, not by Valour.

*Dyes.*

[*JK: There are many times characters sustain mortal wounds but also have death speeches. Try to avoid injuries to the chest that could perforate the lung. Aim below the diaphragm for injuries that can at least partially sever the descending aorta. The internal bleeding can be mixed with the pain of stomach acids or liver bile to give the actor specific actable choices whilst dying.*]

> *Id.* How much thou wrong'st me, heauen be my iudge;
> Die damned Wretch, the curse of her that bare thee:
> And as I thrust thy body in with my sword,
> So wish I, I might thrust thy soule to hell.
> Hence will I dragge thee headlong by the heeles
> Vnto a dunghill, which shall be thy graue,
> And there cut off thy most vngracious head,
> Which I will beare in triumph to the King,
> Leauing thy trunke for Crowes to feed vpon.

*Exit.*

*See Glossary – Carries.*

Dragging from the feet is a little more dangerous. We recommend starting the motion and then fading to black before the actor has to be dragged too far. See Chapter 3 – *Hamlet* (3.4).

## Act 5  Scene 1

*See Glossary – Draws; Ensemble Readiness.*

*Enter Yorke, and his Army of Irish, with Drum and Colours.*

The Irish army should be more organised than Cade's rebels but still have a dangerous feel. Cade's men were unruly and had crude weaponry; York's are professionals with proper equipment and funny haircuts. They can draw and cheer York on – a threatening picture when Buckingham enters. There is a fine line here as there is no direct threat to Buckingham (*i.e.* no soldier should charge), but there should be an air of uncertainty about what is going to happen.

Once York dismisses the soldiers, they should sheath any drawn weapons and depart in peace.

*Enter Iden with Cades head.*

If you don't know your options for bringing on a head, the fourth one in this play, you have not been paying attention and we can't help you.

*See Glossary – Arrests (attempted); Draws (maybe); Ensemble Readiness; Grabs (maybe); Knees (for Iden and Old Clifford, not Somerset's dumbass request); Strikes (maybe); OODLES OF THINGS!!!*

Somerset barks commands to arrest York and, whilst it's unlikely to occur, you must determine how close it gets. If Somerset motions to the guards, do they respect the order enough to begin moving towards York?

You will once again need to decide whether any violence breaks out amongst the lords. Note that the number of wildcards increases here with our introduction to York's most famous kid – the Crookback. He will murder virtually everyone in his way for the next ten acts on the road to becoming Richard 3. Also keep an eye on Young Clifford who gets testier over the next few acts until his demise.

Deeply tense summits like this are the new norm. Most of the participants are highly skilled fighters, as opposed to some in prior parleys, which mostly remained verbal in nature. Be specific with each character's level of training and martial ability. [*JK: I teach Violence Performance Theory to give actors clarity in their choices on training levels. Your fight director has hopefully thought of this as well and can talk the actors through it.*] [*SD: I teach Liver Destruction Theory but the course is currently closed due to the professor having consumed the entirety of the supplies.*]

## Act 5  Scene 2

*[JK: Much to Seth's chagrin, and because you should end the play with a bang, I recommend fully staging this first battle, as it is the official start of the Wars of the Roses.] [SD: The Wars of the Roses started in Chapter 14 – Henry 6 Part 1 (2.4), Jared.] [JK: Um, no, Seth. It's the First Battle of St Albans.] [SD: I suspect, dearest Jared, our disagreement is based on your allergy to politics – you think a war begins with a battle when, in actuality, it begins with plucking flowers.]*

If you want to go big instead of just staging the individual fights, you can bring on troops from both sides to clash centrestage. Amongst the fighting, Warwick can peel away downstage, shouting for Old Clifford. The larger battle can surround the speaking characters and the audience. Maybe Warwick dispatches a few soldiers before Old Clifford finally arrives. As the dialogue ensues, make sure no one relaxes their guard; we've mentioned it from the beginning of this volume – do not stop acting to start a fight, or *vice versa.*

When Warwick and York see Old Clifford, you may want to physicalise the moment. Warwick can start for Old Clifford. York either gets in between them or, if York is behind, he can pull back Warwick's shoulder.

This particular engagement is an opportunity to show York's honourable side. *[SD: Which will be important to set up since it is, contrary to popular belief, his son Richard's primary call to action throughout Chapter 16 – Henry 6 Part 3 and Chapter 17 – Richard 3 rather than just a simplistic resentment of his own deformities. More on that later. A lot more. Because I haven't shut up about it for decades.]* York respects Old Clifford, especially after the pass they just had off stage in which they killed each other's horses, and York wants to win fair and square. Perhaps he disarms Old Clifford and, instead of killing him, York backs away and allows the old man to retrieve his weapon(s) and continue fighting. Something along these lines will make sense of York's eulogy over his elder's corpse.

*See Glossary – Carries.*

Young Clifford enters, speechifies, and takes away pappy's cadaver.

### Enter Richard, and Somerset to fight.

If you're producing this as a standalone production, it will mean little to audiences unfamiliar with the play that a random, disabled fighter can defeat Somerset. But those attending a history play are often nerds and know exactly who the victor here will eventually become. You may as well create a fight to cover all demographics. We'll discuss Richard's fighting style in depth over the next two chapters but you will need to set things up here, particularly if you're producing two or more of these plays in rotating repertory. *[SD: Plenty of options for you to explore. By way of example, I spent the better part of my early adulthood directing and playing the role. I opted for a longsword in my right hand (which doubled as a crutch when sheathed) and a dagger in my left hand (the fingers gnarled around it, with some physical limitations in the wrist and elbow, to justify Richard's later description of his arm as 'a blasted sapling, wither'd up').*]

Somerset doesn't get a final line. If there's anything left you want to reveal about his character, it will have to happen in the fight. Richard's father has held Somerset in little regard over these last ten acts, but this does not mean Somerset is as hideous a fighter as he is a person. And Richard's martial reputation is not necessarily established by this point. [*SD: Play him as 15 in this scene, as he is granted multiple military titles and independent commands from age 17, and I doubt even Somerset would be dumb enough to engage with Richard by that point. Indeed, it says something further of Somerset's cowardice if he actively sought out Richard in the hope he would be an easy kill.*] You could just elect to have Somerset 'fight by the book' and do everything correctly, but then have Richard do something not found in any textbook, taking Somerset (and some of the audience) by surprise. [*SD: If you really want a nice button to the character, and since I previously declared my bias against Somerset, you could have him make fun of Richard before the fight. This choice is very much in line with Somerset's character and will make the audience root for Richard. It will also continue to set up the nobility of the Yorkists, thereby underlining the tragedy in the opening act of the next play when they are systematically tortured and killed.*] [*JK: #spoilers*]

If, miraculously, you still have the budget, and if you want to bring the total headcount in this play to five, feel free to stage the decapitation of Somerset's here (since Richard ventriloquises it in the opening scene of the next play).

*Fight. Excursions.*
*Enter King, Queene, and others.*

The stage direction is clear regarding further battle before the monarchs arrive. As Richard exits, it's time for another big battle moment so the audience do not think things are dying down. As this chaos fades off stage in one direction, have Henry, Margaret, and the others enter fleeing from it. If you make the 'others' referenced here the king's guards, they can continue to fight occasional rebels rushing the stage. Maybe one even gets through and Margaret has to fight whilst Clifford is speaking. Use moments like these to maintain a sense of urgency.

*See Glossary – Grabs (maybe); Strikes (maybe).*

With all that Margaret has endured, she is now at her wits' end. Her disrespect of Henry is open. Margaret can try to strike some sense into her husband. Ensure her violence is in proportion with how much Henry resists leaving. Margaret can push, pull, smack, and slap through all of this. Young Clifford enters (maybe fighting) and agrees the monarchs should flee. Does this convince Henry? If he remains steadfast in his desire to stay put, Clifford can aid Margaret in forcibly removing the king. Alternatively, an enemy can charge at the king, with Clifford yelling 'Away my Lord, away' as he intercepts the enemy.

# Chapter 16

# Henry 6 Part 3

*'But to prevent the tyrant's violence'* – Elizabeth (4.4)

## Act 1  Scene 1[1]

*See Glossary – Draws (maybe); Ensemble Readiness; Strikes (maybe).*

The stakes in this play start at 1,000 per cent and climb. We mentioned some of the wildcards at play in Chapter 15 – *Henry 6 Part 2* (5.1) – Richard and Young Clifford. Continue to track how well (or poorly) they are reined in by their superiors. Others may break with decorum as the scene progresses since King Henry agrees to strip his own line of power upon his death.

*He stampes with his foot, and the Souldiers shew themselues.*

*See Glossary – Draws.*

Warwick, with or without York's knowledge, has been hiding troops in the event verbal negotiations come to an impasse and York requires/desires military backup. Are the soldiers a quiet power whose mere presence is enough to make the point? Or do they enter menacingly, immediately putting the Lancastrians on point? Whichever you choose, it should increase the intensity enough that Henry is forced to think quickly to save his reign.

*See Glossary – Strikes (maybe).*

Westmoreland, Northumberland, and Young Clifford seek out Margaret, knowing full well she's the only Lancastrian left who can knock any sense into Henry. As was the case with her lengthy speech in Chapter 15 – *Henry 6 Part 2* (3.2), your Margaret can deploy several different tactics here in admonishing Henry – slaps, smacks, grabs, spits, pushes, drags. What makes Margaret's bullying of Henry different here from the prior play is the addition of their son – Prince Edward. Margaret now has another weapon in her arsenal to guilt Henry into shape. And she can use him as a teaching tool, to show her son what behaviours to avoid once he is eventually crowned.

## Act 1  Scene 2

*See Glossary – Grabs (maybe); Strikes (maybe).*

Take time to explore the physical dynamic of this family unit. Remember the brothers can be … well … brothers – pushing, prodding, poking. Just because the scene starts here doesn't mean the discussion did. Does their uncle have to break them up? Or does York do so when he arrives? We only have a few scenes left with York; distinguish, as much as you can here, the relationships with his children. York might backhand Richard when he says 'Your Right depends not on his life, or death' since, at first blush, the suggestion seems dishonourable. Edward could come to Richard's defence, jumping in between him and their father.

[*SD: Once Richard has the opportunity to elaborate, his argument is clearly compelling enough to get York on board with the ethics of proceeding, and to get the whole family on the same page. Whilst you've already had a scene in this act (and the final act of the prior play) to set up Richard's idolising of his father, that could have been chalked up to the generic admiration of a teenage boy. It is in this scene that we start to understand the elasticity of Richard's mind, and the specifics behind trying to get his father on the throne – literally or spiritually – for the next nine acts. There are multiple lines in Chapter 17 – Richard 3 that make no sense to an audience when they see the standalone play. Those lines are often cut or just muttered as throwaways. This play makes sense of them, conferring far more dimensionality on Richard than that of some cartoon villain. I'll continue tracking this with you in Richard's ensuing scenes.*]

## Act 1  Scene 3

*See Glossary – Blood; Blood Packs (maybe); Faints (maybe); Knees (maybe).*

Is the tutor armed? If so, how well can he fight? If not, does he try throwing books? He's clearly passionate and desperate to save his pupil. Just because Young Clifford spares the tutor's life doesn't mean he is taken away gently by the soldiers.

Rutland either plays possum or actually faints. Either way, he is on the ground when Young Clifford crosses over to him. You will have to make a series of decisions as to whether your production's Young Clifford is brutal and remorseless, or if there are some chinks in the armour Rutland can target with his pleas.

If the former, you can start the violence right at the top and have Young Clifford kick Rutland to 'wake' him. Young Clifford could continue pushing Rutland down, punching him in the face and guts, and turning the boy into pulp before stabbing him.

If the latter – and this is more interesting – there will be little (if any) violence prior to the kill as Rutland almost prevails in appealing to Young Clifford's conscience. (This trait runs in the family – Rutland's older brother Clarence also has the gift of the gab when faced with murderers of his own, early in the next play, and nearly survives.)

Once Rutland is finally stabbed, feel free to use some stage blood, since it will play such a crucial role in the next scene, but keep the napkin a secret.

*The Murder of Rutland by Lord Clifford.* Charles Robert Leslie, 1815. (*Pennsylvania Academy of the Fine Arts*)

## Act 1  Scene 4

*See Glossary – Binds (maybe); Blood; Blood Packs; Ensemble Readiness; Knees (maybe); Strikes.*

Jaime West as Rutland and Thomas Westphal as Young Clifford. (*The York Shakespeare Company, 2003*)

The fact that York is faint suggests blood loss from injuries sustained in battle. These could be mostly non-life-threatening, but there is probably at least one wound to the body York knows is fatal when he declares his 'Sands are numbred'. A solid cut to the flank or puncture wound to the abdomen would do the trick. This also provides further justification for why he doesn't flee the Lancastrians, besides the fact he was never the type to run away from a fight.

When Margaret enters, Young Clifford and his weapon should still be drenched in Rutland's blood. You may encounter difficulty in keeping regular blood products on a blade this long. Apply some thick blood to the blade, then some wet blood for a good effect.

You will have an opportunity on 'But buckler with thee blowes twice two for one' for Young Clifford to get a few punches in, which might bring York to his knees. If you'd like to get some blood from Young Clifford's punches, have someone slip York a blood pack. After the first punch or two, York can bring his hands up to his face, as part of the reaction, and pop the blood pack in his mouth. On the next hit, York can spit out the blood as he is struck.

Margaret orders Young Clifford to stop, an order which goes unregarded, and so she pleads for Northumberland to intervene. If his words are not enough, he might have to physically restrain Young Clifford. You could take a cue from the language – have one of Young Clifford's punches go to York's face on 'a Curre doth grinne'. This could also be Northumberland's way of getting into the mix. He may very well push Young Clifford off York with those first few lines like a teacher, scolding Young Clifford for using his hands, and then turn to give York a boot to the head on 'spurne him with his Foot away' as the button to his lesson.

*See Glossary – Carries.*

After Margaret commands Young Clifford and Northumberland to pick up York, remember that his injuries will hurt as he is dragged around.

> Where are your Messe of Sonnes, to back you now?
> The wanton *Edward*, and the lustie *George?*
> And where's that valiant Crook-back Prodigie.
> *Dickie*, your Boy, that with his grumbling voyce
> Was wont to cheare his Dad in Mutinies?
> Or with the rest, where is your Darling, *Rutland?*
> Looke *Yorke*, I stayn'd this Napkin with the blood
> That valiant *Clifford*, with his Rapiers point,
> Made issue from the Bosome of the Boy:
> And if thine eyes can water for his death,
> I giue thee this to drie thy Cheekes withall.

You have some options for the reveal of the napkin. A common choice is for Margaret to inquire after Rutland, feigning temporary ignorance; she then retrieves the napkin from wherever it is on her person (or from Young Clifford if still in his possession); slowly savours the reveal; then throws the napkin at York's face.

There is another choice. We have repeatedly mentioned that the impact of a shocking event is diminished if the audience have time to see it coming (see Chapter 1 – *King Lear* (5.3); Chapter 3 – *Hamlet* (5.2); Chapter 4 – *Macbeth* (5.7); Chapter 9 – *Richard 2* (5.5); and Chapter 15 – *Henry 6 Part 2* (4.6)). Try the following: instead of simply binding York and letting him stand in place on the molehill of his own volition, continue to have him restrained by Young Clifford and Northumberland. As Margaret asks after York's children, she can move in to wipe York's face of its sweat in a moment of false sympathy. Don't let the audience see the contents of the napkin, and keep Margaret's back to the audience until after she says Rutland's name. As Margaret steps aside, revealing the nature of her torture device, York and the audience will experience it simultaneously.

York gives Margaret little to work with. She might, out of frustration, pick up the napkin and smear his cheeks with it, if she hadn't done so earlier. If he puts up any struggle, Young Clifford or Northumberland can pull York's head back to keep it still for Margaret.

> Alas poore *Yorke*, but that I hate thee deadly,
> I should lament thy miserable state.
> I prythee grieue, to make me merry, *Yorke*.
> What, hath thy fierie heart so parcht thine entrayles,
> That not a Teare can fall, for *Rutlands* death?
> Why art thou patient, man? thou should'st be mad:
> And I, to make thee mad, doe mock thee thus.

This 'mock' could be the cheek-drying or a separate action, such as probing a finger into York's open wound(s). Still, he gives her nothing.

> Stampe, raue, and fret, that I may sing and dance.
> Thou would'st be fee'd, I see, to make me sport:
> *Yorke* cannot speake, vnlesse he weare a Crowne.
> A Crowne for *Yorke*; and Lords, bow lowe to him:

[*JK: If you chose to have Young Clifford and Northumberland continue to restrain York,*] [*SD: or the soldiers if they've come in as substitutes (and, by the way, make sure you're directing them too even though they're in the background since a few of them may vomit or otherwise react to this horror show),*] [*JK: one could take over and pull York's hands behind his back, or bind his hands in front to make some of the actions with the hanky and crown easier. This way, the other can find something from which to fashion a crown.*] [*SD: **What the hell are you talking about? Is this Arts and Crafts with the Lancastrians?!***] [*JK: Or she could take her own crown off and jam it on his head. Okay? Sure, I guess it's possible that Margaret spent days, weeks, or years eagerly anticipating this moment on her vision board and has a paper crown at the ready in this scene.*] [*SD: Thank you for finally seeing the light.*] [*JK: I'm just saying that, historically, York was slain in battle and a paper crown was not put on his head until after it was cut off, so it doesn't have to be a paper crown in this scene.*] [*SD: But it is a paper crown, Jared.*] [*JK: I know that is convenient, Seth, but it's really strange that Margaret would carry a paper crown around just in case this moment ever came to pass. Looks to me like Shakespeare is conflating two different things from history.*] [*SD: The history plays have little to do with actual history.*] [*JK: FFS, I'm aware but the history they are referencing is interesting to know so we can make other choices. They don't need to do what everyone always does. The crown being paper is not explicitly mentioned in this play.*] [*SD: It's a paper crown in this scene because that's the only way the line in Chapter 17 – Richard 3 (1.3), spoken by the titular character, will make any sense ('When thou didst Crown his Warlike Brows with Paper').*] [*JK: I KNOW AND I AGREE EVEN THOUGH THIS IS THE HUNDREDTH TIME I'VE ASKED YOU TO STOP SAYING 'TITULAR' BUT I'M JUST SAYING THEY DON'T HAVE TO MAKE IT A PAPER CROWN HERE!!!*] [*SD: It's a paper crown.*] [*JK: I hate you.*] [*SD:................*] [*JK:................*] [*SD: It's a paper crown.*]

> Off with the Crowne; and with the Crowne, his Head,
> And whilest we breathe, take time to doe him dead.
>   *Clifford.* That is my Office, for my Fathers sake.

Young Clifford needs to move towards York on this, prompting Margaret's command to stop. This time, the order is followed.

> *Northumb.* Had he been slaughter-man to all my Kinne,
> I should not for my Life but weepe with him,

To see how inly Sorrow gripes his Soule.
 *Queen.* What, weeping ripe, my Lord *Northumberland?*
Thinke but vpon the wrong he did vs all,
And that will quickly drie thy melting Teares.

Depending on your version of Margaret, it's possible she smacks Northumberland here.

 *Clifford.* Heere's for my Oath, heere's for my Fathers Death.
 *Queene.* And heere's to right our gentle-hearted King.
 *Yorke.* Open thy Gate of Mercy, gracious God,
My Soule flyes through these wounds, to seeke out thee.

Young Clifford and Margaret can carve up York with cuts and thrusts.

 *Queene.* Off with his Head, and set it on Yorke Gates,
So *Yorke* may ouer-looke the Towne of Yorke.

If you're feeling particularly bloodthirsty, Margaret could make a final deep cut across York's throat on 'Off with his Head' to start the process. You may choose to show the full beheading here, but remember it usually takes more than one stroke. It would be most effective to have Young Clifford raise his sword to do the deed, go to black, and source a practical sound effect from the stage. This will engage the audience's imagination more powerfully than actually showing the decapitation. Another option is to wait until 2.2 and let Henry's reaction do all the work. If you have a blockbuster-film budget and insist on staging a full beheading, do not do so here. We'll explain why in 2.6.

## Act 2  Scene 1

*See Glossary – Grabs (maybe); Strikes (maybe).*

There are moments here to physicalise some lines. Whilst Edward has no desire to hear the messenger relay the specifics of York's torture and murder, Richard might push Edward out of the way on 'Say how he dy'de, for I will heare it all'. Tensions are high. This is a good way to show how people deal with grief differently: some will remain in a state of shock; some choose to deny it actually happened; some become numb to everything as they don't have the capacity to deal with it yet; some express great anger, not at the incident but at each other. [*SD: Here, Edward immediately wallows in a tragic event he cannot change. This made me gag each evening as Richard. I didn't physically harm Edward, but it's certainly one way I could have played this scene. Which is a crucial one. I mentioned in earlier scenes that Richard's superobjective is not just 'I'm gonna get the crown cuz me iz ugly and peeps be so mean'. Rather, Richard wants to get his father on the throne either literally or spiritually. York's death leaves only the latter option, something which Buckingham in Chapter 17 – Richard 3 (3.7) calls 'the right Idea of your Father', a line that makes little or no sense without the context from this play. This scene also makes clear the moment in 1.2 of the next play, when Richard manipulates Lady Anne by claiming she is the first person to make him 'shed remorsefull teare', something he did not do even upon hearing of the deaths of his brother and father. Whilst his tears with her could be false, I don't think he's lying about failing to shed any here. He will maintain laser focus from here on out in getting a version of his father on the throne. This starts with getting Edward to stop crying and grow the hell up so he can assume the Yorkist mantle. If Richard's true objective the entire time was merely to get the crown for himself, he wouldn't bother grooming Edward at all. And I believe Richard would have backed Clarence after Edward's death if Clarence hadn't gone turncoat later in this play.] [JK: You and the spoilers.]*

## Act 2  Scene 2

*See Glossary – Grabs (maybe); Strikes (maybe).*

Henry's subjects haven't had much of an issue telling him what they think of his ill-suitedness to the throne, particularly in a period like this. Things may move beyond the verbal over the course of this play, given Henry's guards are so disinterested in protecting him that he gets captured. Twice.

There is plenty to explore in your rehearsal room: Young Clifford can get in Henry's face and maybe even push him, shake him, or grab his head and force him to 'Looke on the boy'; and Margaret can do whatever she bloody well pleases since everyone thinks she's the boss anyway.

You also have a potential comedic moment when Margaret makes Henry dub their son a knight – Henry has to lift a sword to perform the ritual, and this could be a five-act tragedy unto itself.

*See Glossary – Draws (super likely); Ensemble Readiness; Strikes (maybe).*

The stakes are high as the Yorkists enter, see the head of their *pater familias* on a spike, and come face to face with some of the murderers who placed it there. There was little reason before to regard the rules of parley and even less so now. A fight could break out at any moment; one or more of these loose cannons might finally place a hand on their sword to draw and get the game of dominoes going.

*[SD: Take the rehearsal time to explore each character's motivation in the scene. Even those dumbass Lancastrians (e.g. Prince Edward is now a knight and wants to impress his mummy; Young Clifford remains thirsty to avenge his father; and Margaret is … well … Margaret). And, for those of you tracking the 'right idea' of York that Richard is pursuing, whilst I harboured an unbearable impatience to 'Breake off the parley' ('for Gods sake Lords*

*giue signall to the fight'), I also recall being very optimistic about Edward in this scene when he finally grows some chest hair. Maybe he'll be a great facsimile of our pappy after all! \*crosses fingers\*]*

## Act 2  Scene 3

The Battle of Towton was one of the largest and bloodiest battles in English history. Some 50,000-65,000 soldiers fought in the middle of a snowstorm and half of them died. The Yorkists were victorious but Henry, Margaret, and Prince Edward all escaped to Scotland.

*Alarum. Excursions. Enter Warwicke.*

This scene kicks off with a battle. You could have the factions charge in from either side of the stage, alternating focus amongst the main characters, and then have Warwick peel downstage as he did in Chapter 15 – *Henry 6 Part 2* (5.2). Or you could keep the battle completely off stage and have Warwick enter breathless, eventually followed by his comrades.

Whilst Warwick has received many blows, this doesn't mean they all landed. Many could have been parried, but it sounds like a few got through. He might be holding a wound shut as he says 'strokes receiu'd' and check on the injury to see how bad it is. As the other sadsack Yorkists enter, decide if any of them have also sustained injuries (remember, if so, these need to be tracked throughout the play).

*[JK: We should have a sense of the brothers' physical relationship whenever they are together. Siblings will mess with each other but will also fiercely protect each other. How do these brothers interact in battle? Does each pursue an individual fighting style and foe, or do they function as a unit?]*

*See Glossary – Grabs (maybe); Strikes (maybe).*

*[SD: By the time Richard enters, it feels like the Yorkists are all but defeated. When playing Richard, I had zero patience for this watercooler whimpering. He only has nine lines to convince them to go back into battle and to win it. Explore physical motivations in addition to linguistic ones – slaps, shakes, grabs, etc.]*

## Act 2  Scene 4

*Excursions. Enter Richard and Clifford.*

There should be no breaks in the battle.

*They Fight, Warwicke comes, Clifford flies.*

Seth Duerr as Richard and Thomas Westphal as Young Clifford. (*The York Shakespeare Company, 2003*)

[*JK: I'm not sure why some productions stage the encounter between Richard and Young Clifford as an unarmed fight. It can and should be a sword fight, one that shows how great both warriors are. It's up to your production whether you have Young Clifford winning when Warwick enters, or if Richard is near victory and about to dispatch Young Clifford once and for all. Either option would anger Richard, but the latter will give Richard more impetus to chastise Warwick.*] [*SD: It only took 223 pages, but I finally agree with Jared. Also note that this is a callback to Chapter 15 – Henry 6 Part 2 (5.2), when York told Warwick to fuck off so that York could have Old Clifford alone. Yet again, Richard is pursuing 'the right idea of [his] father'.*]

## Act 2  Scene 5

*See Glossary – Carries.*

> *Alarum. Enter a Sonne that hath kill'd his Father, at one doore:*
> *and a Father that hath kill'd his Sonne at another doore.*

[*SD: If you've wisely made a drinking game of having a chug whenever 'excursions' are identified, congratulations – you are now several steps closer to requiring an ambulance.*]

> *Alarums.* **Excursions.** *Enter the Queen, the Prince, and Exeter.*

Here we are again – a droopy Henry loitering the battlefield. Use these excursions to snap him (and the audience) back to reality. The queen, prince, and Exeter can enter mid-fight, trying to fend off enemies. This will give urgency to the scene and drive Henry towards his offstage mount.

## Act 2  Scene 6

*A lowd alarum. Enter Clifford Wounded.*

What kind of injury is lethal but would allow Young Clifford to manage twenty-nine lines of mostly stable iambic pentameter? Young Clifford could enter with multiple wounds that slowly shut his body down. By having clarity on how he is injured, your fight director should be able to walk the actor through exactly what is happening to the body as it is dying. One wound could be to the chest cavity but external bleeding has stopped. This means internal bleeding is having a field day and would justify his noting 'much effuse of blood'. If a weapon pierced one chamber of his heart, this would force the other three to pump harder as the pericardium fills with blood, which will cause him to have a seizure and pass out ('doth make me faint') before eventually killing him. Alternatively, he could have a pierced lung, coughing up aerated blood as he delivers this speech, until his lung finally collapses and renders him unconscious. This kind of specificity will give the actor everything he needs to portray these final moments whilst providing a realistic reason for his death rattle later in the scene.

Next, you have the fun task of deciding what the Yorkists do to Young Clifford's corpse. The audience will likely offer you some latitude given that the person in question is a child killer. And the Yorkists are all pretty miffed that Young Clifford died in such an indecisive manner without any particular author getting to enjoy the kill. Keep your choices in line with what would be believable for each Yorkist, some appetites being broader than others.

You also get to choose whether or not to stage the decapitation. If Young Clifford raised his sword to decapitate York in 1.4, followed by a blackout and sound effect, you could repeat this here and have Richard perform the same preliminary tableau. We mentioned that if you have the budget and want to stage a full beheading, not to do so in 1.4. You will have lulled the audience into a false sense of security, forcing the assumption you will jump to black again here. BUT NOW GO FULL OUT!!! That'll keep 'em awake. And possibly soiled. For the mechanics of staging, see Chapter 4 – *Macbeth* (5.7).

## Act 3  Scene 1

*See Glossary – Arrests.*

*Enter Sinklo, and Humfrey, with Crosse-bowes in their hands.*

It doesn't seem like Henry puts up much of a fight here. He continues the play's discussion of oathbreaking for a bit, but ultimately goes with the hunters when they arrest him. [*SD: It's possible he could pull a move here like his spiritual predecessor, the titular character in Chapter 9* – Richard 2 *(5.5).*] [*JK: Go ahead. Say 'titular' one more time. See what happens.*] [*SD: But I suspect this scene is more like Chapter 17* – Richard 3 *(1.4), by which I mean Clarence and not the boobular character.*]

## Act 3  Scene 2

*See Glossary – Grabs (unlikely); Intimacy; Strikes (unlikely).*

We don't anticipate physical violence in this scene. It is far more sinister of a reveal if this remains a polite conversation, headed in the direction of finding a noble solution for the widow's recent loss, right up until the moment it turns into nothing more than Edward wanting to get laid. You should still rehearse with an intimacy coordinator and fight director, as your actors may have physical impulses that could benefit your production.

[*SD: Either way, Elizabeth wisely makes marriage the price for Edward's desires. Whilst Richard might respect the nerve of her gambit in an alternate timeline, Edward has just sacrificed the political gains that would have flowed from marrying Lady Bona of France. Putting the kingdom before himself now takes Edward out of the running in Richard's race to install the right idea of their father. This is what triggers Richard's first great soliloquy. I entertained suspicions about Edward ever since his whingeing in 2.1, but it wasn't until now he fully confirmed himself useless. So, he's gotta go. And I've always harboured disgust for Prince Edward and his spineless father. Those are obvious kills. Clarence, thus far, hasn't particularly shown himself unworthy to assume our father's mantle, but neither did he do much to stand out. His future as a flip-flopper may have been detected by Edward back in 2.1, when he chose to give Clarence a smaller dukedom than me. Since power has clearly been on my mind, developing with each act, the reason to object and request that Edward give Clarence the greater stake was twofold – feigning humility, and testing Clarence's thirst. His silence and Edward's insistence shut the door for me on whether Clarence was a viable candidate for the throne, winnowing the field to Edward and me. Edward only had to royally fuck up once and it would seal his fate. Now he's done it, putting his dick before his country.*]

## Act 3  Scene 3

*See Glossary – Draws (maybe); Ensemble Readiness; Grabs (maybe); Strikes (unlikely).*

*Enter Warwicke.*

*Lewis.* What's hee approacheth boldly to our presence?

Warwick rushes in. The king's guards should react accordingly, based on how close Warwick gets to the king. The same goes for Margaret in her interactions with the king.

What Margaret would do to Warwick, if she could, would take up a greater volume of text than we are allowed. Margaret is vicious but also shrewd. She would probably not attack Warwick, but might be considering a variation on her Duchess of Gloucester schtick (see Chapter 15 – *Henry 6 Part 2* (1.3)).

Oxford and Warwick get heated as well, but are unlikely to get physical in front of Lewis, as this would only alienate his sympathies.

## Act 4  Scene 1

*See Glossary – Ensemble Readiness.*

Clarence and Somerset turn coat against Edward but, as in 3.2, we do not anticipate physical violence as a feature of Edward's court prior to formal battle. You may feel otherwise. Get on with yo bad self.

## Act 4  Scene 2

*See Glossary – Draws (maybe); Ensemble Readiness.*

Out of an abundance of caution, the soldiers should stop Clarence and Somerset as they approach. Once Warwick has determined these are friends rather than foes, the soldiers can stand down.

## Act 4  Scene 3

*See Glossary – Arrests; Binds (maybe); Carries; Ensemble Readiness; Strikes (maybe).*

> *Enter Warwicke, Clarence, Oxford, Somerset, and French Souldiors, silent all.*

> *Warw.* This is his Tent, and see where stand his Guard:
> Courage my Masters: Honor now, or neuer:
> But follow me, and *Edward* shall be ours.
>    1. *Watch.* Who goes there?
>    2. *Watch.* Stay, or thou dyest.

> *Warwicke and the rest cry all, Warwicke, Warwicke, and set vpon the Guard,*
> *who flye, crying, Arme, Arme, Warwicke and the rest following them.*
> *The Drumme playing, and Trumpet sounding.*

[*JK: With the masses flocking to Warwick's side, explore the idea that Warwick is trying to avoid shedding any more English blood. His real problem is with Edward. Whilst the guards must flee after Warwick and company enter, it does not say in what condition the guards depart. The guards can start to fight, then realise it's a lost cause and scatter. Two of Edward's guards can fight as the third runs off to raise the alarm. Drums and trumpets sound, and more guards fly. English soldiers can enter to fight the French soldiers whilst Warwick, Clarence, Oxford, and Somerset are inside the tent.*] [*SD: A different choice is offered to us by Elizabeth in 4.4 when she surmises Edward may have been 'betrayd by falshood of his Guard'. If you pursue this path, maybe two of the watchmen have been paid off. The third proclaims 'stay', running off after the first two to raise the alarm.*]

*Enter Warwicke, Somerset, and the rest, bringing the King out in his Gowne,*
*sitting in a Chaire: Richard and Hastings flyes ouer the Stage.*

You can have Edward already bound in the chair, brought onto stage. Or he could be sitting in the chair, unbound, and then you drag him in and dump him on the ground and cuff him. Right after bringing Edward out, Richard and Hastings flee.

*Warw.* Then for his minde, be *Edward* Englands King,

*Takes off his Crowne.*

But *Henry* now shall weare the English Crowne,
And be true King indeede: thou but the shadow.
My Lord of Somerset, at my request,
See that forthwith Duke *Edward* be conuey'd
Vnto my Brother Arch-Bishop of Yorke:
When I haue fought with *Pembrooke*, and his fellowes,
Ile follow you, and tell what answer
*Lewis* and the Lady *Bona* send to him.
Now for a-while farewell good Duke of Yorke.

*They leade him out forcibly.*

Warwick needn't be gentle when removing Edward's crown. Feel free to throw in a punch to the guts. Edward is directed to be led out forcibly. This gives Warwick and his soldiers some leeway in manhandling Edward. If you tied him to the chair, it would be best to untie him here and lead him away. If two soldiers hook their arms under Edward's shoulders, keeping their chest in front of Edward's, they can support his weight and drag him out roughly.

## Act 4  Scene 5

What happens when the huntsman encounters the rescue party? Richard advises that Edward is 'attended with weake guard', and there is no mention in the scene of a struggle. The huntsman could be surprised and captured before having the chance to put up a fight, then just struggle (or not) against captivity. Or maybe the rescue party goes straight for the huntsman before he can raise his bow, and he ends up on point with a sword or drawn bow. [*JK: If you ever point a loaded weapon at another character, ensure it is not actually aimed at them. It should be directed a bit upstage/downstage. If something goes wrong and the weapon discharges, the projectile will go past the actor.*] [*SD: And hit stage management? I'd rather lose the actor.*] The huntsman may also just be terrified into paralysis or – and this will make sense of his decision to willingly accompany the rescue party, rather than 'tarry and be hang'd' – opt for the most pragmatic choice and offer no resistance.

## Act 4  Scene 7

Between the mayor's guilelessness and Edward's disinterest in asserting himself, we don't expect violence to break out here. Even when Montgomery arrives, delivering his ultimatum to Edward that he step up or shut up, Richard and Hastings probably do not need to beat Edward into reaffirming his claim to the crown. As always, this will depend on your production. If you've taken a farcical approach in your staging, there's room for comical violence between the brothers.

## Act 4  Scene 8

*See Glossary – Arrests; Binds (maybe); Ensemble Readiness; Strikes (maybe).*

Henry, more delusional than ever, thinks he has nothing to worry about regarding Edward or his soldiers. The playwright, more consistent than ever, immediately punishes Henry for this myopia by having him arrested for a second time in the same play. If any of the king's guards remains, they do a piss-poor job and are probably severely outnumbered anyway. Kill them, have them flee, surrender, or whatever else works for you. When Edward orders that Henry not be allowed to speak, Edward's soldiers can bind and gag Henry. As for Exeter, we don't hear from him again. His capture, escape, or murder is entirely up to you.

## Act 5  Scene 1

*See Glossary – Ensemble Readiness.*

We do not anticipate physical violence here, despite the stakes. Besides the distance between the parties, Edward tends to keep parleys above board. If you opted for a farcical production, feel free to ignore us here. Warwick and his Lancastrian army atop the walls could theoretically assault the Yorkists below with rotten fruit, stuffed animals, or neighbourhood children. We won't judge you.

## Act 5  Scene 2

*See Glossary – Blood; Carries; Strikes (maybe).*

If you've spent the last two acts convalescing from the excursions drinking game, hoping it had come to an end, we have some unfortunate news for you. Cheers!

> *Alarum, and Excursions. Enter Edward bringing forth Warwicke wounded.*

Historically, the Battle of Barnet saw Edward's army advance during an early morning mist on Easter, which is how they surprised Warwick. Edward's left flank was routed in battle, but his right and centre were victorious. Warwick was killed as he fled.

*See Glossary – Carries.*

> *Here they beare away his Body. Exeunt.*

## Act 5  Scene 4

The Lancastrian army ran away after the Battle of Barnet, attempting to reach Wales and join forces with Jasper Tudor. Upon getting as far as Tewkesbury, the Lancastrians gave battle to the pursuing Yorkist troops, rather than risk the difficult river crossing. The battle ended when the Lancastrian ranks broke and fled to the river, where they were cut down by the king's troops in an area still known as the Bloody Meadow. Margaret was captured and imprisoned. Prince Edward died, but it is unclear how. Some say the king struck the prince, then several of the leaders stabbed him. Others say the prince died in battle. This marked the end of the second phase of the Wars of the Roses. This historical reference is just to give you a launching point. Shakespeare takes poetic license and so can you. All he offers is the following direction:

*Alarum, Retreat, Excursions. Exeunt.*

*Sláinte!*

The two lines of forces should form and, at the end, the fighting can begin. Show the king's army winning the battle, as well as the capture of Oxford, Somerset, Margaret, and Prince Edward. You can then slide seamlessly into the next scene.

## Act 5  Scene 5

*See Glossary – Arrests; Binds (maybe); Blood; Blood Packs; Ensemble Readiness; Grabs; Strikes.*

After Oxford and Somerset are taken away, the prince is probably escorted in by guards. The level of force should be proportional to how screwed you want the prince to know he is. With either a false sense of security, or boldness in the face of an inevitable death, he systematically diagnoses each of the York brothers – King Edward's wantonness, Clarence's treason, and Richard's self-hatred. Whether it is to prevent the prince from ever speaking again, a need to remove the most significant Lancastrian threat (far more than his father, Henry, who remains imprisoned and has little interest in the crown), or a combination of the two, the Duke of York's children exact further vengeance for Rutland here, cutting off any claims Prince Edward might have via primogeniture. That they can do this, whilst his mother is forced to watch, is bloody icing on the deathcake.

*Edw.* Take that, the likenesse of this Rayler here.

*Stabs him.*

*Rich.* Sprawl'st thou? take that, to end thy agonie.

*Rich. stabs him.*

*Clar.* And ther's for twitting me with periurie.

*Clar. stabs him.*

We highly recommend using a directional blood pack so that some of the more grotesque stabs/slices can hit Margaret with the blood of her son. Decide if you want to have Margaret bound. She is going to fight viciously for her son in this scene so, if you do bind her, do it with her hands in front to give her more violent options. Take time in rehearsal to explore. It should be extraordinarily difficult for her to be restrained by any of the soldiers, and we recommend that they fail. She could knee a guard, elbow another, or otherwise get free of them to hold Prince Edward during his dying breaths.

> *Qu.* Oh, kill me too.
> *Rich.* Marry, and shall.

*Offers to kill her.*

[*SD: Note that King Edward will have to be close enough to Richard to restrain him from killing Margaret. Yet another stupid decision on the king's part, not that Richard needed any more excuses to find him unworthy to fill their father's seat. In my 2003 production, I recall wanting to murder virtually everyone in the scene. But I lingered a bit in the wings on my way to kill Henry so I could watch Deborah "I've Never Done Shakespeare Before" is Something I Tell My Director but Apparently is Meaningless Because I am a Genius' Wallace play this moment, a first draft of Lear over the body of Cordelia. To this day – after Deborah begged King Edward and Clarence to kill her and they failed to oblige – I can recall my spine chill when she called out in a final act of desperation, 'Where is that diuels butcher Richard? / Hard fauor'd Richard? Richard, where art thou?' Once she realised I would not return and she was out of options, the life drained from her face and I had to pick my jaw up off the floor and get myself together for the next scene.*]

## Act 5  Scene 6

Unlike his poetic precursor in Chapter 9 – *Richard 2* (5.5), Henry probably doesn't put up much of a fight here. At least not physically. He's at his most vicious linguistically, but this may just be the freedom that comes with knowing the pain of living will soon be extinguished.

> *Rich.* Ile heare no more:
> Dye Prophet in thy speech,

*Stabbes him.*

For this (among'st the rest) was I ordain'd.
>    *Hen.* I, and for much more slaughter after this,
> O God forgiue my sinnes, and pardon thee.

*Dyes.*

*[JK: I favour Richard coming up behind Henry and sinking the knife behind his collarbone. It is a natural sheath since there is nothing in the way of the knife going in to sever the subclavian artery, chew up the lung, and finish the victim quickly whilst he chokes to death on his own blood.] [SD: You must be fun at parties.] [JK: I am. This is also a highly pressurised artery, so the first spray of blood as the knife comes out can climb many feet in the air. I used a bag of blood and a tube, which the actor playing Henry controlled, so it could spray big at first and then decrease as he nears death, as arterial sprays do. It has the added benefit of hitting Richard in the face so he is a bloody mess during his speech.]*

 *Rich.* What? will the aspiring blood of Lancaster
Sinke in the ground? I thought it would haue mounted.
See how my sword weepes for the poore Kings death.
O may such purple teares be alway shed
From those that wish the downfall of our house.
If any sparke of Life be yet remaining,
Downe, downe to hell, and say I sent thee thither.

     *Stabs him againe.*

The additional gashing can be to finish Henry off, or he can already be dead and Richard just wants some more stabby stabs. Is he methodical or haphazard? What do you want the audience to know about Richard with this additional skewering?

 It will be easy for the actor playing Richard to be in control of the weapon if you choose the methodical approach. *[SD: I was downstage of Henry's body, between it and the audience, and landed the point of the dagger just upstage of the body with each stab.] [JK: Yep, that would be safe, unless the actor playing Richard 'gets into it'.] [SD: I haven't made my actors bleed. Yet.]* If you opt for haphazard, you should stage this so there is no fear of an over-passionate actor harming his scene partner. Richard could turn his back to the audience on 'Downe, downe to hell, and say I sent thee thither', and place the knife in Henry's lap. Richard can then make repeated motions safely, unseen by the audience, if he keeps the stabbing hand masked by his body. *[JK: If there is a chance the audience will see Richard's hand, create a second version of the knife with the blade removed and a hilt made of foam rubber. The audience will see the hilt of the knife in Richard's hand and, if the actions are done quickly, will not notice the blade missing. In the right lighting, you could even have Richard upstage of the corpse.]* This could be particularly effective if you have a blood pack on Henry, allowing Richard to pop it and smear blood all over his hands. When Richard is finished, he can arm himself again, and turn front covered in blood.

 [2]I had no father, I am like no father,
 I haue no brothers, *I* am like no brothers,
 And this word *Loue* which graybeards tearme diuine,
 Be resident in men like one another,
 And not in me, I am my selfe alone,

[*SD: You've probably, by now, picked up on my disinterest in Hamlet. Since you've come this far, I owe you something more than just another cheap shot. He may have spoken to millions of young Shakespearean actors for hundreds of years, but I could never identify with a navel-gazing, paralysed equivocator who makes decisions, even in part, based on what might occur in some absurd idea of an afterlife. I've related, for as long as I can remember, mostly to very angry old farts who say and do whatever they please. Still do. The only character that spoke to me as a fellow young adult was Richard. But this came with its own baggage – namely, childhood circumstances making me want to sever any and all forms of codependency. I longed to rid myself of relatives I had no hand in selecting. Since murder was off the table due to silly things like laws and morals, it took me another fifteen years before I finally went through with it. Perhaps, that was my own variation on the Danish brand of inaction. It was therapeutic getting to try Richard's way for the first few years of my career. I am not a proponent of using substitution as an actor, and never did so beyond these few lines each evening, but it was impossible to resist aiming part of this soliloquy at blood relatives in the audience. My pleas in real life for some breathing room fell on deaf ears, so I doubt they ever picked up on my direct address here. I've thankfully outgrown the role, but I suspect you'll see more young actors gravitate towards the temporary emancipation it offers. There are many reasons new generations are ignoring societal pressures/norms, abandoning poorly conceived traditions, and forming families solely of their choosing. My reason, like many millennials (I'm technically an Xennial, don't @ me), was helicopter parenting. Like Richard, whilst loathing my mother, I idolised my father for a time and had hopes of salvaging paternal and fraternal relationships. Until I realised they were enablers and/or just as toxic as the root of the problem. My only regret about finally severing ties a few years ago is that I didn't do it sooner. It was difficult to turn off the empathy switch; many helicopter parents came from destabilised homes, then overcorrect to prevent the same happening to their children. I never doubted for a day of my life that I was loved. But not all love is healthy. If you're a new parent, I have only two pieces of advice: listen when your children tell you for decades that you're suffocating them; or go all the way and finish the job so they can never mention it in a book. (I might learn forgiveness one day, but it's unlikely to occur before the final chapter of Volume Two – The Winter's Tale.)*]

*See Glossary – Carries.*

Ile throw thy body in another roome,
And Triumph *Henry*, in thy day of Doome.

*Exit.*

[*SD: I didn't pick up the corpse and hurl it elsewhere. We just went to a blackout once I gave Henry a final stab, as it timed out perfectly with the music under the speech, and also because I have the upper-body strength of an inchworm.*]

# from Carman Lacivita

*Whilst doing* Rose Rage *with Chicago Shakespeare Theater, directed by Ed Hall, the production used innards from cows and pigs, which the stage managers would pick up at the slaughterhouses daily. They would come back with bags of the freshest and stinkiest newly bagged innards and store them in refrigerators at the theatre. Ed would use these entrails to signify the amount of blood and guts spilled through his telling of the* Henry 6 *plays, parts 1, 2 and 3, in what he adapted into* Rose Rage. *He also incorporated a LOT of red cabbage for all the beheadings and decapitations.*

*When we transferred to NYC, there were sanitation laws from the health dept that didn't allow for certain innards, so we had to switch them up. During our tech, I was doing Henry 6's molehill speech, one I'd done many times, having just done it for seven months in Chicago, and I was having a hard time getting through it because there were things on my body and feet that I had never felt before. Mainly, that I had pigs' brains stuck in my toes. One of the things that NY allowed, but that Chicago didn't have. These innards were flung about the stage, and slammed on butcher blocks, and slung on hooks, and bashed to bits as the War of the Roses commenced. In this speech, Henry has climbed atop a 'molehill' and offers a contemplative reflection on war, and how he wishes to be a shepherd living life simply, rather than a king. I was trying to do the speech, but all I could think of was what was between my toes. Ed later asked me why I was doing it different, and that it seemed 'off'.*

*I then replied … 'well, I've never had pigs' brains in my toes before, so that's all I was thinking about.' It smelled. It was squishy, it was gross, the experience was an assault, nightly, on the senses. But, one of the best things I have ever been a part of in my career.*

*Bogumil Dawison as Richard III*. Friedrich von Amerling, nineteenth century. (*Public domain*)

Chapter 17

# Richard 3

*'To make an act of tragic violence'* – Elizabeth (2.2)

## Act 1  Scene 1

*See Glossary – Arrests.*

The armed guards need only act as escort for Clarence. He has a powerful title, is not remotely a flight risk, and Richard has probably ensured that Clarence will be made to feel like this is all a comical misunderstanding. Clarence steps into this trap since he is naïve enough to believe his innocence actually matters in the world of this play.

## Act 1  Scene 2

*See Glossary – Blood Packs; Carries; Ensemble Readiness; Grabs (maybe); Strikes (maybe).*

> *Enter the Coarse of Henrie the sixt with Halberds to guard it,*
> *Lady Anne being the Mourner.*

This is a regal procession. Polearms – specifically halberds – were the primary weapon of English guards for centuries, allowing them to strike from farther away and keep the rabble in place. Note that the gentlemen carrying/escorting the body should be separate from the guards with halberds flanking the procession. Not only would it look ridiculous to have the pallbearers bear halberds, it's not practical for them to put the body down and have halberds at the ready during Richard's speech.

When carrying the body in, add a safety line between the carriers' wrists and the platform bearing Henry. If the carriers' hands slip, there is another safety precaution in place. Anne gives the order to take up the coarse, but almost immediately orders the pallbearers to set it down again. Whether this is due to their weariness, or Anne's (who projects it onto the others as a cover so she can rest further), is up to you.

> *Gen*. My Lord stand backe, and let the Coffin passe.
> *Rich*. Vnmanner'd Dogge,
> Stand'st thou when I commaund:
> Aduance thy Halbert higher then my brest,

> Or by S. Paul Ile strike thee to my Foote,
> And spurne vpon thee Begger for thy boldnesse.

By this point, Richard is in charge of most of the nation's military. Whomever is contemplating making a fuller martial threat to Richard likely backs down when ordered. This is inferred from Anne's description of the utter lack of resistance. She might attempt to beat one or two of the gentlemen into compliance, but this isn't going to change matters.

Your production's Anne may turn violent with Richard at the outset. This will come down to the chemistry with your Richard, but we recommend letting the language do the work until later when the stage directions grow harsher. This scene is a replay of Chapter 16 – *Henry 6 Part 3* (3.2). In both, a recently widowed noblewoman is at the mercy of a son of York, in an attempt to salvage some semblance of a future. Edward's wooing was tame and he was easily manipulated. Richard's is a series of scum-ridden funhouse mirrors.

*See Glossary – Blood; Blood Packs.*

Anne tells us that Henry's wounds 'bleed afresh'. You need to decide if this is figurative or literal. Henry has not been dead long, but it's unlikely there is real blood pouring out of the body. In the sixteenth century, a cadaver was typically eviscerated, cleaned, and stuffed with fragrant plants and perfumes. When the preparation was complete, the body would be wrapped in a cerecloth. If Anne is play-acting or hallucinating, then you won't need any blood.

However, if you have been tracking Shakespeare's use of witchcraft and the supernatural over the last few plays, you will know that realism isn't your only option. If blood is coming out of the body, the actor playing your corpse will need to palm a syringe of liquid, and start to push the plunger several lines earlier, so that Anne can see the results and react. If you don't have an actor to spare and instead employ a dummy under the cloth, you could rig a blood pack to the platform. One of the pallbearers upstage would operate the pump.

*See Glossary – Intimacy.*

Richard and Anne spend most of the scene engaging in the act of stichomythia – a theatrical practice in which characters use their dialogue against one another, as though Sanford Meisner were thrown into a time machine and dropped head first into a Greek amphitheatre. The rapid-fire linguistic acrobatics can, for some people, turn intellectual rigour into something sexual. However unlikely it may seem that Anne would have the slightest interest in this prospect, Richard goes full speed ahead. It is for you to decide whether Anne is genuinely taken in by the banter, merely playing along to manipulate Richard, or some combination of the two. Take the rehearsal time with your fight director and intimacy coordinator to really work this scene. Also consider the performative aspects of any given moment since these two are not alone. See Volume Two – *Antony and Cleopatra*.

> *Rich*. Let him thanke me, that holpe to send him thither:
> For he was fitter for that place then earth.
>> *An*. And thou vnfit for any place, but hell.
>> *Rich*. Yes one place else, if you will heare me name it.
>> *An*. Some dungeon.
>> *Rich*. Your Bed-chamber.

This may be a turning point where the scene becomes physical. Richard's reply is disgusting enough to warrant a slap. Rather than be discouraged, Anne's engagement – even if negative, or perhaps especially because of it – lets Richard know he's making headway. He proceeds to counter each of Anne's allegations with endless excuses, cleverly based in half-truths to which any audience of Chapter 16 – *Henry 6 Part 3* are already privy. What will come entirely out of left field for Anne – and the audience – is Richard's claim that Anne was the reason behind all of this.

> *An*. If I thought that, I tell thee Homicide,
> These Nailes should rent that beauty from my Cheekes.

Anne could move to scratch her face here, but Richard would stop her before she could accomplish it. [*SD: Or maybe she draws some blood and he licks it off because we only live once. But let's assume for now he stops her in time and gains a few points that way in this bizarre game.*] Anne's response to Richard's kindness might range from breaking free and slapping him again, to reversing the wrist grab and putting him in an armbar to shove him to the ground. You decide what life she's lived and if Pappy Warwick or Hubby Eddie taught her any tricks before they were slaughtered. [*SD: The only thing she'd have learned from her father-in-law is getting paper cuts from overeager Bible study.*]

Continue exploring how Anne lashes out and Richard reacts. It's a wide-open field until the specifics of bodily fluids.

### Spits at him.

[*JK: This is the point where I tell you to have Anne simply make the sound so that no saliva leaves her mouth and lands on Richard. If you hire Seth to play Richard for the millionth time, however, you can just completely unload and bathe him in the stuff.*] [*SD: Moving on, we reach Richard's most diabolical lie-disguised-in-a-truth – another moment in which knowledge of the prior play significantly deepens the emotional impact of this one.*]

This seems a risky bet but is wisely waged. Whilst the tears Richard now produces may very well be manufactured, the story he just told is true and likely known to Anne.

In Chapter 16 – *Henry 6 Part 3* (2.1), Richard tells Edward to stop being a crybaby. Richard's stoicism in that moment, particularly given how brutally his father and brother were tortured and murdered, would have stuck in Warwick's mind. It is completely plausible he told his daughter Anne. She looks scornfully at Richard, but only after letting him tell that story uninterrupted. This is his moment to go in for the kill.

*He layes his brest open, she offers at with his sword.*

If he sets the sword down at her feet, she can pick it up and charge at him, stopping short because murder is a difficult thing to do for the first time. See Chapter 4 – *Macbeth* (1.7). For safety, remember that if one character is in motion, the other should be in stillness so that the distance does not alter. This will allow Anne to get dangerously close to stabbing Richard, and for the audience to legitimately believe it will happen. Given Anne's circumstances, this is the most dangerous gamble on Richard's part or, as he would call it, a Tuesday.

*She fals the Sword.*

The battle is now over, aside from pleasantries like offering to fall on his sword, giving Anne his ring, and asking to take over the coarse. He requests a proper farewell – possibly a kiss – which Anne demurs, either out of coyness or disgust. Your Richard may opt to ignore Anne's words and steal a kiss, a choice we will revisit in 4.3. His primary objective accomplished, there is nothing left but to order the remaining pallbearers/gentlemen to take the dead king's corpse to a far-less-honourable resting place.

## Act 1  Scene 3

*See Glossary – Ensemble Readiness; Grabs (maybe); Strikes (maybe).*

Richard may get physical with some of these folks, especially the spineless faction under Elizabeth. Richard is stuffed with regal titles and controls most of the military. Snivelling cowards such as Rivers and Gray don't have much recourse here, despite their proximity to the queen. Everyone knows Edward is sick. Several (if not all) of these people can put two and two together, realise their time in power may be running out, and that Richard will very likely be made lord protector until Elizabeth's oldest son comes of age. They also know Plantagenet children often fail to reach adulthood.

Richard is not the only wildcard at court today. If you haven't already, take a gander at the final act of Chapter 15 – *Henry 6 Part 2* and all of Chapter 16 – *Henry 6 Part 3* for earlier encounters between Margaret and the Yorkists. We haven't seen Margaret since Richard slaughtered her son in front of her. Protocol is further spoiled by her status as a former queen – whatever this may or may not be worth – and the fact no one had any idea she was 'at liberty'. She appears deeply unstable, which is to be expected, but the peanut gallery assembled here is hardly equipped to deal with their own mental health issues, let alone Margaret's. See Chapter 7 – *King John* (3.1). Notwithstanding, whilst most of these characters cannot stand each other, it turns out that hating Margaret is the one thing on which all the rest can agree.

As always, how this scene plays out physically comes down to the chemistry of your actors and the universe in which you place them. At the very least, there will be some confused guards with a complete nightmare on their hands. Please dedicate adequate rehearsal time to this scene since it will set up many of the allegiances and betrayals ahead.

*Enter two murtherers.*

Select your murderers carefully. They can be gentlemen (though they are called 'humble' in the next scene and speak in prose), rogues recently pulled from a sewer, or anything in between. Remember that the choice of murderers reflects on their employer. See Chapter 4 – *Macbeth* (3.1).

## Act 1  Scene 4

We had a preview of this scene in Chapter 16 – *Henry 6 Part 3* (1.3) where Rutland attempted to reason with Young Clifford. Here, too, the victim almost escapes his fate.

Before the murderers can come close to committing any physical violence towards Clarence, they have to get past themselves. There is room for some slapstick, depending on your approach. The first murderer is seemingly in charge and tries multiple tactics to knock his accomplice out of a stupor.

Clarence is not so naïve to be unaware of what can happen to people in the tower. At the end of the prior play, he knows full well Richard is headed there to kill King Henry. But Clarence might lack the imaginative leap required to think he would ever be harmed by brother Edward, let alone brother Richard. It makes the presence of the murderers even more confusing, as it is unclear who sent them, or if they are remotely up to the task. This is another scene requiring proper rehearsal time. Clarence deploys one survival tactic after another. Have him test out each possibility, but never the same beat twice.

The murderers make the immediate mistake of allowing Clarence to engage them in conversation, which – as Richard made clear in 1.3 – should not be allowed to happen. Once the first murderer realises the second is losing what little resolve he mustered to begin with, it's time to go a-stabbin'.

> 2 Looke behinde you, my Lord.
> 1 Take that, and that, if all this will not do,

*Stabs him.*

If Richard selected a skilled assassin, the kill should be quick and efficient; if not, the job could get botched and Clarence might suffer a great deal, which would make the kill much harder to watch. We're fans of the latter approach because only deeply damaged individuals would write a book like this.

Ile drowne you in the Malmesey-But within.

*See Glossary – Carries.*

For those interested, a butt is two hogsheads. A hogshead is approximately sixty-three gallons. We mention this because an interesting choice, never seen by either of us, would be to have 126 gallons of wine on stage (to which Clarence can allude at the beginning of the scene when he wants a drink). After stabbing Clarence, the first murderer could dump the body in the vat of wine. If you have the budget for this approach, please invite us to your performance. (We will bring our own goblets.)

Whilst the second murderer rejects payment and just wants to flee, you could have him killed by the first murderer. He is getting full compensation whether or not his colleague remains alive, so you may as well tie up loose ends. If, for whatever reason, your first murderer does not kill the second, continue with the scene as written. [*SD: Richard probably kills any remaining assassins during the act break anyway.*]

## Act 2  Scene 1

*See Glossary – Ensemble Readiness; Falls; Grabs (maybe); Strikes (maybe).*

Let's resume our disturbing game show from Chapter 5 – *All's Well that Ends Well* and Chapter 7 – *King John*, entitled What's Killing the King? Dominic Mancini, an Italian at court during Edward's death, said it was a mix of sadness and a cold caught on a fishing trip on the Thames at Windsor. We can imagine the cold grew into pneumonia, which gives your actor symptoms to play. There also were rumours of the king being slowly poisoned, so you could choose this instead.

Or you can be Shakespearean and replace history with something more hilarious – syphilis! Our inclination towards this choice may be due to the administration in the States at the time of writing this volume, but is bolstered by Edward also being a known womaniser who wouldn't use protection even if he had access to it. Furthermore, the playwright goes out of his way to refer to Edward sharing a mistress with Hastings, and later has Buckingham offer this rumour as leverage in the third act. Buckingham convinces the citizens Richard is the 'right idea' of his father in a way Edward never was, and his children might be bastards, so it's probably better to be safe than sorry and just make Richard king.

Syphilis would allow the actor playing Edward to have skin rashes, swollen glands, hair loss, extreme fatigue, and be out of his goddamned mind. This last bit would also give Richard cover when he gaslights Edward about the choice of messenger sent to reverse Clarence's death warrant.

Your production's Edward is welcome to physically abuse anyone in this scene he finds deserving of it – get in one person's face, grab another by the lapels, push another in the chest, slap, strike, *etc.* – until Edward collapses in a coughing fit and needs to be taken away.

## Act 2  Scene 2

*See Glossary – Ensemble Readiness; Knees (maybe).*

Someone in the mental state to wring her hands, beat her breast, and curse her grandchildren needs to be addressed. Are these just actions the duchess has performed off stage, or does she come on beating herself, or both? Does this self-abuse continue during the scene? How close is she to harming the children? We only have a short time with the duchess in this play and the choices you make here quickly give us a sense of her character.

Similar questions may be asked of Elizabeth when she joins everyone in this very special episode of *The Biggest Griever*™. 'Who shall hinder me' may be a direct response to Rivers and Dorset attempting to calm Elizabeth down. She might physically lash out at Rivers and/or Dorset, rather than just verbally. Whilst the stage directions only state Elizabeth's hair is about her ears, this dishevelled appearance could mean she has been pulling her hair out or otherwise harming herself.

There are multiple permutations of believable physical violence that could ensue amongst this family. Take the time to explore these in rehearsal instead of stereotypical and melodramatic keening.

## Act 2  Scene 4

*See Glossary – Strikes (maybe).*

Elizabeth might smack her son on 'A parlous Boy: go too, you are too shrew'd'. Not out of anger but to caution her son against too quick a wit whilst the Richards of the world are in charge ('Pitchers haue eares').

## Act 3  Scene 1

*See Glossary – Falls (maybe); Grabs (maybe).*

Whether he is naturally obnoxious, or was set on by his mother to taunt Richard as is suggested at the end of the scene, the youngest prince can poke and prod Richard physically, as well as with words. [*SD: Each occasion I've directed and played Richard, I encouraged the actor playing little York to annoy the shit out of me.*]

It starts off pleasantly enough with York's request to play with Richard's dagger, which he grants, but can quickly devolve into attempting to draw his sword out of its sheath, and jumping on his hunchback. Decide whether Richard's type of deformity is light enough that no pain would ensue from the added weight. Or – and this is obviously the choice you should make – does the little bastard cause Richard immense pain and take him down to the ground? Note that if the malformation causes Richard agony in this scene, it could be used against him in battle at the end of the play. (If running in repertory with the earlier plays, did any opponents seize on this potential target?)

## Act 3  Scene 3

*See Glossary – Arrests; Binds; Blood (maybe); Blood Packs (maybe); Strikes (maybe).*

*Enter Sir Richard Ratcliffe, with Halberds, carrying the Nobles to death at Pomfret.*

The First Folio reads as though Ratcliffe enters with a bunch of halberds and prisoners in his octopus arms. The more likely scenario is that Ratcliffe enters, leading guards wielding halberds (similar to 1.2), and those guards in turn are escorting prisoners. Neither Rivers, Vaughan, nor Grey seem particularly acquiescent. One or more of them could struggle and have to be put in their place by the guards. See Chapter 13 – *Henry 5* (2.2).

Whilst these members of Elizabeth's faction are typically taken away, the authors of this book do not much like these prisoners. If you have the budget, you are quite welcome to behead one of these wastes of space on stage. See Chapter 4 – *Macbeth* (5.7). If one has been particularly difficult to deal with – probably Rivers – killing him would lead the others to fall in line and make clear to the audience what will soon happen to the rest.

## Act 3  Scene 4

*See Glossary – Ensemble Readiness; Strikes (maybe).*

>     *Rich.* I pray you all, tell me what they deserue,
> That doe conspire my death with diuellish Plots
> Of damned Witchcraft, and that haue preuail'd
> Vpon my Body with their Hellish Charmes.
>     *Hast.* The tender loue I beare your Grace, my Lord,
> Makes me most forward, in this Princely presence,
> To doome th' Offendors, whosoe're they be:
> I say, my Lord, they haue deserued death.
>     *Rich.* Then be your eyes the witnesse of their euill.
> Looke how I am bewitch'd: behold, mine Arme

Is like a blasted Sapling, wither'd vp:
And this is *Edwards* Wife, that monstrous Witch,
Consorted with that Harlot, Strumpet *Shore*,
That by their Witchcraft thus haue marked me.

[*SD: I remember sticking my deformed left arm in people's faces and beating Hastings with it before ordering his beheading.*]

    *Hast.* If they haue done this deed, my Noble Lord.
    *Rich.* If? thou Protector of this damned Strumpet,
Talk'st thou to me of Ifs: thou art a Traytor,
Off with his Head; now by Saint *Paul* I sweare,
I will not dine, vntill I see the same.
*Louell* and *Ratcliffe*, looke that it be done:
The rest that loue me, rise, and follow me.

      *Exeunt. Manet Louell and Ratcliffe, with the Lord Hastings.*

*See Glossary – Arrests; Binds (maybe); Blood; Blood Packs (maybe).*

    *Hast.* O bloody *Richard:* miserable England,
I prophecie the fearefull'st time to thee,
That euer wretched Age hath look'd vpon.
Come, lead me to the Block, beare him my Head,
They smile at me, who shortly shall be dead.

We recommend using this time to express more about Hastings' character through violence. He could run after Richard as he exits, or run the other way to flee. Before getting too far, Lovell or Ratcliffe could sucker-punch Hastings, dropping him to the ground as he starts his speech. Lovell or Ratcliffe eventually grab Hastings to drag him away. He can struggle and even break free, only to be kicked by Lovell on 'Come, come, dispatch, 'tis bootlesse to exclaime'. Hastings comes to terms with his sentence before exiting. Decide if Lovell and Ratcliffe drag Hastings from the room, or if he collects himself on his final five lines and peacefully exits with Lovell and Ratcliffe.

    If you're into showing beheadings on stage, here is another opportunity. You might also consider interspersing the end of this scene with the beginning of the next one (*i.e.* decapitate Hastings on stage in 3.4 and have Lovell and Ratcliffe walk the head over to Richard, who has already commenced 3.5 somewhere else on stage). Further flow can be achieved by having the scrivener in 3.6 speak over the remains of Hastings' body, which has yet to leave the stage.

    If you opt to show the beheading, work with your design team and/or hire a magician as a consultant. If you can't afford the full magician's rig but want to add a little levity on a slim budget, have Lovell and/or Ratcliffe drag Hastings off stage, play a beheading sound effect, and have Hastings' head roll on stage so it has to be chased after. Or it can just roll to Richard's feet if you have an expert bocce ball specialist on staff. You can also go with our suggestion in Chapter 4 – *Macbeth* (5.7).

## Act 3  Scene 5[1]

> *Enter Richard, and Buckingham, in rotten Armour, maruellous ill-fauoured.*

The rotten armour is to remind people, particularly the mayor, that Richard and Buckingham have seen battle and protected the country. It would also serve to instil fear in the people that war may break out again soon. With Edward dead, another civil war would not be surprising. The citizenry will want a battle-tested warrior at the helm, not another child like they had under Henry 6.

*See Glossary – Ensemble Readiness; Falls (maybe).*

> *Enter Louell and Ratcliffe, with Hastings Head.*

We've mentioned before that your approach might tend towards the farcical with some of these plays. If so, how does the mayor react to Hastings' severed head? Does the mayor vomit and/or faint? [*SD: Even if the mayor puts on a brave front, it is your task to unsettle him as much as possible so that he becomes easier to manipulate. This process begins with the 'ill-fauored' armour, continues with caressing/kissing Hastings' severed head, and finishes with the forced choice between an allegedly holy Richard or a bunch of infidels.*]

## Act 4  Scene 1

*See Glossary – Ensemble Readiness; Strikes (maybe).*

Follow through with your choices for the duchess and the queen in prior scenes. If they were physical earlier, they need little excuse here to lash out at the men around them, each of whom are more useless than the next.

## Act 4  Scene 2

*See Glossary – Ensemble Readiness; Grabs (maybe); Strikes (maybe).*

Now that he has what he was gunning for, like Chapter 4 – *Macbeth* (3.1), Richard has absolutely no bloody idea what to do with it, and will spend the remainder of his little time left alive looking over his shoulder, tyrannically slaughtering his enemies, whether perceived or actual. Your Richard has unlimited leeway – he has been the most powerful person in the kingdom for months and now it's been made official. Explore over these next few scenes how his paranoia manifests, and how quickly he turns his friends into enemies. [*SD: I recall using the shared lines to their fullest extent. No sooner does Richard ask a question than he jumps on the respondent. It is his method of exacting the truth – the longer it takes his subjects to answer him, the more likely they're full of shit. Buckingham, who has spent the entire play getting Richard the crown, even has to beg for 'some little breath, some pawse'.*]

> *Rich.* Come hither *Catesby*, rumor it abroad,
> That *Anne* my Wife is very grieuous sicke,
> I will take order for her keeping close.

If you've been cross-staging scenes, this practice could continue here. Anne is alive at the beginning of this scene and apparently dead by the end of it. She died of tuberculosis in real life but, for the purposes of this play, Shakespeare has Richard arrange a murder so he can marry Elizabeth's daughter, thereby consolidating his power by blocking Richmond's claim.

You may also choose to stage Dighton and Forrest murdering the two boys in the background during Tyrrel's speech. However, when Shakespeare wants to murder children on stage, he has no problem doing so. See Chapter 16 – *Henry 6 Part 3* (1.3). There is a reason he gives us this speech instead – trust the audience to do some of the work. [*JK: I don't. It's a history play. If we don't show the audience what's going on, they won't know what's going on. Remember?*] [*SD: Have you tried hiring more competent actors in the productions you direct? Or … ya know … replacing the director?*]

*See Glossary – Intimacy.*

[*SD: Consider the sexuality of your production's Richard. In playing him, I never sensed any of his claimed attraction to Anne in 1.2 was legitimate. Indeed, he makes it clear to the audience that the marriage was 'not all so much for loue' and he 'will not keepe her long'. I also did not find any genuine desire in Richard's request to spend private time with Tyrrel after dinner. I merely got a read on Tyrrel and exploited it – my supposed friends were proving incompetent left and right, and I wanted Tyrrel on retainer for any future kills. My Richard used sexual advances/harassment only as an excuse/tool/threat where he thought it might serve his purposes, either to seduce or distract his marks from the real objective. You should work with your intimacy coordinator if you want to have a moment here with Tyrrel, whether Richard actually feels anything or not. I haven't felt anything in years.*]

## Act 4  Scene 3

*See Glossary – Grabs (maybe); Strikes (maybe).*

If your duchess was violent in her earlier scenes, you may want to continue. If she wasn't, here may be a good place to start as it would be even more jarring. Richard wants nothing to do with this conversation, and the duchess is getting nowhere with her linguistic vitriol. Richard either drowns her out with military fanfare, or with retorts too clever by half. If you do have her slap him silly, it could happen on/after 'Heare me a word', which then is bolstered by her promise never to speak to him again. This results in his shortest reply in the scene. Either the slap shocked him, her pledge did, or some combination of the two. [*SD: For added terror, I suggest you break with whichever tradition you established throughout the play: if she had been physically violent before, use only words here; if not, go for the slap. Richard's conscience, which has been sleeping since midway through the last play, slowly starts to wake in this act and will torture him in the next. Whilst his mother's existence will always disgust him, she is now the last living tie to his father. Also, we know from the last scene that prophecies are on his mind and that he lends them credence. This gives the duchess power.*]

*See Glossary – Grabs (maybe); Intimacy; Strikes (maybe).*

Richard reruns some plays here from 1.2 – reprising the stichomythic posture – but Elizabeth navigates these tactics more expertly than Anne was able. Elizabeth not only catches onto Richard's act, she also manages to fool him into believing he has won. This is the first time anyone intellectually bests Richard in the course of the three plays in which he appears. The scene is lengthy and we ask you to allocate serious rehearsal hours with your intimacy coordinator and fight director to explore the strongest dynamics for your production's battle between the two smartest people in the play.

[*SD: This is the third and final exploration of Richard's sexual psychopathy. I recall my Richard, for the first time in nine acts, bordering on exhaustion attempting one abhorrent tactic after another and seemingly getting nowhere. I had one of the most formidable scene partners of my life in Jenne Vath, who came from a polar opposite acting universe than I did. She kept me on my toes, as I had no bloody idea what she would try next in rehearsals. There are countless moments where things could get physical. Elizabeth might attempt to achieve 'Nayles … anchor'd in [Richard's] eyes', and he then has to stop her. When Richard asks how to woo her daughter, Elizabeth might take a play out of Richard's book and commence a seduction on 'And wilt thou learne of me?', only to taunt him with clinically detailed descriptions of murdered family members. Jenne did this each evening and it was very unsettling. By this point, I was tired of coming up with tactics of my own and decided to steal hers, physicalising the offer 'If I haue kill'd the issue of your wombe, / To quicken your encrease, I will beget / Mine yssue of your blood' with what nowadays might be dubbed a Presidential Pussygrab. For safety, see Chapter 4 – Macbeth (3.1). Jenne's Elizabeth maintained a lethal poker face, but your version might consider letting loose a few of 'The liquid drops of Teares', which Richard could wipe away – with his hands or in some other way, depending on the sodium content in his diet. Richard ultimately presents his terms in the same manner Elizabeth requested of Edward in the prior play, when all of this madness started – make the person in question a queen, or bugger off and die. Jenne eventually could no longer brook my proposals and twists of truth. She guilt-tripped*] *me for a bit, starting on 'O no, my Reasons are too deepe and dead.' Your Elizabeth may want to knock Richard to the ground, and/or shove his face in it in the ensuing exchanges. Whether or not Elizabeth is legitimately persuaded by Richard's final argument is up to you, but I think it's play-acting as a survival tactic. It buys her enough time to get her daughter safely to Richmond, a plot Richard should be able to suss out under normal circumstances, but he hasn't experienced any of those since donning the crown and slowly losing his mind. I recall having a bit of healthy suspicion, which I ignored once Jenne passed my final test of 'Beare her my true loues kiss, and so farewell' by not vomiting on me.]*

Next up is a cavalcade of messengers with bad news – reminiscent of *Richard 2* (3.2). Richard might react in any number of ways, including physically lashing out at the few people who remain in his employ. He probably doesn't beat Stanley senseless since threatening his son's life is harsh enough. Or the first two messengers because there is barely any time to process the news. But the third messenger is fair game.

### *He striketh him.*

Whilst there is only one explicit strike in the stage directions, Richard is growing increasingly violent as his sanity unravels. Explore in rehearsal whether he harms anyone else before realising he needs to get the hell out of here and onto the battlefield.

## Act 5  Scene 1

*See Glossary – Arrests.*

### *Enter Buckingham with Halberds, led to Execution.*

Maybe we should have made a drinking game about halberds in this play. To clear up any confusion, Buckingham does not have any halberds in his possession, but rather is being led to execution by guards wielding halberds. We'll make up for the lost pints in a few paragraphs with the return of 'excursions'.

Unlike those wimps Rivers, Vaughan, and Grey, we view Buckingham as maintaining some sense of grace in facing death. As such, there is probably no struggle here. We leave you the choice of whether or not to show the execution on stage. [*JK: DO IT!!!!*]

## Act 5  Scene 3

*See Glossary – Ensemble Readiness; Grabs (maybe); Strikes (maybe).*

Continue tracking the relationship between Richard's mental decline and physical abuse of others before, during, and after his version of a Crispin's Day speech drenched in toxic acid.

## Act 5  Scene 4

*Alarum, excursions. Enter Catesby.*

The Battle of Bosworth Field was effectively the last battle of the Wars of the Roses. When Henry Tudor, Earl of Richmond, defeats Richard in battle, it ends the Plantagenet stranglehold on the monarchy and establishes the Tudor dynasty. The actual battle took place on 22 August 1485, lasting a few hours. Richard had a large arsenal of cannons, and two-to-three times the troops. It was somewhat surprising Richmond won. The historical battle was relatively short, so maybe Shakespeare decided for once to stick with history. [*JK: I recommend a full battle here – all-out war on stage will be exciting and make the climax … climactic. Have the armies flooding in from their respective sides. Let's see Richard and his troops losing.*] [*SD: Richard, in a final (accidental) tribute to his father, finds himself horseless. See Chapter 15 –* Henry 6 Part 2 *(5.2).*]

*Alarum, Enter Richard and Richmond, they fight, Richard is slaine.*

The battle between Richard and Richmond should be of epic proportions. Richard is an incredibly proficient fighter, so Richmond needs to find a way to be just a little better. Now that the actual body of Richard has been unearthed, we know it was riddled with nearly a dozen wounds. The fatal blows were two delivered to the back of the head. This is not necessarily important in creating the choreography for the fight, but could be interesting to include for the final blows. Moreover, there can be multiple wounds before actually ending the fight. We know so much about Richard by this point in the play that it's more difficult to reveal character through the fight, but it's still important the audience discover something new as our antihero goes down. Is he partly the author of his own demise? See Chapter 4 – *Macbeth* (5.7). This would explain how someone like Richmond, who has been on the run most his life, could defeat Richard. Also consider Richmond's training – he could have studied with foreign masters, learned to fight in a more unorthodox manner, and adopted tricks Richard has never seen before. These choices will give your fight director a way to structure the fight and reveal character through the choreography.

*Retreat, and Flourish. Enter Richmond, Derby bearing the Crowne,*
*with diuers other Lords.*

If this stage direction were altered in production, there could be some torture of the corpse of the 'bloody Dogge'. Or not. Depends on what your Richmond is like, and the feeling with which you want to leave the audience. As in Chapter 4 – *Macbeth* (5.7), the question at the end of the play for Malcolm is the same for Richmond here – despite their purported anti-tyranny stances, what kind of rulers will they actually become?

# *from Antony Sher*

*In 1984, when I did* Richard III *for the RSC, I played him on crutches. At first they were simply intended to convey the extent of his disability, but Malcolm Ranson, the fight director, and I quickly discovered they had other uses. As well as making Richard the fastest man in court – I could cross the stage in just a couple of stretching, scooping bounds – they were formidable weapons: swatting away swords, gripping Hastings by the neck, silencing a room by a slam on the table. Malcolm Ranson wasn't just an inspiration to me in his inventiveness with the crutches, but he also has a very dark sense of humour (maybe because he spends his life devising ways of wounding and killing people) and his wicked chuckles in rehearsals helped me understand that Richard could be funny as well as frightening.*

# Chapter 18

# Sir Thomas More[1]

*'Where they intend to offer violence'* – More (2.3)

## Act 1  Scene 1

*See Glossary – Grabs; Strikes (maybe).*

*[JK: You gotta love a play that starts with a little violence.] [SD: I'm so tired, Jared.] [JK: It's okay. Shakespeare didn't spend much time on this play, so neither will we.]*

Your immediate task is to set up the increasingly physical conflicts between the natives and the foreigners, something that has no relevance today and never will again because we have evolved as a species and we really can't continue this sentence with a straight face.

> [*London. A Street. Enter, at one end, John Lincoln, with the two Bettses together; at the other end, enters Francis de Barde and Doll a lusty woman, he haling her by the arm.*]

De Barde grabs Doll right away, assuming she is a prostitute. [*JK: Maybe because 'de Barde' has access to the stage directions of 'the Bard'?] [SD: This will be Exhibit A for the defence at my trial for your murder.*] Doll then rips away from him. Remember that when it comes to grabs, pulls, and pushes, the actor playing the victim should always be in control. *See Appendix – Bursting the Bubble.* Most of this scene should be de Barde continuing to grab Doll, then her breaking free and smacking him away. Depending on the escalation of violence, Doll might also play with slaps or other strikes (*e.g.* on 'Compel me, ye dog's face').

*See Glossary –Ensemble Readiness; Grabs (maybe); Intimacy (maybe); Strikes (maybe).*

There is a law that the male Londoners are not allowed to physically harm the foreigners, so Lincoln may have to physically restrain George from attacking the Lombards. The reverse does not appear to be true, since we will learn in 1.3 that Caveler beat Williamson. Whilst you can choose to have that happen off stage, you could include the beating as part of this discourse. Caveler can turn on Williamson and start pushing/punching him on 'If he paid for them'. If you want some laughs, have Caveler beat Williamson with

*Sir Thomas More.* Hans Holbein, 1527. (*The Frick Collection*)

one or both doves. [*SD: We'll explore further ornithological comedy in Volume Two –* Titus Andronicus *(4.3). You should probably pre-order Volume Two now, yes?*]

[*JK: By staging this, the audience will get a sense of what is inciting George to attack the 'strangers', and will lead to some sympathy for the Londoners.*] [*SD: Which could be useful not just because Jared is a xenophobe, but also because the audience should fall into this racist trap at the outset – much like Volume Two –* The Merchant of Venice *(1.2) (the book you've just purchased), during which we laugh along with Portia and Nerissa's nativist jokes – until the play progresses, and some of us realise we were assholes for doing that.*]

Once this physical assault is complete, Doll can get right in her husband's face, verbally and possibly physically. This will depend on the type of marriage you are portraying. Does Doll smack Williamson? Does he take it, or return it in kind?

You also can decide whether Doll assaults de Barde on 'Touch not Doll Williamson', or grabs/punches Caveler's junk on 'will not leave one inch untorn of thee'. See Chapter 4 – *Macbeth* (3.1), Chapter 10 – *Henry 4 Part 1* (2.3), and Chapter 17 – *Richard 3* (4.3).

Each of these decisions should be based on your production's casting, particularly of Doll. Set aside proper rehearsal time to explore these choices with your fight director and an intimacy consultant. For More's showstopping number in 2.4 to really soar, you'll have to spend each preceding scene ratcheting up the tension.

## Act 1  Scene 2

*See Glossary – Arrests; Binds; Draws (hand on hilt maybe); Ensemble Readiness.*

[*London. The Sessions House. An arras is drawn, and behind it as in sessions sit the Lord Mayor, Justice Suresby, and other Justices; Sheriff More and the other Sheriff sitting by. Smart is the plaintiff, Lifter the prisoner at the bar. Recorder, Officers.*]

This scene is clearly meant for levity, and to show how witty More is. Play with options that can entertain (*e.g.* Lifter is quick with his hands, so maybe he is shackled or bound but keeps getting out of it and the officers have to shackle/bind him again).

Decide how you want the audience to feel about More in his first scene. If Lifter is relaxed with More, we might presume More's reputation for kindness is well known and that More is doing this to help Lifter. If Lifter is nervous and circled menacingly by More, Lifter may respond out of fear. More could lay hand on his sword to keep Lifter on notice; a threat sometimes motivates more powerfully than actual violence.

Lifter is then left alone to pick Suresby's purse. [*JK: The actual lifting of the purse can be done easily if it is kept on the belt by a small piece of tape. Experiment with exactly how much to use so Lifter won't need to pull too hard.*] [*SD: It is at this point in our first volume I get to inform you that Jared is not a magician. Go hire one. Then rehire them when you work on Volume Two –* The Winter's Tale. *Did you order it yet?*]

## Act 2  Scene 1

*See Glossary – Ensemble Readiness; Grabs (maybe); Strikes (maybe).*

[*Cheapside. Enter three or four Apprentices of trades, with a pair of cudgels.*]

The stage directions note three or four apprentices but only a pair of cudgels. Several apprentices want to take matters into their own hands. Harry is trying to get them to stop. When do they decide to start getting physical? You'll want to be specific so that the violence grows from a point of pushing each other first, then escalates.

[*JK: The scholar referenced is a rank in the English fencing guild, the Company of the Maisters of the Science of Defence of London. Granted their official charter in 1540 by Henry 8, this is the guild that taught fencing to the common man. The mention of backsword further supports this as it was the weapon used by many Englishmen, of which they were very proud. The rapier was being taught in the Blackfriars area during this time by Italians (Rocco Bonetti and Vincentio Saviolo).*] [*SD: You're seriously going to mention that bloody book again?*] [*JK: No. I won't mention that book again. For a good idea of what the backsword looked like, see the below image from* THE Expert Sword-Man's Companion: Or the True Art of SELF-DEFENCE. WITH An ACCOUNT of the Authors LIFE, and his Transactions during the Wars with France: To which is Annexed, The ART of GUNNERIE *by Donald McBane, edited by Jared Kirby.*] [*SD: You are completely without shame.*]

N. 18

Instead of fighting the foreigners, Kit and Harry turn on each other. Whilst they do not break into a full fight here, there can be some generic macho bullroar (pushing, chest-bumping, *etc.*) to get them to a point of challenging each other to a fight/duel with sharps.

## Act 2  Scene 2

[*Saint Martins-le-Grand. Enter Lincoln, two Bettses, Williamson, Sherwin, and other, armed; Doll in a shirt of mail, a headpiece, sword, and buckler; a crew attending.*]

For these next few scenes, you are faced with the question we posed repeatedly during the fourth act of Chapter 15 – *Henry 6 Part 2*: how much of the rioting and chaos amongst the commoners do you stage? This will come down to your budget, and the amount of menace you want to foment leading up to More's quashing of the issue, which ultimately will leave these characters behind as the play shifts into vastly different territory.

*See Glossary – Ensemble Readiness; Strikes (maybe).*

We know from the stage direction that Doll is ready and raring to go.

Already incensed, Doll is only further aggravated by her husband. She's welcome to make this verbal beating of Williamson physical as well.

It's possible some folks get trigger happy and begin attacking Sherwin's party, but this quickly comes to a stop.

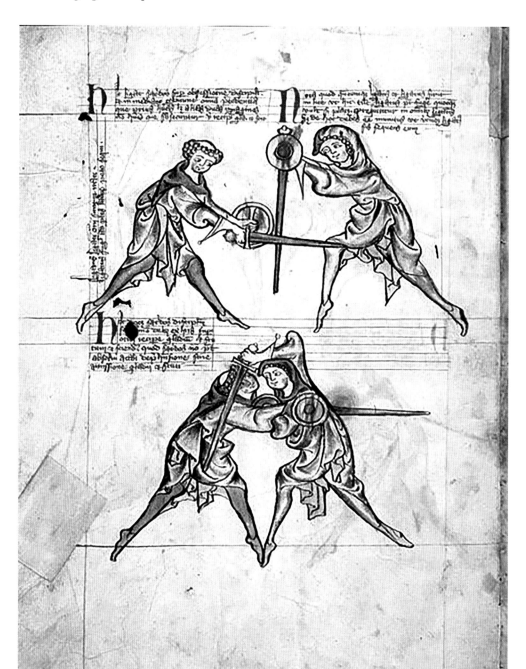

Manuscript illustration of two men fencing with sword and buckler. Tower Fechtbuch, late-thirteenth century. (*The Board of Trustees of the Armouries Royal Armouries Museum, Leeds*)

Finally, if you want to set a bunch of stuff on fire, here's your shot! Make sure to properly research your jurisdiction's laws, theatrical rental agreements, union rules, blah blah blah.

## Act 2  Scene 3

*See Glossary – Blood (maybe); Blood Packs (maybe).*

[*The Guildhall. Enter at one door Sir Thomas More and Lord Mayor; at another door Sir John Munday hurt.*]

If Munday stepped into the middle of a cudgel fight and got injured, it is most likely to the head. This may be a big lump or a laceration of the scalp. If the latter, there would be a lot of blood, especially from the crown. There are many blood vessels in this area because the brain requires a tremendous amount of oxygen; roughly a fifth of the body's blood goes to the brain. If Munday had time to get the wound patched up, he can enter with a bandage on his head and proceed to bore us all with this less-interesting choice.

## Act 2  Scene 4

*See Glossary – Ensemble Readiness.*

Fighting does not break out as far as the stage directions are concerned, but the threat is very real. Each and every character is in full battle mode. Many are armed. Their level of volatility is nothing short of domestic terrorism. Entire neighbourhoods are on fire. A failure from More today will result in the streets flowing with blood. Work carefully with your fight director to orchestrate this bedlam since actors sometimes get 'lost in the moment' – the politest euphemism we can muster – and have the potential to cause real-world injury.

[*St. Martin's Gate. Enter Lincoln, Doll, Clown, George Betts, Williamson, others; and a Sergeant at Arms.*]

You will need more than just a 'Sergeant at Arms' here to contain the rabble, and arrest several of them at scene's end. The officers aren't exactly doing a bang-up job at the outset. The lord mayor's calls to hold are treated with more respect, so perhaps he has some more intimidating guards.

[*They lay by their weapons.*]

Little danger exists in laying down the weapons, but there needs to be a clear path for all the characters to travel. Otherwise, there is a real danger of a weapon being kicked into another actor. [*JK: Or into the audience, which is worse.*] [*SD: Debatable.*] If it makes sense for your production, have an upstage area in which each character can deposit their weapon, and ensure none of the actors toss the bloody things. This is not only harmful to the weapons, but could force them to flip up and hit one or more performers.

*See Glossary – Arrests.*

[*They are led away.*]

## Act 3 Scene 1

Whilst staging the hangings of Cordelia in Chapter 1 – *King Lear* (5.3) and Bardolph in Chapter 13 – *Henry 5* (3.6) were optional, the onstage hanging of Lincoln is explicitly called for here.

Hangings would historically gather a large crowd. There should be as many people as you can muster to watch and cheer as Lincoln hangs. This can be a mixed bag of cheers for his death but also cries for the injustice of it.

*[Exit some severally; others set up the gibbet.]*

The gibbet is a platform from which to hang people. Your design team will have to build this. Whilst you can wheel it in completely built, it could also be in several pieces brought in from different sides of the stage that click together. It seems impossible to build it from scratch during the scene and it would be very noisy work. If you are keen to prove us wrong, please invite us to see your performance!

*See Glossary – Arrests; Binds (in front should something go wrong).*

*[The prisoners are brought in, well guarded.]*

You will need to hire a rigger to ensure everything is set up correctly each night before this moment is executed. The actor playing Lincoln should have a harness under his costume. The device from which he will hang is a straight piece of rope, which will go down the back of his costume and be connected to a pick-point, so that the actor will actually be suspended by his harness. The neck loop will be a breakaway (*i.e.* it cannot bear any weight without breaking off the main rope), lightly affixed higher on the rope to give the illusion of a hangman's noose. This ensures that the actor playing Lincoln won't actually be hanged if something goes wrong. Remember that the goal of a hanging isn't the asphyxiation we often see in film and television. If done properly, the neck will snap for an immediate kill. Only if that goes wrong would a victim wait to die by strangulation.

*[He leaps off]*

When Lincoln jumps to his death, you'll need a sound effect for the break of his neck. A rebreakable Karate board works, as does crushing a plastic water bottle. Either way, this should be done by someone in the cast near Lincoln's body; the sound should be localised, not piped through the speakers. Alternatively, you may decide not to have Lincoln's neck snap so he takes longer to die via asphyxiation, tragically expiring just as Surrey arrives with notice of pardon.

Note that suspension trauma is also a concern. Please do not leave your actor in the harness for long lengths of time (particularly in rehearsals). Make sure to describe this scene clearly in your breakdown notice, and discuss the process in depth with the actor you eventually decide to cast.

## Act 3  Scene 2

*See Glossary – Arrests; Carries; Ensemble Readiness.*

The sheriff and officers drag in Faulkner. Is this a serious affair, or meant to introduce some comedy? [*JK: Rhetorical question. This play needs comedy wherever you can find it. Have a big Faulkner and smaller guards. Faulkner follows the guards on stage, but stops moving when he starts speaking. This jerks the guards back, and they fall onto their backsides. As the guards get up, Faulkner walks past them whilst they are on all fours, patting their heads on 'all the dogs'. Faulkner can keep walking forward, dragging the guards with him. The sheriff may or may not get involved on 'Bring him forward'.*]

When More commands 'Away!', do the sheriff and/or officers move towards Faulkner? They could hesitate when Faulkner says 'I appeal' because More may change his mind. Or the sheriff and/or officers can drag Faulkner out, forcing him to struggle and shout the last two lines at More.

*See Glossary – Knees (maybe); Strikes (maybe).*

What is your production's particular master/servant relationship? Morris is clearly frustrated with Faulkner but does he get physical with pushing, beating, or the like? And how desperately does Faulkner follow to reverse his firing (crawling, latching onto Morris' leg, *etc.*)?

## Act 4  Scene 1

*See Glossary – Draws.*

The dagger might be wood or cardboard in a period production so that the threat doesn't seem real enough for the nobles to fear the performers. If your troupe is particularly eccentric on this front, or you set the play in another period, something more realistic could be used. The flourish of the dagger just needs to show that Inclination knows how to handle a knife. Your fight director should be able to guide the actor through a simple routine.

[*Flourishing a dagger.*]

*See Glossary – Grabs (maybe); Strikes (maybe).*

Once the nobles leave, the actors can revert to being themselves. One of them – likely Wit – could smack Luggins for being late and almost screwing up the entire gig.

More sanctions the players to rough up the servingman in order to get the last two angels. You will need to decide if they go right into it (allowing More to watch and get one more laugh from them), or if they wait. The stage direction notes that the attendants exit with More but nothing about this servingman, whom they will have to grab if he tries to flee. Maybe they follow More's direction to the letter ('pull his coat over his ears'). Or maybe they just take the servant's coat. And his shoes. And his undergarments.

## Act 4  Scene 2

*See Glossary – Arrests; Binds (maybe).*

Palmer is not truly giving the nobles a choice, regardless of how this sounds. The king has already decided the fate of each noble who fails to comply. Palmer's treatment of Rochester after he declines to sign is a veiled threat to everyone else. More declines next, and Palmer has another prepared order from the king. Palmer can send a clearer signal to the other lords that this isn't really a decision by calling in the guards to flank Rochester and More. This would shock Rochester, whilst More would probably remain outwardly tranquil. It would also explain why the rest of the lords immediately consent to the king; with Rochester and More guarded, Palmer's 'Will you subscribe, my lords?' is threatening, and the reply of 'Instantly' makes sense.

## Act 4  Scene 3

*See Glossary – Knees.*

[*Daughters kneel.*]

## Act 4  Scene 4

*See Glossary – Arrests.*

[*The Tower. Enter the Bishop of Rochester, Surrey, Shrewsbury, Lieutenant of the Tower, and Warders with weapons.*]

Rochester is led to prison. How is he treated? Whilst it is standard to treat nobility well, this does not mean your Henry 8 or his officers bother to do so. Is Rochester malnourished/dehydrated? Or, as we proposed in Chapter 6 – *As You Like It* (3.1) with Oliver, is Rochester being tortured? Depending on what the never-seen king is like in your production, this could set up a threat for More in later scenes. If so, there are a few common tortures you can consider. The rack was a device that a prisoner would be strapped to, restrained by the wrists and ankles. The prisoner would be stretched, often leading to dislocated limbs that eventually would be torn from the sockets. This was known to be used by Henry 8 and other sixteenth-century monarchs. The wounds would be clearly visible on Rochester's wrists.

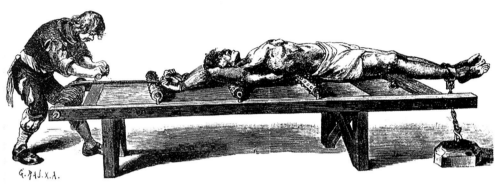

(*Wikimedia Commons*)

The Scavenger's Daughter (or Skeffington's Irons) was actually created during the reign of Henry 8. It worked in the opposite manner, by compressing the person into a foetal position. The wounds would be clearly visible on Rochester's neck.

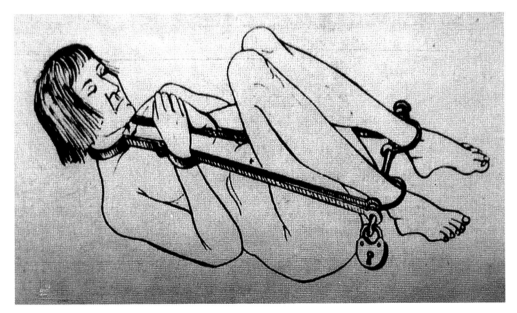

*Cigüeña (instrumento de tortura). Exposición Inquisición en el Palacio de los Olvidados de Granada.* (*Dorieo, Wikimedia Commons* (*License CC-BY-SA 4.0*))

## Act 4  Scene 5

*See Glossary – Arrests; Binds (maybe); Knees.*

There is little room for violence here. Whilst Downes is clearly armed and arresting More, it's important to remember the history More has with Downes. This would give any man pause; so long as More is not resisting arrest, Downes can struggle with his conscience, and possibly never lay a finger on More beyond any obligatory binding/cuffing/*etc.*

## Act 5  Scene 1

*See Glossary – Arrests; Ensemble Readiness.*

[*The Tower Gate. Enter the Warders of the Tower, with halbards.*]

If you've been missing crowd scenes these last few acts, we've got good news. This is a scene you can pack to the brim, such that it requires warders for crowd control. Whilst the halberd is a great range weapon and a symbol of the office the warders hold, see Chapter 17 – *Richard 3* (1.2), halberds won't help much up close. Pick a moment or two to insert a little fight or pushing match with people in the crowd. This is not just gratuitous violence but to help the audience understand how dangerous these times are. We see a mob form, burn London, disperse, then form again even faster. More is elevated to, and dropped from, glory in the blink of an eye. The capriciousness of Henry's reign is a character unto itself. This will up the stakes for the warders, making it clear why they are concerned for the poor woman's safety.

The play is ultimately building towards More walking off to a death that the audience will not actually be shown. Therefore, we encourage you to fully stage the preceding horrors so that the final moment of the play gains its power entirely from taking place in the audience's imagination.

## Act 5  Scene 3

[*The Tower. Enter Sir Thomas More, the Lieutenant, and a Servant attending, as in his chamber in the Tower.*]

How has More been treated in the tower? If you chose a violent path for the imprisonment of Rochester, increase the intensity here. The more brutal you go – torture, starvation, open cuts, bruises, a broken bone or two – a larger amount of More's fortitude will be on display, thereby increasing the tragedy of his eventual removal from the world.

*See Glossary – Ensemble Readiness; Grabs (maybe); Knees (maybe).*

There are opportunities for More's family to physicalise their pleas that he fight against his own execution: dropping to their knees as in earlier scenes; grabbing one of his legs to stop him from moving; an embrace from which he has to free himself, *etc.*

The lieutenant is watching all of this, but it's unlikely he would intervene. He is sympathetic to the Mores, even crying in the next scene over More's execution. The lieutenant is the one person assigned to interact with More. Keep any other guards off stage.

## Act 5  Scene 4

[*Tower Hill. Enter the Sheriffs of London and their Officers at one door, the Warders with their halbards at another.*]

*See Glossary – Arrests; Binds; Ensemble Readiness.*

More should probably be bound when escorted to the hangman, at least for show to the public. The text is clear that no one is doing harm to More, so don't add any. When More arrives at the top of the gallows platform, the hangman should undo the bindings, allowing More to hand over his gown and purse.

# Chapter 19

# Henry 8

*'You ask with such a violence'* – Wolsey (3.2)

If you've reached peak British monarch fatigue, we're happy to announce this is the last we'll write about these folks.

## Act 1  Scene 1

*See Glossary – Arrests; Binds (maybe).*

> *Enter Brandon, a Sergeant at Armes before him, and two or three of the Guard.*

Brandon performs a respectful arrest. Buckingham acknowledges it is pointless to resist. If Buckingham's comments about Wolsey are offensive to any of the arresting officers, there might be room to threaten or outright punish Buckingham for the insult. This seems unlikely to us. (Abergavenny also must 'bear [Buckingham] company', but we expect this quasi-arrest is also a snooze.) If you choose to shackle/bind here, use restraints that are period to your production. The sixteenth century gives you standard shackles for the wrist and bilboes for the ankles (though these will make it difficult to exit).

*Curious Punishments of Bygone Days.* Alice Morse Earle, 1896. Colonial Williamsburg. (*Public domain*)

## Act 2  Scene 1

*See Glossary – Arrests; Binds (maybe); Grabs (maybe); Strikes (maybe).*

> *Enter Buckingham from his Arraignment, Tipstaues before him, the Axe with the edge towards him, Halberds on each side, accompanied with Sir Thomas Louell, Sir Nicholas Vaux, Sir Walter Sands, and common people, &c.*

The procession is armed, with tipstaves and halberds to keep the common people away, not to keep Buckingham in line (that's the axe's job). There should be peasants on stage

*Dame Ellen Terry as Queen Katherine of Aragon.* Unidentified painter (after Window & Grove), 1892.

for the guards to move out of the way. To drive home the need for all the weapons, you can have a commoner get in the way of the process (if they are in support of Buckingham), or throw something at Buckingham (if they are not). A guard can make an example of said commoner with a boot to the face, or a strike to the guts with the butt of the halberd. As for Buckingham, he again seems to be treated respectfully since he is allowed to speak.

## Act 2  Scene 2

*See Glossary – Ensemble Readiness; Grabs (maybe); Strikes (maybe).*

How does Henry lash out physically, if at all? He's extremely upset when disturbed by Suffolk and Norfolk. Does Henry push them out of the way? Grab them? Bark lines in their faces? Explore the possibilities as this is an avenue to reveal character through violence. Not too much of it, mind you, but whatever amount your Henry employs as a probe for truth-telling. We won't point out every scene in which this might be conceivable, but rather suggest you keep an eye on it throughout the play. It may serve a particular purpose in your version of the story.

## Act 2  Scene 4

*See Glossary – Binds (maybe); Ensemble Readiness; Grabs (maybe); Strikes (maybe).*

There is probably little violence, despite great desire for it. Given the calibre of the human chess pieces at issue here, we should examine where protocol may be enforced/ ignored. You'll likely go bankrupt from the opening stage direction alone, so please invite us to see your production whilst it is still possible.

> *Car.* Whil'st our Commission from Rome is read,
> Let silence be commanded.
> *King.*                              What's the need?

We'll illustrate again how your choices matter. Wolsey calls for silence either because the room is fantastically unruly, or the crowd is already so silent they could hear a pin drop and Wolsey is just being a drama queen. If you opt for the former, Henry's query is a result of his trademark impatience; if the latter, it's a laugh line at Wolsey's expense. [*JK: Please take the laugh. Your audience need it by now. Especially if I'm your audience.*]

*See Glossary – Knees.*

> *The Queene makes no answer, rises out of her Chaire, goes about the Court, comes to the King, and kneeles at his Feete. Then speakes.*

Always scrutinise stage directions. Before the queen has even uttered a word, she ignores the protocol of being in the proverbial 'witness box' and moves to the king. It is strange that everyone allows this, and for as long as they do. It's especially a(nother) slap to Wolsey's face. You'll have to decide why he restrains himself from ordering Katherine back to the chair. Wolsey could very well try to have Katherine grabbed and returned to her seat. Depending on her ability to intimidate, and/or the guards' level of pity or confusion, such a physical manoeuvre may prove impossible without the king's orders. Does he intervene? He may want this to be over as soon as humanly possible but struggle with a desire to appear impartial, and removed from any harm that comes to Katherine.

It's unlikely Katherine strikes, spits, or physically harms Wolsey. But she could get very close to doing so, and might have some acolytes in the crowd willing to cross the line.

As we've implored in earlier chapters with major crowd scenes, please take the rehearsal time to explore all permutations, based on the chemistry of your cast and universe. Find your strongest version of this stunner – a sort of love child of the deposition in Chapter 9 – *Richard 2* (4.1) and Hermione's trial in Volume Two – *The Winter's Tale* (3.2).

## Act 3  Scene 1

*See Glossary – Grabs (maybe); Strikes (maybe).*

We've already floated the idea of private battles between a king's representatives and a queen with whom they disagree. See Chapter 9 – *Richard 2* (2.2). We have more to work with here: Wolsey established an intimidating presence in other scenes – just ask Buckingham; and Katherine made mincemeat of Wolsey during the trial. Finding themselves in a less-public setting, how far might the cardinals retaliate against Katherine for that humiliation, and/or the queen's ladies as proxies?

## Act 3  Scene 2

*See Glossary – Draws (maybe); Ensemble Readiness; Grabs (maybe); Strikes (maybe).*

Henry may be tempted to physically intimidate Wolsey during the interrogation, but we advise against this. We are meant to experience the scene through Wolsey's eyes. A normally violent Henry could terrify here merely by being calm. See Volume Two – *Titus Andronicus* (5.2).

A lack of violence where expected also opens up an opportunity after Henry leaves – potential violence with Surrey, whose father-in-law Wolsey had killed. Surrey states the only thing stopping him from running Wolsey through is his office. Does Surrey's sword or dagger come out of its sheath? Is it pressed to Wolsey's throat? It's possible that Surrey is just enough of a hothead to punch Wolsey in the guts. [*JK: Keep in mind how many lines would be crossed when striking a holy man.*] [*SD: Now you're just encouraging me.*] Do the other lords participate before Wolsey finally breaks down to the point they feel enough is enough?

## Act 4  Scene 2

There are a few possibilities to explore for Katherine's illness. There was an illness of this time known as the sweating sickness, which became an epidemic on five different occasions in the first half of the sixteenth century. It began with a feeling that something was off, followed by a violent headache, aching limbs, and shivers. An extreme fever would be followed by irregularities in the heart, and finally death. This could all take place within a day or two. If Katherine had this disease and spat in Wolsey's face earlier in the play, it's possible she gave him the disease and he dies of it just a day before she will. Whilst this timeline may sound off, Wolsey could have comorbidities that would accelerate the disease for him. Can you tell we're writing this during COVID-19?

It's also possible the king had both of them poisoned. Just food for thought, as being specific about what is killing Katherine will help the actress stay true to the physical maladies of that particular choice. There is a great description of how she looks. Let your makeup department have a field day.

*See Glossary – Carries.*

*Enter Katherine Dowager, sicke, lead betweene Griffith, her Gentleman Vsher, and Patience her Woman.*

## Act 5  Scene 2

*See Glossary – Ensemble Readiness; Grabs (maybe); Strikes (maybe).*

This scene's taunting of Cranmer is a mirror to Wolsey's scene (not dissimilar to Bolingbroke's fourth-act crisis in Chapter 9 – *Richard 2* versus Richard's in the first act). What physical violence do the lords threaten/achieve before the lord chamberlain stops them?

*See Glossary – Arrests (almost).*

How far does the guard get in arresting Cranmer before he produces the ring?

## Act 5  Scene 3

*Noyse and Tumult within: Enter Porter and his man.*

The rabble theoretically remains off stage, but you might have an impulse for some of the folks to get through and for the porter and/or his man to deal with them. The audience are asked to envision all of this, which does seem the funnier route, but maybe a well-timed sight gag could add something. Up to you. The play is terribly verbose, even for Shakespeare, with virtually no physical violence contemplated.

Thus endeth our exploration of *Henry 8*, a journey so brief we failed even to make an obligatory joke about Doctor Butts.

Part 5

# Vienna Sausages

*Mariana in the South*. John William Waterhouse, circa 1897. (*Public domain*)

# Chapter 20

# Measure for Measure

*'And blown with restless violence round about / The pendent world'* – Claudio (3.1)

## Act 1  Scene 2

*See Glossary – Ensemble Readiness; Grabs (maybe); Intimacy (maybe); Strikes (maybe).*

To balance out the strictness of the leading characters (what Lucio calls Claudio's 'restraint' later in the scene), you can get pretty freewheeling with the comedic ensemble. Lucio and the two gentlemen may engage in some horseplay at the outset. And this dynamic could develop with the entry of Mistress Overdone – pushes, grabs, slaps, *etc.* Lucio may also try to loosen up Claudio.

## Act 1  Scene 3[1]

*See Glossary – Arrests; Binds.*

We do not anticipate violence in this scene. The provost has no ill will towards Claudio, and this frog march was ordered by Angelo. Notwithstanding, since this is all for show, Claudio should probably be bound ('Whence comes this restraint'). Claudio could struggle a bit, but his verse is relatively stable and the provost allows him conversation with the others despite their ill repute.

## Act 2  Scene 1

*See Glossary – Arrests; Binds; Grabs (maybe); Ensemble Readiness; Strikes (maybe).*

Remember that no actor should be truly bound. The same goes for gags. [*JK: Creating a prop gag is done by tying the knot behind the victim's head like normal. Take it off, then cut the cloth in the middle (where it was in line with the nose when worn). Insert both ends into the victim's mouth and it will look like the victim has been gagged.*]

  Elbow has not been kind to his prisoners, so they should be dishevelled. The more Pompey questions, the more crazed Elbow can get. There may be comedy in Elbow physicalising his interactions with Froth and Pompey even though Escalus is there. Elbow has been at this for seven-and-a-half years. He would be used to gentlemen not caring what happens to commoners in prison. Elbow could grab his prisoners' hair or ears. There is even mention of a Shakespearean favourite – box o'th' eare – so take the time with your fight director to explore. See Chapter 13 – *Henry 5* (4.8).

## Act 2  Scene 2

Of the many activities your production's Angelo might partake, self-flagellation on religious grounds is somewhat fitting, given all the threats of whipping faced by other characters up until this point. Your Angelo may choose a whip with which to punish himself (see Chapter 15 – *Henry 6 Part 2* (2.1)), or another instrument entirely. Work with your props department to create a stage-safe version of whichever you choose.

## Act 2  Scene 4

*Isabella and Angelo, Measure for Measure.* Stephen Reid, 1909.

Angelo, like the play at large, is locked in the psychological intersections of power, sex, and faith corrupted. Angelo's auto-erotic abuse could also start/continue here before Isabella's arrival.

*See Glossary – Grabs (maybe); Intimacy; Strikes (maybe).*

Have your intimacy coordinator and fight director on hand to explore this encounter. It is somewhat reminiscent of the dynamic in Edward's wooing of Elizabeth from Chapter 16 – *Henry 6 Part 3* (3.2), but with more opportunities for the encounter to become physically violent, as in Chapter 17 – *Richard 3* (1.2; 4.3).

Angelo is likely unpractised in seduction [*JK: as opposed to your authors*] [*SD: *gag**], despite having been betrothed to Mariana, whom he only desired for her family money. Assuming little skill to begin with, plus all of his religious hangups, the innate creepiness of using a brother's life or death as collateral in propositioning his sister, and the fact that said sister is a novice to the order of Saint Clare, how does Angelo interact with someone he actually desires? [*SD: Especially when there is virtually no one but himself (and some invisible douchebag on a cloud) to restrain him.*] How much does Isabella perceive Angelo's struggle early on? Once she fully comprehends Angelo's ultimatum, how will she keep him at bay whilst still pleading for Claudio's reprieve? As with each of the loathsome courtships in the canon, take the rehearsal time to flesh this scene out; continually explore new tactics, so you don't end up playing the same beats over and over.

## Act 3  Scene 1

*See Glossary – Grabs (maybe); Knees (maybe); Strikes (maybe).*

How physical are Claudio's pleas and, in turn, Isabella's denials? Does Claudio feel compelled to beg on his knees? Does he have to grab Isabella to keep her from leaving? How does she react? Something to explore in rehearsal – this scene is not altogether different from Isabella's encounter with Angelo.

## Act 3  Scene 2[2]

*See Glossary – Arrests; Binds; Ensemble Readiness; Grabs (maybe); Knees.*

Elbow has arrested Pompey – again – in order to bring him to the whipping Escalus promised in 2.1, in the event Pompey turned recidivist. Elbow probably binds Pompey in some manner. This could be elaborate – it sounds like Elbow made a leash out of the binding ('a Cord sir'). It appears that Elbow, himself or via officers, forces Pompey to kneel ('his necke will come to your wast' and 'at the wheels of Caesar'). Pompey could crawl to Lucio for salvation when he enters. Then, Elbow could pull on Pompey's leash, making him fall backwards. The more desperate Pompey gets, the more he can crawl after Lucio and be ripped backwards. The canine treatment continues with Lucio telling Pompey to 'Goe to kennell'. Maybe Pompey clings to Lucio's leg, gets dragged for a bit, then is tossed off or kicked.

[*JK: Lucio slanders the duke without knowing the friar is the duke in disguise. In 5.1, Lucio says a plucking of the nose happened in this scene. It could be a bald-faced lie, but explore the possibility of the friar pulling Lucio's nose whilst saying 'imagine me to vnhurtfull an opposite'. Another possibility is that Lucio is lying about who was the plucker and the pluckee.*]

Later, Escalus arrests Mistress Overdone. How much does she resist? 'Goe too, no more words' may suggest she is attempting to further interject vocally and/or physically. Overdone is a force to be reckoned with. Explore options for at least the threat of violence. For example, the officers escorting her could be frightened to death to touch her. We explored self-arrest with Eleanor in Chapter 15 – *Henry 6 Part 2* (1.4). Here, maybe Mistress Overdone stares down the grabby officers, scares them into backing off, then marches out as they confusedly follow.

## Act 5  Scene 1

*See Glossary – Binds (maybe); Ensemble Readiness; Knees (maybe).*

> *Duke.*　　　　　　Away with her: poore soule
> She speakes this, in th' infirmity of sence.

The duke orders Isabella to be taken away but the scene continues. Do the officers attempt to remove her and she pulls away? Does the duke motion for them to stand down, or do the officers restrain Isabella throughout? She is making severe allegations against the very person appointed to preside over her matter and doing so publicly. The duke likely gave her room to plead her case without restraint, given that he has to call for an officer to bring her to prison later in the scene.

> *Duke.* I know you'd faine be gone: An Officer:
> To prison with her:

*See Glossary – Strikes (maybe).*

There also needs to be an officer near Lucio. The officer tries a variety of ways to stop Lucio from speaking. [*JK: This could start with a stern look, escalate to kicking him in the foot/shin, a slap, even covering his mouth from behind. On this last bit of violence, do not actually cover the mouth/nose as it would restrict the actor's airway. Have your officer make contact with the blade of his hand on Lucio's mandible, but keep the top open so that the actor can breathe regularly. If the officer attempts this from the front, his hand will probably be upside down (i.e. the blade of the hand on the nose) so make contact with the thenar (the pad of the thumb).]*

*See Glossary – Knees.*

> *Mar.* Noble Prince,
> As there comes light from heauen, and words from breath,
> As there is sence in truth, and truth in vertue,
> I am affianced this mans wife, as strongly
> As words could make vp vowes: And my good Lord,
> But Tuesday night last gon, in's garden house,
> He knew me as a wife. As this is true,
> Let me in safety raise me from my knees,
> Or else for euer be confixed here
> A Marble Monument.

Mariana does her best impression of Helena from Chapter 5 – *All's Show Well that Ends Well* (1.3), as will Isabella later on, but we now return to The Lucio Show. Depending on how many officers are around, it may be comically difficult to follow Escalus' next order to apprehend the disguised duke.

There is a scuffle here with the provost, duke, and Lucio. Consider including the officers, as it might be funnier to have them trying to get into the mix, but failing as the trio struggles. Alternatively, you can go full schtick and have the officers, provost, and Lucio surround the duke, who then squeezes out of the swarm and peels downstage, leaving his disguise behind him. In this scenario, if the duke turns upstage, the audience will experience the reveal from his perspective as everyone upstage soils themselves. Similar to Polixenes' loss of disguise in Volume Two – *The Winter's Tale* (4.4) [*SD and JK in disturbing harmony: BUY VOLUME TWO!!!*], the subjects would drop to their knees. This could happen in a sudden and simultaneous drop into full prostration, but that seems more appropriate for a sheep-shearing festival full of peasants fearing execution. Here, the subjects are from multiple classes and differing degrees of guilt. Also, they are probably not all focused in the same direction yet, as not everyone will have figured out that the duke is no longer in the pile-on. One person could realise they're standing in the duke's presence and react, then two others see the first person kneeling and join in, then the rest catch on quickly.

Lucio attempts to sneak away, but is apprehended by your overworked officers, each of whom deserve medals for their efforts in this scene.

We'll see you again in Volume Two. Until then, we advise you to remain on your best behaviour. This should help tide you over.

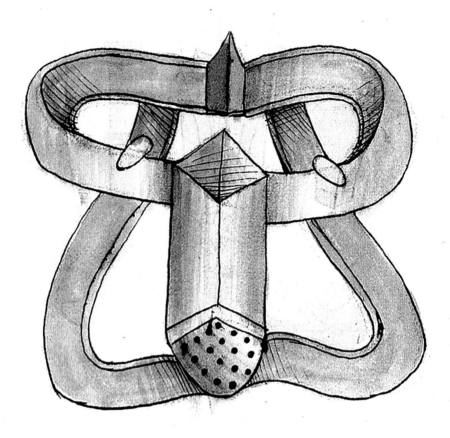

Chastity belt. Kyeser von Eichstadt, circa 1405. (*Public domain*)

# Glossary of Recurring Concepts

**Arrests** – There are a variety of ways characters get arrested, but each should reveal more about the characters at that moment in the play. Some will be simple escorts out of the room, so there is no need to touch the prisoner. It's important guards are not lackadaisical (unless they're incompetent); the alertness of guards will heighten the tension in any scene. Review *Ensemble Readiness,* because there are no small parts, only lazy actors. If the guards grab the prisoner, *see Appendix – Bursting the Bubble.* There should only be acted violence, always with the victim in control. If the prisoner is being driven to their knees, the prisoner leads the action, the guard follows, and both sell the struggle. If the prisoner is struggling, guards need to remember 'distance is not your friend'. Did we mention *see Appendix – Bursting the Bubble*?

**Binds** – When binding a prisoner, it's important that the victim is always in control. The actors should not be bound for real. The victim will palm both ends of the rope, and there are many ways to make it look realistic. [*JK: Fight director Ruth Cooper-Brown, who was a magician's assistant once upon a time, taught me a bunch.*] If your production is modern and uses handcuffs, the fake ones have a lever to release them. These rules apply whether you are binding the hands to each other or to an object.

**Blood** – There are plenty of products available online. [*JK: Contact me for my preferences.*]

- *Stage Blood* – This deep-red blood uses a biodegradable detergent base, which helps it wash out of most fabrics and surfaces, but it is not edible.
- *Thick Blood* – This imitates abrasions and wounds that are starting to congeal. It's thick enough to plant on stage (*e.g.* under the lip of a table), so an actor can access it without needing to carry a blood pack.
- *Magic Blood* – This two-part compound comes with a powder and a liquid. Apply the powder to the body and the liquid to the knife. When the two parts meet, the compound turns red.
- *Homemade Edible Blood* – Homemade blood is much cheaper. A simple recipe uses a light golden syrup, mixed with red and blue food dyes. Using the syrup as the base, add one drop of blue food dye, then add red food dye until the colour becomes correct for your blood effect.
- *Homemade Clothing Blood* – A simple recipe is laundry detergent mixed with red and blue food dyes. Using the detergent as the base, add one drop of blue food dye, then

red food dye until the colour becomes correct for your blood effect. [*JK: A good trick discovered by a director I worked with – Cindy Blades – is to use a pale blue detergent so only red food dye is needed.*]

Make sure to test any blood product on the fabric or surface prior to using it in large quantities. And confirm the lighting with your design team. [*JK: One time as Banquo's ghost, I found out during tech week that the lighting would all be red. Since red blood would not play, I used chocolate syrup. It looked amazing.*] Also factor in the colour of clothing. If characters are wearing blacks or dark greys, red will not show up. [*JK: Use something viscous.*]

**Blood Packs –**

• *Regular Pack* – Blood packs can be created relatively easily with a little practice. You will need your blood mixture, gaffer tape, and small cheap plastic bags. Do not use high quality bags; they do not break easily. Using a spoon or turkey baster or syringe, get the blood into one corner of the bag. Try to avoid touching the sides, as it will increase the mess. Once you have an appropriate amount of blood in the corner, twist the bag until it is airtight. Adhere the gaffer tape in the same direction. If the pack is not firm, use more tape to tighten the pack. Finally, trim the top of the bag so that there is a quarter-to-half-inch stem remaining. This will help actors palm the bag or tape it to themselves for body blood.
• *Rehearsal Pack* – Starting a bit before tech week, actors should work with rehearsal blood packs. Everything is the same as above, but use water instead of blood mixture. It will splash more than blood but keep you from having to do laundry after every run during tech.
• *Directional* – [*JK: This is a trick I learned from fight director Kyle Rowling.*] Tape around the whole bag, leaving just the corner open. The spray of blood will generally go where you want.
• *Squibs* – These are miniature devices commonly used for gunshot-wound effects. You MUST hire a professional; these are explosives which require a certified operator. There is a way to create the effect using $CO_2$ cartridges, but the sound they make will destroy the theatrical illusion.
• *Advanced Blood Delivery* – You may want more blood than can be released by a standard blood pack. To get a large spray of blood, use tubing and a bag. There are too many variants to list here. [*JK: Okay, but here's a great idea I got from a talented VFX artist – Stephanie Cox-Williams. Use a sports bra to keep the bag of blood higher and in place.*]

There are many more tricks of the trade, so look to your fight director for more. [*SD: Or email jared@jaredkirby.com to hire him.*] [*JK: Thanks, Seth!*] [*SD: It wasn't a compliment. Just trying to unload you onto someone else.*]

**Carries** – There are myriad ways to carry someone. More often than not, you'll be carrying a dead body. Make sure your performer(s) can support the full weight of the person being carried. Work within your actors' abilities. For less-able carriers (whether due to age, disability, or history of previous injury), you may have to find a creative way to execute the action. The most common (and easiest) carries are cradling and the fireman's carry.

It is important to get the victim's centre mass as close as possible to the lifter's body. Make sure to utilise the legs for the lift, and do not bend over at an awkward angle that would require the lower back muscles to engage.

The same principles apply to drags. When dragging an unconscious or dead character, avoid jerking actions. Make sure the drag is fluid in order to avoid injury to the victim's joints. Pay attention to the playing space and make sure it is free of debris.

**Draws** – Drawing any weapon should carry the weight that drawing a gun would in a modern context. Do not draw until prepared to use the weapon (unless the character is incompetent). The moment one or more weapons come out, everyone needs to tense up as the stakes have raised. Your fight director should be able to help the actors understand this.

**Ensemble Readiness** – The best productions we have seen and worked on ensured that all the actors understood the dangers of the time period in which the stagings were set: how the people of that era would consider death, dying, and killing; or how quickly one could die at the hands of another with no consequences due to class differences. Consider this story recounted by Vincentio Saviolo in his 1595 publication:

> It happened that the Duke of Mantua and his brother Rodomont being in the same Emperor Charles his Court about certain affairs of their own, they walked in a great chamber on a time expecting the Emperor should send for them when his Majesty was at leisure. Into this chamber at the same time came a certain Spanish Captain who, without any greeting or salvation, came by them and bravely walked between the Duke and his brother, nothing respecting the greatness of that prince and so braved them three or four times. Wherewith Rodomont being greatly offended with the discourtesy of this proud and insolent Captain went to a window which he perceived to be open and, staying till the captain came that way, took him by the collar with one hand and putting the other under his breech thrust him out at the window and broke his neck. Whereupon he fled from the Court with all speed he could. But the Emperor being informed of the matter blamed not Rodomont, considering the Spanish Captain had so insolently behaved himself to Rodomont's brother the Duke of Mantua. – *A Gentleman's Guide to Duelling: Of Honour and Honourable Quarrels.* [*JK: Edited by Jared Kirby.*] [*SD: Gross.*]

Death could be right around the corner, for no other reason than walking between two gentlemen. And various rulers would find this an acceptable recourse for the perceived wrong. Your ensemble, every single member of it, should consider the kind of danger just one unsanctioned move or word could garner. This will give your production a kind of gravitas rarely seen outside of the professional level, and often not even inside of it.

When we speak about ensemble readiness to heighten the tensions of a scene, a perfect example is the beginning of a battle. This is some of the highest stress a warrior will be under. Each character needs to consider the anxiety they've endured prior to battle. Dig into the intensity, struggle, and doubts actual fighters go through. Channel this kind of energy before the battle begins.

**Faints** – Follow the rules of falls. It should look like the body is crumpling, so bring the knees together and essentially do a squat. Wobble on the way down, then shift onto one buttock. Finish by rolling onto the back or side.

**Falls** – *See Appendix – Bursting the Bubble.* Remove as much distance between your body and the ground as possible before gravity takes control. Less distance means less velocity, which means less pain. Gravity can aid the fall but, if you rely on it, you may get hurt when something goes wrong. There is no singular way to fall safely. If your performer has studied martial arts, they will have ways to get to the ground such as a breakfall, sidefall, or frontfall. Dancers will have a different method, and clowns another entirely. If your actors have basic stage combat training, they most likely learned a basic sitfall.

**Grabs** – *See Appendix – Bursting the Bubble.* Whilst seemingly forceful, it's important that there is no actual force in the hand. The aggressor's fingers should be relaxed (*i.e.* the victim should be able to turn their arm easily), whilst the aggressor's arm is tense. Even if the audience can't see the arm (*e.g.* due to a costume), that tension must exist so the aggressor's body moves correctly. If the aggressor is moving the victim, make sure they stay close together. The closer they are, the safer this will be, and the more violent the grab can look.

**Intimacy** – Intimacy direction creates choreography for intimate scenes so they can be performed in a way which is both safe and replicable. There are many organisations worldwide where you can find a qualified professional. There is also a new book – *Staging Sex* by Chelsea Pace, who is the founder of Theatrical Intimacy Education at theatricalintimacyed.com.

**Knees** – As in falling to your knees, not kneeing someone in the stomach. Similar to falls, *see Appendix – Bursting the Bubble.* The victim is in control of getting to the ground, even though it looks like the aggressor is pushing the victim down or taking their knees out from behind. The main difference from falls is that, when going to the knees, there are no muscle groups on which to land. We always recommend knee pads unless the costume will not allow for them. There are low-profile knee pads available.

**Strikes** – *See Appendix – On the Bubble.* To make it look realistic, you will need to find the angle that hides the air from the audience.

# Appendix

Stage Combat Primer
by Jared Kirby

**Two Minutes and Two Hundred Hours**

I often say it takes two minutes to understand how to perform stage combat safely and realistically, but it takes 200 hours of practice to get any good at it. This is not an exact science. The goal of this statement is to help people understand that stage combat is an independent art form, which requires as much practice as any other artistic discipline.

It is generally accepted that, when taking up an instrument, painting, dance or a martial art, these skills will take time to acquire and hone. It's no different with stage combat. Actors sometimes think 'I'll learn that when I'm cast in the part.' This is tantamount to learning dance *after* being cast in a role with three dance numbers. Rarely will someone excel in that performance if they start to learn a skill at the beginning of rehearsal. If you're seeking leading roles in Shakespeare, it's wise to invest in stage-combat training. By developing these skills in advance, you will have the opportunity to truly express your character through violence.

There's also a misconception that having skill in tangential disciples, such as dance or martial arts, will make it easy to pick up stage combat. These can offer some advantages, but are akin to knowing ballet when wanting to learn tap. It might not hurt, but it requires an entirely different, and sometimes contradictory, skill set.

This is further exacerbated by productions waiting until the eleventh hour to stage the fights. When this occurs, you can only create a fraction of what would have been an engaging and enthralling part of the show. The best productions will involve the fight director from the beginning of the process.

In my method, the art of stage combat is divided into two categories. All actions are performed 'on the bubble' or 'bursting the bubble'. Within each are simple tenets. The bubble refers to an imaginary force field that surrounds each performer. This force field gives you a specific place to target your energy, in order to perform actions at full speed and intensity, without endangering your partner. The 'bubble' varies in distance based on what you are performing.

**On the Bubble**

Actions performed on the bubble are any violent events in which the partners are out of distance from each other and the space between them is hidden by proper angulation.

These tend to be strikes – a punch, slap, kick, or use of an object. When working on the bubble, the two principles to remember are: distance is your friend; and planar geometry.

**Distance is your friend**: Proximity to your partner is relatively irrelevant when working on the bubble. Whether you're one foot or three feet away, it will usually not matter. That said, start training with a larger amount of distance between partners. This is safer and also puts the focus on proper targeting in conjunction with the correct timing of the action/reaction to make everything look realistic. The *proximity* to your partner is rarely important; it's all about the *angle*. The strike will 'sell' if the performers are at the correct angle in relation to the audience. That is why planar geometry is so important.

**Planar geometry**: Planar geometry is used to hide the air from the audience by staging the action at the correct angle. Once you line up a strike with the target and aim at your partner's bubble, you have created a pocket of air that keeps your partner safe. If the audience see that air, the action will not be believable. To find the correct angle, take that pocket of air and turn it into a line. If that line is parallel to the audience's sightline, they will see that no strike actually occurred. By placing that line of air perpendicular to the audience's sightline, you will be able to create the illusion of a believable strike. Another way to look at this is to draw a line from the audience's eyes to the object being struck. The person doing the striking must intersect the audience's sightline for it to look like a realistic punch. The audience lose depth perception in the theatre, so it will look like the hit actually landed.

As an example, let's look at a straight punch to the face. If the victim is facing the audience, and the aggressor's back is to the audience, draw a line from the audience's eyes to the victim's head. The aggressor will be several feet downstage of the victim and will make a punch to the bubble. As long as this intersects the audience's sightline and the victim reacts, we have a believable punch. If the audience are looking at the victim from behind, so the aggressor is upstage, then the aggressor's fist must disappear from the audience's sightline upstage of the victim's head. This is because that sightline is then drawn from the audience's eyes through the victim's head. As long as they see the fist disappear behind the head, and reappear as the victim reacts to the punch, it will be believable. In either of these scenarios, the aggressor may need to punch to the right or left of the actual head to make it look like a hit. This may feel strange to the actor but the geometry of this is exact.

Planar geometry always needs to be considered to make the actions look realistic. If the audience see the air, you are relying on them to suspend their disbelief to make the fight work. Never pull the audience out of the show like that.

## Bursting the Bubble

Actions performed by bursting the bubble are violent events in which you come into contact with your partner. This can be anything from grabbing and pushing to hair pulls, chokes, and pain-compliance positions, such as armbars. The two main rules to follow now are: distance is not your friend; and the victim is always in control.

**Distance is not your friend**: It's important, when performing actions in this category, that you remove as much distance as possible between the partners. This will not only be safer, it will be more realistic. Many times, an injury occurs when there is distance between the partners that shouldn't exist. In a choke from behind, the most common injury is the aggressor getting headbutted in the nose or mouth because there is a gap between the actors' heads. If the aggressor simply brings their head into contact with the victim's head, no headbutt can occur. My simple adage – distance creates velocity, velocity creates pain. If there is no distance between two people, then no velocity can be created, and thus no pain.

Find all the points of physical contact that can be maintained. This connection provides a safe way to communicate physically with one another and grounds the actors as one, making the actions safer for both. It is also easier for the partners to communicate through non-verbal cues in the body. A subtle weight shift to one foot can be the victim's way of telling the aggressor to start moving in that direction. By being in contact, sharing weight and energy, the partners will sell the illusion of violence whilst creating safe actions that look realistic.

**The victim is always in control**: In reality, the actions in this category are designed to impede the free movement of your adversary. We cannot do that in stage combat. We have to make certain that the victim is in control of each action. At any point, the victim should be able to break out of the technique if something is going wrong.

As an example, let's look at a hair pull. The aggressor will grab right above the hair and, at the same time, the victim will grab the aggressor's hand to place it onto the victim's scalp. This will create the illusion of the hair being pulled, but the victim can let go at any time and be free of the grab. There is never a moment when the aggressor actually grasps a clump of hair.

When we get to chokes and pain-compliance actions, any pressure being applied needs to transfer away from somewhere dangerous to somewhere safe. A good example is the two-handed choke from the front. The aggressor will make a 'v' with their hands, layering the thumbs in line with the opposite hand's index finger. The aggressor will then place the heel of their hands on the victim's sternum/collarbone, so that all the aggressor's fingertips are lightly placed on the victim's jugular. The palms should face each other, to create about three-to-four inches of space between the victim's oesophagus and the aggressor's hands. The victim will grab the aggressor's wrist and pull down, whilst the aggressor concurrently applies pressure into the sternum, through the heel of their hands. This will create a solid connection between the partners and keep the victim safe. Finally, the victim will move their head forward, so the bottom of their chin meets the 'v' shape of the aggressor's hands, hiding the pocket of air that keeps the victim safe.

Transferring pressure from somewhere dangerous to somewhere safe will make actions such as grabs, pushes, chokes from behind or in front, armbars or any kind of joint manipulation harmless whilst looking realistic.

## Conclusion

The concept of the bubble (on it or bursting it) is an integral part of performing safe and effective violence. You'll find that many approaches to stage combat follow these same rules, even if they do not codify things this way. The important thing is to have safety measures in place that will allow for realistic-looking violence, which creates an illusion of danger for the audience. When using the bubble approach to stage combat, it becomes easy to determine which actions need to be on the bubble or burst the bubble. Each keeps the performers free from harm by focusing on the correct application of the bubble. On the bubble utilises distance to keep performers safe, whilst bursting the bubble eliminates that distance to accomplish the same goal. By following the appropriate rules, you will be able to make the action safe for the performers, whilst maintaining a realistic story through violence for the audience.

# Notes

### Chapter 1 – *King Lear*

1. Despite all the discussion of the First Folio in the Introduction, we use the First Quarto for this play. It is, however, quite miserly about scene numbers. We provide the ones most other editions offer because we're not complete monsters. Bear in mind that, due to the popularity of the play, modern versions of the text tend to be a mixture of the folio and two quarto versions. [*SD: The quartos have some moments the folio does not, which are worth keeping. However, the final scene plays better in folio, and the assignment of the final lines to Edgar rather than Albany makes more sense to me, but it does not affect the topics on which we are focused in this book so I'll stop writing now.*]
2. This is mentioned in the First Folio but not in either quarto.

### Chapter 5 – *All's Well that Ends Well*

1. The First Folio only lists act breaks for this play. For ease of reference, we provide scene numbers where it is reasonable to conclude the action complete.

### Chapter 8 – *Edward 3*

1. This play does not appear in the First Folio. We have selected the 1596 Quarto printing. It contains no act/scene numbers. We have resorted to commonly accepted numbering for ease of reference.

### Chapter 13 – *Henry 5*

1. There is a paucity of act/scene numbers in the First Folio version of this play and we have decided to follow common designations for ease of reference.

## Chapter 14 – *Henry 6 Part 1*

1. There is a paucity of scene numbers in the first two acts of the First Folio version of the play and unstable listings in the fifth act.

## Chapter 15 – *Henry 6 Part 2*

1. There is a paucity of scene numbers in the First Folio version of the play for all but the opening act and scene. We have resorted to commonly accepted numbering for ease of reference.

## Chapter 16 – *Henry 6 Part 3*

1. There is a paucity of scene numbers in the First Folio version of the play for all but the opening act and scene. We have resorted to commonly accepted numbering for ease of reference.
2. This is taken from the 1595 Octavo version.

## Chapter 17 – *Richard 3*

1. There are no scene numbers in the First Folio for 3.5, 3.6, 3.7, 5.3, 5.4, or 5.5. We include most of them for ease of reference. [*SD: But not 5.5 because it's particularly stupid.*]

## Chapter 18 – *Sir Thomas More*

1. This play does not appear in the First Folio. We have selected the initial 1844 printing based on a manuscript written in several hands dating back to 1728.

## Chapter 20 – *Measure for Measure*

1. This is how the First Folio labels the scene but it is merely a continuation of 1.2.
2. This scene number is not listed in the First Folio but a break in the action is strongly implied.

# Bibliography

**Books**

Berry, Herbert, *The Noble Science: A Study and Transcription of Sloane Ms. 2530, Papers of the Masters of Defence of London, Temp. Henry VIII to 1590*, (University of Delaware Press, Delaware, 1991)

Dal Vera, Rocco, *The Voice in Violence*, (VASTA/Applause Books, New York, 2001)

Drew, Katherine, F; Peters, Edward, *The Lombard Laws*, (University of Pennsylvania Press, Philadelphia, 1973)

Edelman, Charles, *Brawl Ridiculous*, (Manchester University Press, UK, 1992)

Freeman, Neil, *Shakespeare's First Texts*, (Folio Scripts, Vancouver, 1994)

Grossman, Dave, *On Killing: The Psychological Cost of Learning to Kill in War and Society*, (Little, Brown & Company, Boston, 1995)

Hazlitt, William, *Characters of Shakespear's Plays*, (C. H. Reynell, London, 1817)

Inouye, Kevin, *The Theatrical Firearms Handbook*, (Focal Press, Massachusetts, 2014)

Kirby, Jared (ed.), *A Gentleman's Guide to Duelling: Vincentio Saviolo's Of Honour and Honourable Quarrels*, (Frontline Books, London, 2013)

Kirby, Jared (ed.), *Italian Rapier Combat: Ridolfo Capo Ferro's 'Gran Simulacro'*, (Greenhill Books, London 2004)

Kirby, Jared (ed.), *THE Expert Sword-Man's Companion: Or the True Art of SELF-DEFENCE. WITH An ACCOUNT of the Authors LIFE, and his Transactions during the Wars with France*, (Createspace, USA, 2017)

Lennox, Dr John, *A History of Stage Swordplay*, (Lambert Academic Publishing, Germany, 2011)

Pace, Chelsea, *Staging Sex: Best Practices, Tools, and Techniques for Theatrical Intimacy*, (Routledge, New York, 2020)

Sher, Antony, *Beside Myself: An Actor's Life*, (Nick Hern Books, London, 2001, www.nickhernbooks.co.uk)

Talhoffer, Hans, *Fechtbuch*, (Unpublished manuscript, 1459)

Woodstock, Thomas of, *The Ordenaunce and Fourme of Fightyng within Lists*, (1389). In *The Black Book of Admirality*, edited by Sir Travers Twiss, (Longman, London, 1871)

**Dissertations**

Elema, Ariella, *Trial by Battle in France and England*, (Centre for Medieval Studies, University of Toronto, Toronto, 2012)